# It Gets Foggy at Mossy Creek

## Dr. Chris Jones

# Mossy Creek Press

**It Gets Foggy at Mossy Creek**

Copyright © 2012 by Chris Jones

**ISBN:** 978-1-936912-55-1  **Hardcover**

All rights reserved. No part of this book may be reproduced or transmitted in any form or by any means, electronic or mechanical, including photocopying, recording, or by any information storage and retrieval system, without permission in writing from the publisher.

This book was printed in the United States of America.

**To order additional copies of this book, contact:**

**Mossy Creek Press**

## Table of Contents

I. Introduction 13

II. Early History 24

III. The Transition Period 53

IV. The War Years and a Period of Growth 105

V. National Acclaim in Athletics 137

VI. Outstanding Athletes and Coaches in Carson-Newman Sports History 185

VII. Outstanding Athletic Teams in the History of Carson-Newman Sport 268

VIII. The Modern Era and Future 317

IX. Appendix A 373

X. Appendix B 376

XI. Bibliography 379

XII. About the Author 382

# PERSONAL INTRODUCTION TO THIS BOOK

The idea for the book, IT GETS FOGGY AT MOSSY CHEEK, was born in 1969. In order to complete my Doctorate at the University of Georgia I had to write a dissertation. I did not want to select a subject that would not have any meaning or future value. So many people write on something like "How Many Push-Ups a Rat Can Do" and it is placed in File 13 never to be heard from again.

I love history. The events that have taken place in the past help mold our future. What made great people tick helps us find ourselves and improve our own lives. In light of this, I decided to do a historical study involving the Origin and Development of Carson-Newman College Athletics since 1851. Except for changing the order of certain chapters and the addition of numerous pictures the actual dissertation has stayed the same to my regret. I wanted very much to write and tell events in a more creative way but lack of time and dissertation style would not permit.

Many athletes, teams and events have probably been left out but this was not intentional I assure you.

My main reasons for writing this book centered on my love for Carson-Newman College, its principles, intangible characteristics and especially its athletic program.

I have tried to bring out these points:

      1. The background of sport and especially the beginning of Carson-Newman athletics.
      2. The importance of athletics to a college or university.
      3. The importance of physical exercise, intramurals, or athletics to you as an individual.
      4. To bring alive events of the past.
      5. To link the past events with the future.
      6. To create more interest and pride of former athletes and students in C - N's total athletic and over-all program.
      7. To look ahead to what the future holds for CNC athletics.

For four long years I researched the many events, teams and people that appear in this writing. It now feels like I was in the huddle when a young quarterback named "Frosty" called the plays in the early twenties, or jumped for joy when 7' 3" Slim Shoun knocked the ball from the opposition's goal in 1927. I saw Ira Dance slug that guy in the football game of 1921 to give us the name of "Fighting Parsons"; was there during the construction of Butler Blanc; and as we went undefeated in football in the fall of 1936. I feel like I was there when the school bus of 1937 slammed into that trailer killing two basketball players. And was proud when the V-12 guys came in to guard our athletic heritage during the war stricken years of the middle forties.

## *It Gets Foggy at Mossy Creek*

The book's name itself came from the ole' master himself, "Frosty" Holt. I heard him say to us in the early sixties, "Boys, they might beat us over there, but it will be foggy at Mossy Creek." This meant that it was hard to beat the Eagles at Carson-Newman. It meant that the fog would roll into Burke-Tarr Stadium at just the right time; it would be hard to see our pitchers in the ninth inning because of the fog, or it would be hard for the visitors to see their goal in the fourth quarter at Holt Field House.

I would like to thank many people for making this book possible; Reece Tallent, who made the pictures on the cover showing the Old and New Administration Building, the Old Gymnasium (Butler Blanc) and Holt Field House with a double exposure of some fog and Mossy Creek rolling onto the campus; Mr. Tom Gentry and his staff (Paul Young, Pat Young, and Bonnie Spencer) at the Standard Publishing Company. Many other people are responsible for this book (see Acknowledgement Page) but present and former athletes, coaches, fans and you the reader are the real reasons this book could be possible. I want to thank most of all the Almighty Coach, God, for giving me a sound body and mind plus a lot of determination to finish this book.

The actual dissertation was finished in 1972 so the years of 1973 and 1974 are included in only pictures and bulletin form. I hope to write another volume every 5 or 10 years so the 73 and 74 statistics will be updated more in the next volume.

The Epic (located in the back of this book) which I have written tells some of the key events that have happened from 1851 to the present time. I feel that it will help tie together in summary form what you will read in this writing,

I hope you will enjoy reading this book as much as I have enjoyed researching and writing it and that your respect and appreciation for the athletic program will be elevated.

Sincerely,

Chris Jones


P. S. Let the "Fog" roll in!

## ACKNOWLEDGMENTS

I would like to thank all those who have helped in any way in the gathering of the data for this paper and especially the following persons; Dr. Ralph Johnson, my major professor, for the advice and assistance he has given; Dr. Robert Bowen, Dr. Marilyn Vincent, and Dr. Clifford Lewis for the support and help they have given as members of my committee; Miss Mildred Iddins and her staff in the help they have given in allowing the use of old records and books located in the Treasury Room of Carson-Newman College library; Coach "Frosty" Holt and Miss Mae Iddins for the scrapbooks and personal information they have given; Miss Helen Smithson for the assistance she has given in typing this paper; my parents, Mr. and Mrs. John H. Jones, for their influence and encouragement; my wife, Diane and our children Kip and Whitney for the support and love they have given during this writing; and last but not least all those athletes and coaches who have given of their time, energy and talents to make this paper possible.

*But they that wait upon the Lord shall renew their strength; they shall mount up with wings as EAGLES; they shall run, and not be weary; and they shall walk, and not faint.*

Isaiah 40: 31

# PREFACE

Competition, drive, goal striving, dedication, hard work, pride, enthusiasm, initiative, team work, the will to win, desire to excel, sacrifice, discipline, self-respect and respect for others are but a few components derived from athletics. Americans are competitive people by nature. They love to see a winner, a good fight or a hero. Athletics are a reminder to us as Americans why we have such a great nation today. A team begins to crumble when it has no togetherness, discipline, hard work or pride. A team that takes an apathetic attitude instead of a desire to excel approach will soon fall. This is true of our nation or any nation. This is also true of an individual life.

Hopefully, through these pages you will see the sacrifice and hard work of many C-N athletes, coaches and teams striving for victory, a better Carson-Newman and a better America.

Thousands of former Carson-Newman College athletes have and still are contributing in high style to our American society.

I firmly believe that those hot August football practices, those second half basketball comebacks, those extra inning baseball games, those grueling cross country and track practices, those long all-day tennis tournaments, those 2 ft. birdie putts to win or lose and the tough competition in wrestling, soccer and other sports have given these athletes something extra to face this tough game of life.

Paul put it this way in I Corinthians 9:24-27. In a race, everyone runs but only one person gets first prize. So run your race to win. To win the contest you must deny' yourselves many things that would keep you from doing your best. An athlete goes to all this trouble just to win a blue ribbon or a silver cup, but we do it for a heavenly reward that never disappears. So I run straight to the goal with purpose in every step. I fight to win. I'm not just shadow-boxing or playing around. Like an athlete I punish my body, treating it roughly, training it to do what it should, not what it wants to. Otherwise I fear that after enlisting others for the race, I myself might be declared unfit and ordered to stand aside.

## Presidents of Carson-Newman College | 1851 – 1974

Rev. R. R. Bryan
1851-1853; 1866-1888

Matthew Hillsman
1857-1859

Jessie Baker
1869-1870

N. B. Goforth
1871- 1871

W. T. Russell
1882-1889
Newman College

W. A. Montgomery
1888-1893

*It Gets Foggy at Mossy Creek*

John T. Henderson
1892-1903

M. D. Jeffries
1903-1912

J. M. Burnett
1912-1917

W. L. Gentry
1917-1919

Oscar L. Sams
1920-1927

James T. Warren
1927-1948

# *A History of Sports at Carson-Newman College 1851-1974*

Daniel Harley Fite
1948-1968

John A. Fincher
1968-1977

# CHAPTER I
# INTRODUCTION
# HISTORICAL BACKGROUND

Athletics or sports have developed over a period of many years to become an important part of our way of life. Our country has become a sports loving nation and nearly every family is in some way involved in sports. In many cases, athletics have been the one factor that has unified and built pride in schools and colleges, Today the average American male will turn first to the sports section of the newspaper; athletic events are regularly shown on television; and many athletes effectively advertise products since they are admired by the American public.

Never before in the history of our nation has the role of sports been as important as it is today, In a setting such as we have today, school athletics can make a positive contribution to physical well-being through skillful performance and through relaxation as well as by the inculcation of sound values. The achievement of such outcomes requires effective leadership, appropriate activities, good organization, and sound policies. Prior to the late nineteenth century and the early years of the twentieth century, such an administrative organization was virtually unknown (Bucher and Dupree, 1965: v).

The development of sports in the United States dates back to Colonial America. Since most of the population was rural, organized gymnastics and athletics found no place in the daily lives .of people. The colonists, with the exception of the group known as the Puritans, engaged in the games and recreational activities of their motherlands as time permitted. The significance of play and its possibilities as an important phase of the educational process were not understood; in fact, those who determined educational policies were opposed to the idea of physical education and sports (Rice, Hutchinson, Lee, 1969:137-38).

The character of education in the Colonial school in America was not conducive to development of competitive sports. For the most part, the schools were conducted by religious groups which had as their primary purpose to teach the student how to read the Bible and to understand and participate in the religious activities of the community. Public schools as a function of government were as yet unknown except in the pauper schools of some- of the colonies, where the community assumed some responsibility for the education of orphans and paupers. During the period of the Revolutionary War most of the schools were closed; other problems were more pressing than education. As the war years faded into the past and the newly formed Union began to gain a foothold and establish itself, there was a growing agitation for establishment of tax-supported schools (Scott, 1951:11). Although not tax-supported, the most important school to emerge out of this time was the academy. The people were beginning to separate civic responsibilities from religious beliefs and activities. The newly found democratic philosophy was filtering into the minds and institutions of the people. The academy at that time represented a more liberal and democratic educational philosophy and offered a much broader curriculum than other schools of the period. While the academies continued to reflect the religious interest of the community, they were non-denominational. Their purpose was to prepare the student for social life in the community. Consequently, good health, physical work, play, and recreation were considered

# *A History of Sports at Carson-Newman College 1851-1974*

to be relatively important phases of the curriculum. By the time the Union was formed, there were a number of such schools, including Andover and Exeter. Probably the first school actually to incorporate games and sports into its curriculum was the Dummer Grammer School at Byfield, Massachusetts, in 1782. It is also quite likely that Benjamin Franklin's Academy in Philadelphia encouraged considerable participation in sports and games, since Franklin himself was an ardent advocate of swimming and other physical recreation (Scott, 1951: 11-12),

The development of education in institutions of higher learning in America followed the same general pattern established in the lower schools. Harvard, founded in 1636, was the first of the colleges to be established in the new world. The federal government, although not directly responsible for public education, saw the wisdom of establishing state institutions of higher learning. Accordingly they found a way to provide grants of land to be used by territories seeking statehood to found systems of public education. The move to establish state universities was slow in gaining headway, however, as many felt that colleges were only for the well-to-do and relatively few students could meet the college requirements. Despite the assistance from the federal government, only 17 out of 246 colleges existing in 1860 were state institutions. In 1862 Congress passed the Morrill Act which gave grants in aid to the land-grant colleges to stimulate the development of agriculture and engineering. This act was to exert a profound influence upon the development of state universities and agricultural and mechanical colleges (Scott, 1951: 13).

In 1820, the first college gymnasium was constructed at Harvard University. Although privately owned, it was maintained for the use of Harvard students. It was well equipped with German apparatus of the day. Other gymnasiums followed: Williams College in 1851—a gymnasium with baths, owned and controlled by the students; University of Virginia in 1852--a building destroyed during the Civil War; Miami University (Ohio) in 1857--a building renting for $60 per year. Harvard University, in 1859 constructed a building that cost $8,000 including the cost of equipment. The new Harvard gymnasium was an octagonal building of brick and was a gift of the class of 1882. It had two bowling alleys and dressing rooms but no baths, and was opened in 1860 to all students for a two dollar fee per term. This was the beginning of gymnasiums/, as each college began to add this facility to its campus to meet the demands of the student body (Rice, Hutchinson, Lee, 1969:167).

American sports, as we know them, originated in the period of internal conflict after the Civil War. Baseball and tennis became popular in that order. Golf, bowling, Swimming, basketball, and a multitude of other so-called minor sports made their appearance in the latter half of the nineteenth century. American football also started its rise to popularity during that period. The Amateur Athletic Union, organized in 1888, gave invaluable service toward the promotion of legitimate amateur sport (Scott, 1951:14).

From the outset, colleges took the position that games and sports were not necessarily a part of the educational program. Interest was so intense, however, that the wishes of the students could not be denied. They were anxious to demonstrate their abilities in the various sports against young men from other institutions; thus from 1850 to 1880 the rise of interest in intercollegiate sports was phenomenal. Rowing, baseball, track and field, football, and later basketball, were the major sports (Scott, 1951:14-15).

## It Gets Foggy at Mossy Creek

The first intercollegiate contest recorded in the United States was a race between the boat clubs of Harvard and Yale on Lake Winnipesaukee in New Hampshire on August 2, 1852. The .match was won by Harvard. This first intercollegiate event received little notice in the papers, although it was advertised by circulars distributed widely by the railroad company which sponsored the event in the interest of bringing vacationers to the area. Excursion trains were run for the contest and a brass band was hired to add a festive note to the occasion. In 1855 the two schools held another rowing match, this time in Springfield, Massachusetts, and again Harvard won. In 1859 the four schools that had organized the College Regatta Association (Amherst, Brown, Bowdoin, and Harvard) staged the first intercollegiate regatta on Lake Quinsigamond at Worcester, Massachusetts. By this time much public interest had arisen in these rowing matches and over 15,000 spectators turned out for the event. THE NEW YORK HERALD gave-three and one-half columns on the front page to the story, and postgame enthusiasm got out of control to the point that a battle developed between the students and police which ended in the calling off of all contests for the next five years (Rice, Hutchinson, Lee, 1969:155).

The second sport to enter the intercollegiate arena was baseball. The earliest record of an intercollegiate match is of a game in Pittsfield, Massachusetts, in July 1859, when Amherst won over Williams by a score of 66 to 32 (Scott, 1951:16),

From their beginning, the women's academies and colleges favored participation of their women in sports and games as well as in gymnastics and dancing. By the 1870's American college women were skating, riding sidesaddle, forming walking clubs, and playing tennis. The girls at Vassar were even playing baseball. Also at this time, gymnastic demonstrations and gymnastic-drill contests became popular, especially with college women.

Intercollegiate competition for women began soon after the game of basketball was created. Several women's colleges in the East located near each other began playing the game in interschool contests, but Miss Berenson, the originator of the women's game, was opposed to such contests (Rice, Hutchinson, Lee, 1969:197).

Since team sports were so new for girls and women, competition between teams was chaotic at first; college teams; high school teams, and out-of-school women's teams all played against each other indiscriminately, perhaps not so much because of a failure to understand the need for discrimination as from inability to find teams of one's own age group to challenge. Except in the colleges, practically all teams were coached by men, showing the great lack of women physical education teachers around 1900 (Williams, 1930; 114).

Today the athletic successes of women from other countries are reflected in Olympic competition and resulted in a renewed desire on the part of many educators and public-minded citizens to stress sports for the gifted women athletes. The trend would appear to be in the direction of providing more opportunities for girls and women to participate in school and college competitive sports (Rice, Hutchinson, Lee, 1969: 360).

Because intercollegiate competition in sports was inevitable from the start, it was logical that colleges of similar size, ideals, and geographical location should form an association for intercollegiate control. Similarly, when competition commenced to go outside of a rather

# *A History of Sports at Carson-Newman College 1851-1974*

narrowly defined geographical area, some organization of a national character was equally inevitable (Cozens and Stumpf, 1953:89).

Wars, terrible as they are, often cause an accelerated development in many fields of human endeavor-- in medicine, in industrial production, and certainly in sports. It may be that professional educators would have succeeded eventually in setting up compulsory physical education programs in American schools had there been no World War I, It is a matter of record, however, that preparation for participation in World War I produced cultural pressures which resulted in the passage of such state legislation (Cozens and Stumpf, 1953:79),

No one thing or no one set of circumstances produced the sports program in the schools. Rather, such programs came from a combination of circumstances sparked by almost universal physical education requirements throughout the nation. In other words, had it not been for the requirement, the millions of boys and girls of school age would not have had the exposure to the program which was afforded them. Schools found themselves lacking in personnel, equipment, and facilities. But almost immediately a number of states followed the example of California in introducing into the program of physical education sports skills and tests for these skills to motivate progress in their acquisition. Thus a gradual change from a gymnastic to a sports program developed in the years between World War I and the early 1930's (Cozens and Stumpf, 1953:80).

The depression of 1929 did not immediately affect the school situation, but by 1932 the schools were hard hit. Budgets were cut, teachers' salaries were lowered, and teaching loads were heavier due to increases in student enrollment. Physical education along with art and music experienced some difficulty. Equipment and facilities were drastically curtailed, and expenditures were carefully checked. Interschool competition involving out-of-town trips was often eliminated. Smaller schools, in order to economize, adopted a new type of football--six man football. Competition in this activity spread rapidly and by 1941 it was played in forty-five states. Intercollegiate football attendance reached its lowest level in 1932 but thereafter started to increase. The sale of sporting goods declined 57 percent from 1929 to 1933, partly due to export and partly to the financial condition of the nation as a whole (Cozens and Stumpf, 1953:82).

However, out of the depression came some things favorable to the development of sports in the schools. A considerable share of WPA and PWA funds was used for the building of school sports facilities--gymnasiums, swimming pools, tennis courts, and athletic fields. By 1937 it was estimated that $75,000,000 had been spent for such projects. It appears to be a reasonable assumption that the inclusion of many individual sports in the school program of physical education came as a direct result of cultural pressures during the 1930's (Cozens and Stumpf, 1953:83).

At the beginning of World War II, the talk of physical fitness centered around the value of sports in the building of morale as well as in the building of physical stamina necessary to successful prosecution of the war. Interscholastic and intercollegiate competition were very definitely handicapped during the war period. The depletion of manpower in many colleges and universities resulted in the abandonment of competitive schedules. Other institutions, particularly those which were training Navy personnel, played a limited schedule with a reduction in long trips and time given to practice (Cozens and Stumpf, 1953:87).

Long before the end of World War II, leaders in all aspects of our culture were giving serious consideration to what should be done in postwar America. Physical fitness continued to receive a considerable share of attention; swimming programs were emphasized; the question was raised as to whether a game program was sufficient to obtain physical fitness; the needs of the veterans returning to college were considered to be of particular importance; the old question of too much time spent on the stars to the neglect of the masses was given attention; the broadening of the competitive athletic program for boys and girls received special consideration (Cozens and Stumpf, 1953:88-89).

Without question the sports program that developed slowly during the nineteenth century had by the middle of the twentieth century crowded the traditional and formal required physical education program out of the schools. Although there was a tremendous increase in participation in sports since World War II, there was still a great interest throughout the country in watching sports competition, both professional and amateur, so that sports coverage took up much of both radio and television time, as well as much space in the newspapers. Also, many new periodicals were established which catered exclusively to the sports scene (Cozens and Stumpf, 1953:151-152).

Since World War II, the United States has used athletes as goodwill ambassadors to various foreign countries and has sent athletic coaches to backward countries to help them set up athletic programs a. prepare teams for Olympic and other international competition (Menke, 1960:761).
There is much international competition in sports going on all over the world, promoted by a variety of organizations and sponsored by a variety of interests. Of all these international contests, none arouses as much national interest as the Olympic Games that are held every four years. These games date back to the early Greeks and the modern Olympics which began in 1912 have become an important part of our society today (Menke, 1953:757).

## CARSON—NEWMAN, ITS PROGRESS AND DEVELOPMENT

In Tennessee, as in nearly all the Atlantic Seaboard states, academies flourished and furnished educational opportunities which were later offered on a much broader base by public elementary and high schools. The academies were usually private and tuition was charged for most students. There was ample evidence that Baptists felt they were not performing their full duty unless they, too, set up an educational institution. The founding of Mossy Creek Baptist Seminary which later became Carson-Newman College was an outgrowth of the ideals and dreams of people who lived in the eastern section of Tennessee (Hall, unpublished Master's thesis, 1937:3).

In September of 1851, the college, Mossy Creek, opened its first session in the Baptist church building of Mossy Creek. People of the surrounding area had furnished most of the money and plans were developed for the construction of the three original buildings. Bricks were to be burned in a local kiln and there was adequate soil nearby for making them with much of

# *A History of Sports at Carson-Newman College 1851-1974*

the labor for this task and that of construction work being donated. Money was used to purchase hardware, books, apparatus, and other necessary equipment (Carr, 1959:11, 17).

The original leaders were men of courage and vision, planning for the future of the Baptist denomination and the East Tennessee area. Financing a college was a great undertaking and they found themselves with a difficult task, but a beginning had to be made. They persevered and were able to carry out the plans which had been formulated. After President Rogers' death, Professor Bryan gook charge of the institution as both president and teacher through the period of 1851-1853. "More than once he had to teach all courses offered." In 1853, he was succeeded in the President's office by Dr. Samuel Anderson and Professor Bryan remained as a teacher until the institution was closed in 1862 (Carr, 1959:17-18).

The name of the institution was changed on December 5, 1855, to "Mossy Creek Baptist College." This was done by the Legislature of Tennessee as an amendment of the original charter. This act made no other significant change in the status of the college. The reason for the change given by several older people was that the college was a liberal arts institution and not a seminary devoted to the special training of ministers. The curriculum had been expanded, and it was felt that the college was well on the road toward academic recognition and stability (Carr, 1959:18).

The college progressed and there was an increase in the number of students until the effects of the Civil War were felt. The Mossy Creek Institution was in the geographic center of the war-torn area. The war completed the disintegration of the college as the students, one by one, and sometimes in groups, put on uniforms and went away to contribute their part in the war. Since it was a college for men only, there were no students left after the commencement in 1862 and the doors of the college were closed. Soon after, all the college buildings were converted into quarters and barracks for Union soldiers. During their stay of approximately three years, the three brick structures were almost entirely dismantled. The doors, windows, window casings and many joists, with some flooring, were destroyed or badly damaged. The walls of the building had large-sized holes battered through them (Hall, 1937:25).

The college reopened in September of 1868 and the prospects were bright, provided financial needs could be met. At the time the college was closed in 1862, it was practically bankrupt with a considerable debt. In 1869, Dr. Jesse Baker, an alumnus of the college and an associate professor since 1868, was chosen by the Board of Trustees as president. The total indebtedness of the college was found to be approximately $6,000. Dr. Baker secured the aid of William T. Russell as a faculty member who operated the college while Dr. Baker left to solicit the money. During the session 1869-1870, Dr. Baker rode 3,500 miles on horseback and secured $5,250 in cash and pledges. By the end of the year, Dr. Baker had paid the debts, and the college was free from indebtedness for the first time in its history (Carr, 1959:24-25).

On January 23, 1880, the name of the college was changed by resolution of the Board of Trustees to that Of Carson College. The change was to become effective at the beginning of the spring semester of 1880 (Carr, 1959:32).

In June of 1882, the community and college experienced a terrible epidemic of smallpox. Many became seriously ill and there were several deaths. It was reported that a large number of townspeople died. As the number of victims daily became greater, many students went home with the hope of avoiding the contagious malady. Illness struck down at least one faculty member. President Manard's courage reached a low level and both he and Professor S. E. Jones resigned and left the college in haste. President Manard never returned. The epidemic was practically over by the beginning of the second semester. Later, Professor Jones returned to the college to continue teaching. Despite the ravages of the epidemic, the college opened in the fall of 1883 with a normal enrollment (Carr, 1959:35).

Newman College, a college for young women, was founded during this period since much interest had been manifested in educating girls and young women in the area. Nineteen students graduated from the college during the six years of its existence, and twenty-four students remained in the college for the first year the school operated as united coeducational institution. Some twenty students from the preparatory division entered the college division at the same time (Carr, 1959: 36).

In August of 1889, Carson College for men and Newman College for women became united and were called Carson and Newman College. The future college was planned on property which Newman College purchased. The colleges continued their preparatory department but enlarged the curriculum (Carr, 1959:52).

## THE COLLEGE - SPORTS

In the early days, college athletic activities at Carson-Newman were organized to allow every student who was interested an opportunity to participate. Teams were chosen by student leaders, who divided the student body into equal groups in terms of ability. Soon after the college was organized, all young men participated in various sports on an informal intramural basis. These sports included baseball, and a little later, a "rough and tumble" type of football. The recreational program was often unorganized, but included hunting, fishing, and swimming. Young men whose homes were in the community sometimes invited other students to their homes on weekends and on week nights for fox chasing, using both trained and untrained hound dogs. Many times these hunts would extend into the nearby Smokies or the Cumberlands. Both fishing and swimming groups visited the Holston River which was about three miles away or the French River some ten miles from the campus (Carr, 1959:259).

On April 27, 1895, Carson-Newman had its first intercollegiate contest when the baseball team of Carson-Newman met The University of Tennessee and defeated them 4 to 3. That same year organized football also appeared on the campus and a game was also played with The University of Tennessee. The University was leading by a wide margin at the half, but during the second half they were unable to score on Carson-Newman. By the session of 1911, basketball was established with a men's team that was undefeated (Carr, 1959:259-68). Since that time Carson-Newman has reached a point of national recognition in nearly all sports.

On December 13, 1916, a campus fire completely destroyed the Administration Building. Destruction included the library laboratory, art and business department equipment. Some permanent records were preserved but many were destroyed in the fire. Included in some of these records were those relating to athletics at the college (Carr, 1959:76).

## CONCLUSION

Historical research in education may include studies of individuals (biographies), studies of school systems or institutions; studies of ideas and patterns; legal studies involving constitutional provisions for schools, charters, and court decisions (Bledsoe, 1953:52). This research was a study of the sports program from its beginning at Carson-Newman College to the present year, 1972, and the role it has played in the advancement of the college.

The discussion of the history of sports in the United States and Carson-Newman College provided the background for the statement of the problem of this research. The statement of the problem with the specific objectives, limitations, and basic assumptions follow in the next section of this chapter.

## STATEMENT OF THE PROBLEM

The purpose of this research was to investigate and record the history of Carson-Newman College athletics from 1851 to the present time (1972). The specific objectives of this study were: (1) to determine the early development, administration, and organization of intercollegiate athletics at Carson-Newman College; (2) to include the Modern period (1970-1972) and a look at what many of the former coaches, faculty, and athletes think the future holds for Carson-Newman College; (3) to trace the history of the following programs within Carson-Newman College: football, basketball, baseball, track, cross country, tennis, golf, wrestling and soccer; (4) to refer to outstanding athletes, coaches, and teams of Carson-Newman College, including the outstanding women athletes especially during the earlier years when Carson-Newman provided an intercollegiate program for women.

This study was limited to the athletic program at Carson-Newman College and included only those events dealing with the athletic program. Four specific limitations were included: (1) the study was limited to athletics at Carson-Newman College and did not include the program of the other schools in the Smoky Mountain Athletic Conference or the National Association of Intercollegiate Athletics; (2) it did not include any other activities at the college such as the intramural program for men; (3) the athletic program for women was included and their intramural program after the college discontinued intercollegiate athletics for women was included; (4) teams, individuals, playing facilities and other pertinent material were included.

The basic assumptions of this study were: (1) that there would be educational value in conducting research in the history of athletics at Carson-Newman College; and (2) that the data were available to conduct the research.

## SIGNIFICANCE OF THE PROBLEM

The progress of any program can be measured by its history. The data can be used to compare the present with the past with respect to the importance and influences of the program. This constitutes a record of experiments and achievements and also demonstrates the relationship which exists between certain elements in civilization and the role of the subject in a particular society. Through the study of history, a broad and appreciative view of the subject can be obtained (Rice, Hutchinson, and Lee, 1969: iii).

The athletic program has made a substantial contribution to the progress of Carson-Newman College. Football, basketball, baseball, tennis, golf, and wrestling teams have received national recognition which has helped to publicize the college and to attract more students. Athletics at Carson-Newman have created a unity and school spirit which have helped to draw the student body closer together. While many of the early leaders are deceased or retire, a few of the outstanding ones were able to provide an account of the early events in Carson-Newman athletics.

This study then becomes significant, relevant, and opportune in order that the history of the athletic program at this liberal arts college be recorded for posterity. Athletes who attend the college in future years will be able to review the history of the athletic program and realize the pride and tradition that has preceded them. The principles established by the former athletes will serve as examples for these young men and help them to formulate desirable goals. It will also be a source of reference for newspapers, coaches, athletes, alumni, and the public.

## REVIEW OF RELATED LITERATURE

THE CARSON-NEWMAN COLLEGE COLLEGIAN was issued monthly, September to June, by the students and in it was found athletic information about events that occurred during that period of time.

THE CARSON INDEX was published monthly during the collegiate year by the literary societies of Carson College and told of the events which took place on the campus, including athletics.

THE CARSON-NEWMAN MAGAZINE was published monthly after the union of Carson College and Newman College. It was published by the literary societies and provided accounts of events which took place on the campus.

The CARSON-NEWMAN COLLEGE CATALOGUE, published by the college, provided pertinent information dealing with the students. The catalogue contains information such as eligibility of students, required courses and requirements the students must meet to attend Carson-Newman.

The APPALACHIAN is the college yearbook in which can be found the athletic section with write-ups and pictures of each sport for that school year.

In 1959 Dr. Isaac Newton Carr published HISTORY OF CARSON-NEWMAN COLLEGE which gives a comprehensive history of the college. He included in his book a brief sketch of the early athletic program. An unpublished Master's thesis by W.F. Hall on the history of Carson-Newman College was completed in 1937.

# *A History of Sports at Carson-Newman College 1851-1974*

John Billing-ton wrote a Master's thesis in 1953 about the life of Sam B. "Frosty" Holt. In the study he related the life of Coach Holt while at Carson-Newman for a period of nearly fifty years. This included the time he spent as a student as well as his coaching years at Carson-Newman.

**METHODS AND PROCEDURES**

Three sources were used to collect data--interview, questionnaire, and printed material:

1. Questionnaire study - The various categories of persons to be sent questionnaires concerning the historical incidents, characteristics, trends, progress and influences of the athletic program of Carson-Newman College were:

    (a) Persons living in Jefferson City, Tennessee
    (b) Former and present faculty members of Carson-Newman College
    (c) Former and present coaches at Carson-Newman
    (d) Former and present students who did not participate in athletics at Carson-Newman
    (e) Former and present athletes of Carson-Newman
    (a) Former and present opponent coaches of Carson-Newman
    (b) Former and present women involved in intramurals of intercollegiate athletics at Carson-Newman.

Separate questionnaire forms were prepared for each category with questions that persons could logically answer. A form letter was sent with the questionnaire explaining the scope and purpose of the study and giving the types of general information most desired.

2. Interview study. Thirteen categories of persons were interviewed in connection with this study. The first seven categories were the same as those of the seven categories listed under the questionnaire classifications, with questions identical with those used in the questionnaires.

The other sources were as follows:

    (a) Coach Sam B. "Frosty" bolt
    (a) Coach Lake Russell
    (b) Miss Mae Iddins
    (c) Bus driver, Arkie Jarnigan
    (d) Eugene Wright, Charlie Bryant, and Maurice Joyce

Present and former staff members.

The interviewing of Coach Holt, Coach Russell and Miss Iddins consisted of questions of a historical nature. They were asked their philosophy of life and of physical education and athletics. Eugene Wright and Maurice Joyce were asked question concerning their part in starting the golf and rugby teams on the Carson-Newman campus. Charlie Bryant was asked questions pertaining to the renewal of track on the campus... The bus driver, Arkie Jarnigan, was interviewed concerning the 1937 bus accident in which two players were killed.

3. The historical method,

   (a) Newspaper accounts. Significant historical data were taken from the KNOXVILLE, NEWS SENTINEL and the KNOXVILLE JOURNAL, Knoxville, Tennessee; CHATTANOOGA TIMES, Chattanooga, Tennessee: WASHINGTON HERALD (presently the TIMES-HERALD), Washington. D.C.: and MORRISTOWN TRIBUNE. Morristown. Tennessee.

   (b) Carson-Newman College publications. Various data of historical significance were taken from the CARSON-NEWMAN COLLEGE BULLETIN, CARSON-NEWMAN COLLEGE CATALOGUES, THE ORANGE AND BLUE (the school paper), and numerous copies of the APPALACHIAN (the school yearbook),

   (c) Other sources:

   (1) Scrapbooks of Miss Mae Iddins and Coach "Frosty" Holt
   (2) THE HISTORY OF CARSON—NEWMAN COLLEGE by Isaac Newton Carr
   (3) A Biography of S. B. Holt by John E. Billington (Master's thesis)
   (4) A History of Carson-Newman College by W.F. Hall (Master's thesis)
   (5) Minutes, Board of Trustees, Carson-Newman College.

## CHAPTER II

## EARLY HISTORY

## 1881 - 1919

Before Carson College united with Newman College, some attention was turned to the physical concerns of the students. Professor B.G. Manard emphasized the laws of hygiene and discussed the types and amount of food to be eaten. He stated that ability to study depended upon the state of one's physical constitution. Students were quoted in the CARSON INDEX (published monthly during the collegiate year by the literary societies of Carson College) (December, 1882:52) as saying that it required more self-denial than many of them possessed,

The CARSON INDEX (October: 4) of 1882 1883 stated that it was of the highest importance for students to have correct ideas of the "laws of health" and that they should take exercises that would be "conducive to physical and mental vigor." The freshmen class members were required to attend lectures on physiology and hygiene. The hope was expressed that the college would soon have a suitable gymnasium and that regular and systematic exercise would be a part of the program offered the students.

The idea of the physical in education was mentioned again in the spring of 1883 when one of the first graduation speakers, J. T. Henderson presented his subject, "True Culture" which included physical, mental, moral, and spiritual attributes. He dwelt especially on the physical as he felt it was being neglected in many colleges in spite of its importance (CARSON INDEX, June, 1883:4).

The CARSON INDEX (April, 1883:3, 9) also mentioned certain skills which could be used in athletic events. An example was given of a student, C.E. Harris, who told how he killed a rabbit by hitting it in the head with a rock. Also, the same reference mentioned the organization of three local baseball teams in Jefferson City. College men could participate, but the team was not connected with the college in any way.

The first time Carson College for men specifically encouraged physical exercise was in the 1886 1887 edition of the CARSON CATALOGUE (Catalogue published yearly by Carson College) (13). It stated that the relationship between body and mind emphasized physical health as being essential to proper mental growth. Because of this, each student was required to take daily exercise in calisthenics.

In 1889, a merger between Carson College for men and Newman College for women was completed. Both colleges were located in Jefferson City, Tennessee, but it was not until the two boards of trustees voted for merger that they united to become one (Carr, 1959). Athletics prior to that time was non-existent. Most of the competition was mental instead of physical and recognition, awards, and trophies were won for lectures and debates (CARSON INDEX, December, 1882:45), but not for athletics. There was a ,time when a student delighted in looking "thing, pale, and hollow eyed" for the sake of having someone compliment him for his so called "studious appearance" (CARSON NEWMAN

COLLEGIAN, September, 1912:52). The feeling was that all work must precede play (CARSON INDEX, September, 1882:4).

The first required physical exercise after the merger of the two schools was conducted in 1891 in one of the halls of the new building on campus. A half hour each day was devoted to exercise with dumb-bells.

In 1892-1893, the administration began a push for athletics and physical education. This was recognized in the catalogue for that year, as indicated by the mention of: Athletic Association President, girls and boys required physical culture, Field Day, equipment for the physical education program and the hiring of Directors for the Physical Exercise program. R.A. Henderson was named Director for the men and Mrs. Hassie Brown for the women. Baseball, running, jumping, and all other athletic sports were encouraged (CARSON-NEWMAN CATALOGUE, 1892-1893:32-33). Other faculty members who were responsible for directing the young ladies' physical drill during the next few years were Mrs. L.D. Phillips (1895-1897), a teacher of elocution; Miss Lavina Tennessee Jenkins (1897-1902), a full time teacher of history; and Miss Mattie LeGrande (1902-1903), a teacher of elocution and art.

All students, except the few who were excused because of physical disability, engaged in the exercises. The young ladies met in the large halls of the new college, and young men met on the campus when the weather would permit (CARSON-NEWMAN CATALOGUE. 1892-1893:2). It was thought that the exercise program was beneficial to the health of the students and the progress they showed in their studies was considered to be gratifying. It was reported that there had never before been so little sickness among so many students (CARSON-NEWMAN CATALOGUE, 1892-1893:3)

## FIRST ORGANIZED COMPETITION

The first organized athletic event held on the campus was a field day held on June 3, 1893, with prizes given by the local merchants. The Athletic Association of that year, with L.B. DeArmond as its president, was regarded as an important organization, and was encouraged by the administration in every way. There were eleven prizes awarded by the Association to the several winners in the athletic contest and were listed as (CARSON-NEWMAN CATALOGUE, 1892-1893:32-33):

| | |
|---|---|
| Two Hundred and Twenty Yard Dash | W.S. Wilson |
| One Hundred Yard Dash | W.S. Wilson |
| Three legged Race | C. Fairfield and W. DeVault |
| Long distance throw | Luther Shanks |
| One mile walk | W.D. Devault |
| High Jump | J.B. Bundren |
| High Kick | J.B. Bundren |
| Running Jump | Luther Shanks |
| Hurdle Race | E.L. Edington |

# A History of Sports at Carson-Newman College 1851-1974

Participation in Field Day Showed track to be as popular as baseball and both were encouraged on an intramural basis.

In 1894-1895, the college catalogue (CARSON-NEWMAN CATALOGUE, 31) suggested that the administration still felt that school duties must come before play. Baseball, running, jumping, and all other athletic sports were encouraged but athletics had to be subordinate to the regular school duties.

Many of the skills used by the student in athletics were learned as they grew up on the farm. The CARSON AND NEWMAN MAGAZINE (published monthly by the Literary Societies of Carson-Newman College from 1896 to 1902) of 1896 (June: 105) stated that Thomas Granville Davis spent his early days on the farm and that before his teens were over he had distinguished himself as a good horseman. The magazine also related that Branford Dougherty was an expert ox-driver and could manage six yoke at one time.

## FIRST INTERCOLLEGIATE ATHLETIC TEAM

By 1895 the ground work was laid for Carson-Newnan's first intercollegiate athletics and on April 27, 1895, Carson-Newman won a baseball game against The University of Tennessee by a score of 4 to 3.

The members of the team were (ALUMNI BULLETIN, October, 1948:12):

| | |
|---|---|
| L. E. Hill | Left Field |
| Frank Rhoton | Right Field |
| Nelson | Pitcher |
| James Johnson | Catcher |
| Claude Godwin | 3rd Base |
| Gus Gowers | Umpire |
| Ramsey | Left Field |
| L.M. Beeler | 2nd Base |
| James Floyd | Shortstop |
| Ray Godwin | 1st Base |
| James Moreland | Mascot |

In referring to baseball games played during that time, it was stated that the catcher had neither mask nor glove and usually caught balls behind the bat on the first bounce. The players on bases and in the field frequently did not possess gloves and caught the ball with bare hands. To many of them a glove signified a tenderfoot, and most of them wished to be regarded as tough or as real "he-men" (Carr, 1959:259).

## ORGANIZED FOOTBALL

Organized football also appeared on the campus in the fall of the same year when the game was instituted by Luther M. Beeler and a student, James S. Floyd. Beeler had completed his

## It Gets Foggy at Mossy Creek

training at Carson College and had entered Yale University, where he studied for two years. While a student at Yale, he also studied the game of football and after returning to his home in Jefferson City, he became a volunteer coach of the new Carson-Newman team. Floyd was the captain and quarterback of the first Carson-Newman College football team (Carr, 1959:260).

After a few seasons, when some football enthusiasts had graduated, interest dropped. The next team was organized in 1903 under the leadership of Professor Luther Birdwell DeArmond, manager, director of athletics, and teacher of business courses. Claude Taylor of Bristol, Tennessee, was coach; and Clarence A. Bales, a student, was captain (CARSON-NEWMAN CATALOGUE, 1903-1904: 8-9).

The college participated as a member of the East Tennessee Football Association, an organization which included some secondary schools, such as the Tennessee School for Deaf and Dumb and the Baker-Himel School. The Knoxville Y.M.C.A. was also included on the schedule, The association issued an announcement that the bulletin "affords an excellent keepsake as showing the brawny men who struggled on the field for their college during the year 1903 but it will serve to furnish, to a large degree, an idea of the composite of the teams of 1904 which will struggle again for supremacy" (Bulletin of East Tennessee Football Association, published for Members, 1903: 11).

Even though the 1903 team did not win the Championship, they played creditable football and otherwise did well considering their limitations (Carr, 1959:261).
A player had to have endurance, and he was trained to take hard knocks. Nose guards, outside shoulder pads, cleats in regular shoes, and a baseball uniform constituted regular equipment. If a player did not have a baseball suit, he could obtain a pair of khaki trousers used by the United States Army (Carr, 1 959:262).

Much emphasis was placed on conditioning the players as they had to play the whole game, which were two forty-five minute periods. A substitution could be made only for an injury or other good reason. A man removed from the game could not be returned during the game. The forward pass had not come into existence but the drop kick was much in vogue. The game was rough and it took a good man to play an hour and a half (BULLETIN OF CARSON-NEWMAN COLLEGE, October, 1948:5).

During the following years at Carson-Newman, conditions remained almost static, In the 1907-1908 season, a new rule was made for athletics which stated that if any student failed to pass or make conditional marks in two studies he would not be eligible to play on any team during' the next term that he attended the college. The football schedule remained much the same and the interest of the students grew as they learned more about the game. But, because of the fatal injury of a football player in a game with Bingham Military Institute, Asheville, North Carolina, during the 1907-1908 season, "the sport was reluctantly discontinued by the college community" and was not brought back until 1913. During the time football was not played, the athletic program centered on baseball and basketball (Carr, 1959:263).

# *A History of Sports at Carson-Newman College 1851-1974*

## TENNIS AND BASKETBALL INTRODUCED

In 1908 both tennis and basketball were introduced as recognized college sports, Basketball was first played on outside courts but this was changed under President J.M. Burnett's administration. The platform of the college auditorium was used as a basketball court by the varsity teams of both men and women. Since the same platform was used for dramatics and nearly all public programs of the college. It was necessary to maintain a rigid schedule for its use" (Carr, 1959:263).

Around 1911, a movement was started among the college classes which resulted in the organization of teams in basketball, baseball, tennis and track to compete for a cup that would be offered to the class winning the most points. The faculty heartily endorsed the movement and promised to give one day in May for the college field-day at which time the final contests would be arranged. It was felt this movement would help create a college spirit which was necessary for the success of the college (CARSON -NEWMAN COLLEGIAN, Issued monthly, September to June, by the students of Carson-Newman, April, 1911:39).

THE CARSON-NEWMAN COLLEGIAN (April, 1911: 39-40) devoted a special article to tennis and its advantages. It mentioned tennis as the "universal game" which "afforded the best physical exercise." It stated that football and baseball were only for boys but that both boys and girls could participate in tennis. Tennis was described as providing better physical exercise than either of the other games as every muscle of the body was brought into use and it also had the advantages of open air exercise without the disadvantage of the rougher games. Tennis was also said to be the most scientific game on campus, unless it was the "highly perfected" baseball game. The article made mention of the complex situations a player was placed in when playing tennis and stated that "only the quickest action of the brain could relieve the strain and save the game." Taking everything into consideration, "it was the most beneficial game on campus and if everyone would become aware of its many advantages there would be more tennis enthusiasts.

The Tennis Club on campus was organized at the beginning of the 1911 school term with thirty-five members. There was such a demand for the tennis courts that assignments had to be made. It was proposed that each student select a partner and locate a court and clear it off. The courts would then be theirs until the end of the term. Enough courts for thirty-four players were developed. Only members of the Tennis Club were permitted to play on the courts and the club had to support itself financially (CARSON-NEWMAN COLLEGIAN, April, 1911; 37).

In order to have athletics at Carson Newman for the 1912 session, a proposition was placed before the students asking for an athletic fee of one dollar, which would entitle them to free admission to all athletic contests during the spring term. Prior to that time athletics had been financed by whatever means the managers of the teams could devise and teams were usually found to be in arrears every season (CARSON- NEWMAN COLLEGIAN, April, 1911:37).

It was felt that all students be required to pay something each year for athletics because an athletic program would be impossible without funds. To the student who felt it unfair because he never attended an athletic contest, the argument was advanced that a library fee was charged and that some people never read the books, papers, and magazines in the library. Also, it was noted that other schools in the area were charging the athletic fee (CARSON-NEWMAN COLLEGIAN, December, 1911:37).

Dana X. Bible, while a student wrote in the school paper (CARSON-NEWMAN COLLEGIAN, September, 1911: 33).

> People have ever realized the need of the physical as well as the moral and the intellectual development of the races. Athletics are not, as some say, a time killer but they stand for that which develops muscle; that which intensifies speed and power of muscular action.
>
> The successful students are the ones who not only study hard during the school hours but also allow for recreation. A part of each day should be devoted to physical exercise, and the best physical exercise is some kind of game. This would release the mind from worry, and worry and study together would make a physical wreck of any man. Study and play, however, would put one's name on the honor roll. Studying all day the brain would likely recall the thoughts that had been passing through it during the day; a review of these thoughts could produce worry. But if part of the afternoon was given to play then one would be ready to undertake the difficult tasks. Play was made to rest the brain. When the time for retiring comes one would sleep better and the mind would be clearer on arising in the morning. A proper amount of study, well spiced with sunny sport, is almost absolutely necessary for the formation of firm, hardy physical constitution and a cheerful and happy mind.

It was reported in 1911 that basketball seemed to be showing progress in college class competition and that never before had there been so much interest taken in the game. The teams were representing each class and a suggestion was made that the four college classes-- freshman, sophomore, junior, seniors-- play a series of eight games and that the winner be presented a large class pennant by the three losing teams (CARSON-NEWMAN COLLEGIAN, December, 1911:35).

The girls were not to be overlooked for they were said to be more athletic than the boys during the year of 1912. Many of them would arise around five o'clock to play basketball; their devotion resulted in over forty girls with the ability to pass the ball and make goals as skillfully as any boy in college. It was said that a selection from the group would make a team from other colleges look like "thirty cents" (CARSON- NEWMAN COLLEGIAN, December, 1911:36).

Since the athletic fee was enforced, a college basketball team was made possible. It was at first felt to be a disadvantage as there had not been a college team the previous year. Later when the men showed up for the season, things looked promising. The students and faculty showed much interest in the possibility of a creditable team for the college. For those who did not make the college basketball team, there were class teams on which they could participate and each class organized a team to try to beat the other teams (CARSON-NEWMAN COLLEGIAN, October, 1912:52).

# *A History of Sports at Carson-Newman College 1851-1974*

## UNDEFEATED TEAMS

By the session of 1911- 1912, basketball was well established and the men's team was undefeated. Oscar L. McMahan, a student, was captain and manager. The other players were B. Carroll Reece, Dana X. Bible, Clyde Hale, Roy Shipley, Theron Sams, and Hugh Hayworth (THE SWANN, First College Year- book, 1912: 13).

During the same year, Frank Crowder was student manager of the undefeated baseball team called the "Invincibles." The squad included, among others, Mayford Cusack, pitcher; Clyde Hale, E .B. Booth, Clyde Wheeler, John Kilpatrick, Hugh Hayworth, Dana X. Bible, and Lee McElveen (THE SWANN, 1912:12).

The following year the prospects for the baseball team looked good. The students and faculty showed more interest than had been shown for several years, and the indications pointed toward a baseball team that would bring credit to the institution. A most commendable thing mentioned was that the better students were the ones trying to make the team and not the loafers. The season opened in North Carolina the last week of March with teams representing Mars Hill College, Asheville School, and Bingham College. Other trips included Tusculum, Washington College, the University of Chattanooga, and Cumberland University. McElveen was the coach of the team (CARSON-NEWMAN COLLEGIAN, March, 1912:35).

In 1911 a movement had been started among the students to have a Field Day. The program was carried out and proved to be a great success. The same event was held again in 1912. The boys who entered had not had sufficient training to attain the highest efficiency but did well in some of the events. Prizes were well distributed among the contestants and first honors were shared by Caldwell and Squibb, who made twenty points each (CARSON-NEWMAN COLLEGIAN, May, 1912:38).

A track meet was held in the spring of 1913 with King College. As a preliminary to the meet, there was to be a Field Day on the campus. The Field Day meant more than any previous one as there were prizes awarded and the winner had the privilege of going to Bristol to the main track meet. Each student was encouraged to practice and to enter as many events as possible (CARSON -NEWMAN COLLEGIAN, December, 1912:40).

Athletics had slowly become a part of the college. The student who was "thin, pale, and hollow-eyed was no longer thought of as being studious but was an object of contempt." Such a condition was neither a sign of studiousness nor of scholarship. But, rather an acceptance of the idea that a sufficient amount of physical exercise was necessary to develop muscles and rest the mind and was a "prerequisite both to scholarship and to studiousness" (CARSON-NEWMAN COLLEGIAN, September, 1912:52).

The local Y.M.C.A. began to realize more fully the place of athletics in college life around 1912 and began a special activity program. Members of the faculty were ready and eager to promote good, clean athletics and backed the Y.M .C.A. program (CARSON-NEWMAN COLLEGIAN, September, 1912:53).

*It Gets Foggy at Mossy Creek*

## ATHLETIC ASSOCIATION ORGANIZED

In the spring of 1912, a movement was initiated for the organization of an East Tennessee Athletic Association. The association was headed by Professor W. L. Gentry and was composed of the following schools: Grant University, Maryville, Carson-Newman, T'usculurn, Johnson Bible and King Colleges. The association directed and regulated football, baseball, basketball, and track meets, with each college deciding which contests it would enter. There were regulations as to scholarship and attendance that governed the participation of any student in the contest. A college pennant was to be given in each form of athletics (CARSON-NEWMAN COLLEGIAN, September, 1912:53).

Girls were encouraged to continue athletics even though they could not participate in the intercollegiate contests. It was suggested that there were plenty of games suitable for them, with tennis being the most excellent for boys and girls alike (CARSON-NEWMAN COLLEGIAN, September, 1912:54).

## FOOTBALL REVIVED

The football program was reactivated in 1912 as this statement was found in one of the college papers, "Although football has lain dormant at this place for six years, she has a wakened this year with renewed vigor, and taken her place in the stand of college athletics, and bids fair to make this a banner year" (CARSON-NEWMAN COLLEGIAN, September, 1913:35). Petitions favoring the renewal of football were circulated among the student body; they were signed by at least 80 percent of the students and presented to the college authorities, President J. M. Burnett later announced that the student request had been granted (Carr, 1959:236).

The student leaders in the movement to renew football were Spencer M. Tunnell, who was ably assisted by Charles L. Conrad, Bert W. Wills, and E, G. McMahan. Mr. Tunnell, who arranged the schedule for the fall of 1913, was appointed football manager and president of the athletic cabinet. He worked at the program as though he knew it was going to be a success, while others were skeptical. He managed the finances of the team (Carr, 1959:263), made arrangements to have showers and lockers in the clubhouse, and ran training table for the athletes (CARSON-NEWMAN COLLEGIAN, May, 1913:36).

The game proved popular. Expenses, including the purchase of new football uniforms and other necessary equipment, were met satisfactorily. Standards in athletics were improved, and Manager Tunnell became well known in the field of athletics in East Tennessee (Carr, 1959:263).

Manager Tunnell was so highly thought of that the CARSON-NEWMAN COMMENCEMENT of 1013-1014 (62) had this to say:

> There is no other person in college and we could say in the country who could have done such a thing as Tunnell has--putting football in at Carson-Newman when the faculty to a certain extent were opposed to it, and all others were very skeptic as to the success of it if started. But he, like in everything else worked at it like it was the

only thing to do and you who have been here have seen what he has done and the way he has gone about it. Here we must mention his keen business ability. The day of the Cumberland game we had 3 inches of snow, but it did not faze him -- he built log heaps all around the field, got the stores to close, and advertised that there would be fires. Did we have a crowd, did you say?--well, it was the largest of the season. Not only this, but in every way he proved more than master of the situation. If his successor fails to make a success of it next year it will not be because he did not have the chance to learn, for Tunnell gave the people the game 'as it should be did.' He is the best known man in athletic circles in East Tennessee. As president of the Athletic Cabinet he had caused the standard of athletics to be raised to a remarkable degree. The precedent he has set in football will live long. At the close of the season the faculty and students presented him a beautiful silver loving cup as an appreciation of his work.

Dana X. Bible also aided in bringing football to the campus by helping coach the team. During his years as a student he had written articles in the school newspaper telling of the value of sports to the individual. He had been outstanding football player in high school and naturally encouraged the renewal of the program at Carson-Newman. Dana X. Bible had entered Carson-Newman in 1908, the year after football was discontinued. He played baseball and basketball and would have been an asset to the football program had there been a team. He was a fine athlete and coach and was an addition to the college. Bible assisted with the 1913 football team only, then accepted a football coaching position at Mississippi College the following year. The CARSON -NEWMAN COMMENCEMENT (1913-1914:35) had this to say:

Dana is the best all-round man we have ever turned out. Mr. Bible goes to Mississippi College this year. Will he have a good team? Well, if they don't it won't be because they haven't got the material. We think D. X. to be the best in the South--some others think the same.

The KNOXVILLE JOURNAL AND TRIBUNE. May 8, 1914, spoke of Bible in the same manner:

Coach Bible of Mississippi College, Jackson, Mississippi should put out the best team in Dixie. Bible has made a wonderful record in Tennessee Athletics, being mentioned as the best football player in the state. He not only can play football, but he can teach it. He has only one superior in our state--Dan McGugin of Vanderbilt.

Coach Bible later became known as one of the outstanding football coaches in the country. He is a member of the Football Hall of Fame and is presently retired Athletic Director at the University of Texas.

**FIRST FULL-TIME COACH**

In order to continue the football program, a full-time coach was needed. President J. M. Burnett and the trustees felt a three dollar per student fee would make this possible. The first person employed primarily as a coach was Phil M. Utley, a young man who had been graduated from Wake Forest College. It was late in the summer when he was employed, but he came to the college in time to coach football in 1913. The Athletic Council consisted of Dean Horace L. Ellis, Professor William L. Gentry, Professor A.P. Van Dusen, P, M. McElveen, and students Spencer M. Tunnell (chairman), B. W. Willis, C.L. Conrad and E .C. McMahan (Carr, 1959:263).

The football schedule and scores for the 1913 team were (CARSON-NEWMAN COLLEGIAN, 1913-1914:6):

| | | | |
|---|---|---|---|
| Carson-Newman | 0 | 54 | University of Tennessee |
| Carson-Newman | 7 | 13 | King College |
| Carson-Newman | 22 | 13 | Asheville College |
| Carson-Newman | 34 | 6 | Bingham School |
| Carson-Newman | 60 | 0 | Maryville Polytechnical |
| Carson-Newman | 6 | 0 | Tusculum |
| Carson-Newman | 6 | 6 | Cumberland |
| Carson-Newman | 19 | 0 | Athens University |
| Carson-Newman | 22 | 3 | Maryville College |
| Carson-Newman | 34 | 0 | Washington University |

The home games were with King College, Maryville Polytechnical, Cumberland College, and Athens University (CARSON -NEWMAN COMMENCEMENT, 1913-1914:64).

An amusing incident was related in the CARSON-NEWMAN COMMENCEMENT (1914:62) of that year. When the team went to Knoxville to play The University of Tennessee, E. C. Greer, a guard, had his life insurance written out before the game. "This may sound like a fairy tale, but it isn't; it's nothing but the truth."

According to the COLLEGIAN, the success of the 1913 basketball team was due to the earnest, hard work of the players and to the excellent coaching of Mr. McElveen and its financial success was due to the skillful planning and excellent arrangement of the schedule by Mr. McMahan. At the end of the season the finances were "in the black," for Mr. McMahan had been a capable businessman. Music had been furnished by the college orchestra at the home games. Spectators supported the team with their cheers. "If there ever was such a thing as desire to see our boys defeat our rivals and do it in a fair way, it was shown this year'." During the entire season, the college spirit ran high and large crowds attended the games, Carson-Newman won all but one of thirteen scheduled games, losing only to The University of Tennessee. This outstanding basketball squad included L. Reece, Crosby, John Kilpatrick, Davis, Willis, S. C. Reece, Foster and Burnett (CARSON-NEWMAN COLLEGIAN. March, 1914:43).

An article in the commencement program of 1913-1914 stated that some claimed that it was the electrical age, others that it was the Iron Age, and by a professor of science that it was the age of insects.

# A History of Sports at Carson-Newman College 1851-1974

While all had good arguments to back up their theory, others felt it was the age of athletics. University, college, and even high school men were coming to realize more and more the advantage of athletics in schools, and were giving more of their time and attention toward the development of clean athletics; some turned to football and basketball, while others were interested in baseball and tennis (Carr, 1959:266).

Three students, Robert E. Humphrey, Clyde N. Wheeler, and J. Paul Phillips, led a movement among the students, faculty, and townspeople to construct seating for the athletic field. The movement was so successful that adequate bleachers for three hundred spectators were constructed and were enjoyed for many years (Carr, 1959:81).

After the football season of 1914, Coach Utley resigned to accept a better-paying job at Wake Forest, his alma mater. He coached there and in later years became the director of athletics. He was succeeded at Carson-Newman by an able and promising young man, James H. Barnett, who had received an A.B. degree from Richmond University. He came to Carson-Newman in the middle of the session as director of athletics and instructor in the Preparatory Department (CARSON-NEWMAN COLLEGIAN, November, 1913:34).

## ATHLETIC CABINET

Under Coach Barnett, all athletic interests were placed under the direction of the athletic association and were subject to the supervision and guidance of the Faculty Committee on Athletics. The athletics cabinet, which was composed of the faculty committee and the managers of the various teams, ruled on all games, trips and expeditions. The college author-Ities took an interest in and encouraged the sports program and an attempt was made to keep athletics on a sane basis, not usurping undue importance in college affairs, as was often true in college life (Carr, 1959:267).

A high standard of scholarship was required of all athletes and regulations were established to secure the best results, both physical and moral. Every effort was made to eliminate professionalism. Only bonafide students were allowed to play on intercollegiate teams. To that end, the following regulations were enforced (CARSON-NEWMAN CATALOGUE, 1914-1915:39).

> 1. No student would be eligible for membership on any intercollegiate team that did not carry an amount of work equal to twelve hours a week.
>
> 2. No student whose work was not satisfactory-to the faculty could participate on any intercollegiate team.
>
> 3. It was the duty of the manager of any intercollegiate team to report to the athletic committee the names of members of the teams. If a person's name was not reported, he was not eligible to play.
>
> 4. If a student entered college later than the beginning of the second month of the term he would not be allowed to play on any intercollegiate team.

*It Gets Foggy at Mossy Creek*

The 1914 football season began with Professor Barnett as the coach, Mr. Foster, as manager, and Bunch as captain. It was said that nothing added more to the college spirit than a good football team, and that nothing added more life to a team than a live, loyal group of fans who were willing to support the team and the manager.

Carson-Newman lost only one game to King College, 0-12. The victories Included Washington College, 73-0; Mars Hill, 39-0; Central High School, 76-0; and Maryville, 3-0. A train was chartered for the Maryville game and two hundred supporters went to see Utley win the game 3 to 0 with a fifty yard drop kick in the third quarter (CARSON-NEWMAN COLLEGIAN, September, 1914:30).

The basketball team of 1914 had more players than Coach Barnett could successfully coach. In fact, it was necessary to stagger practice from six to eight in the evening in order to accommodate all of the players who had come out for the team (Carr, 1959:263). The team lost to The University of Tennessee, Elon, Trinity, North Carolina A. & M. Wake Forest and Guilford. "The team was not as successful in the number of games won" but things looked better for the coming year (CARSON-NEWMAN COLLEGIAN, September, 1914:30).

There was a continued need for a better place to play. The team was handicapped by playing on the small home court and then playing on larger courts on the road. It was believed that teams which had adequate gymnasiums were able to show their superiority over the schools which did not have similar facilities. There was a feeling that Carson-Newman had comparable material to the other schools, but that the lack of a gymnasium prevented the development of good team work. The students were asked to get behind the project to build a new gymnasium and not let up until the task was completed (CARSON- NEWMAN COLLEGIAN, March, 1915:46). The gymnasium did not become a reality, however, until the early 1920's.

The girls' basketball team for 1914 was coached by Mrs. Clayton. She was considered a good coach, something the girls had needed for some time. The girls mentioned as members of the team were Misses Joe Catlett, Ethel Snelson, forwards; Miss Basquette, center; and Misses McDonald, Pangle, and Henderson, guards. There was an interest in intercollegiate basketball for the girls, but a schedule was not worked out for 1914 (CARSON-NEWMAN COLLEGIAN, November, 1915:40.)

**LETTER CLUB ORGANIZED**

A Letter Club to promote closer fellowship among the athletes was organized in 1914. It was composed of young men who earned letters on varsity athletic teams. All team members had to meet the academic standards required by the college and the Smoky Mountain Athletic Conference (SMAC). Members entered the organization by election and by completing an initiation, which might include long hikes from a point of deposit to their homes, sleeping out overnight; or after performing other chores, being made the butt of jokes and frivolity. Coaches were the sponsors of the organization, The Club had various methods of earning money, including the operation of concessions at games played at home (Carr, 1951:301). The Letter Club has continued through the years and has not been changed much, Members do not have to be voted into the club now since it is open to any varsity athlete. However, if an athlete chooses to become a member he must go through an initiation.

In the autumn of 1915, a new coach, John Kilpatrick, took over full duties in the athletic department. The new coach, a native of East Tennessee, had an excellent academic record. He was also a member of the college basketball team for four years, and in addition played baseball and football (CARSON-NEWMAN COMMENCEMENT, 1915:40).

Coach Kilpatrick enforced the college rules and allowed only bona fide students to participate. A student had to follow the regulations or was removed from the team. Students were urged to participate if at all possible; those who could not, were asked to support the team.

When the new coach called for his first football practice, he was greeted by inexperienced candidates with which to build a team. The season was not as good in the number of games won as the previous season had been, but it was a success in one way--students represented the college. The students were proud of the team because it did not have any salaried "ringers," or ineligible players. There was general opposition to players receiving compensation for playing. Playing football was considered to be worthwhile, but the school was opposed to giving aid to men who made football a specialty. Men were wanted who were succeeding scholastically and making themselves a part of the college by entering into the school spirit (CARSON-NEWMAN COLLEGIAN, September, 1915:30).

The basketball season made a good start as Coach Barnett had a group of husky "goal tossers" on his squad. The men playing most extensively were: Carter, Burnett, Shipley, Wood, Philips, Davis, Jackson, Reese, Smith, and Kilpatrick. The team, however, was handicapped by the injury of several players during the season. Carson-Newman should build good teams in future years from among the young players (CARSON -NEWMAN COLLEGIAN, February, 1915:42).

The baseball season of 1915 was a great success in every sense of the word. The team was composed of an alert group ready to "take on" any team composed of bonafide students. Manager Wheeler, Coach Kilpatrick, and the team members attributed much of the success to the town for its support--financial and otherwise. Hays, Plemons, Acuff, and Loy were among members of the team credited with much of the success (CARSON-NEWMAN COMMENCEMENT, 1913-1914:62)

During 1915, tennis had one of the most successful years in the history of the school. Due to the energetic work of the manager, the number of interested students almost doubled and the courts were regraded. These two factors engendered a desire to make tennis one of the leading college sports. The tournament sponsored by the business men of the town was very successful. Humphrey won the men's singles, Humphrey and Dale the men's doubles and Misses Huff and White the ladies' doubles (CARSON-NEWMAN COMMENCEMENT, 1915:43).

*It Gets Foggy at Mossy Creek*

## THE FIRE OF 1916

Tragedy struck the campus on December 13, 1916, when fire swept the campus and destroyed the Administration Building which housed most of the classrooms. The trustees and faculty came to the close of the session on June 2, 1917, with "much apprehension about the future of the college" (Carr, 1959:268).

At the April meeting of the trustees in 1917, the Executive Committee recommended to the entire Board of Trustees "that no coach be employed for the next session." This recommendation was approved by everyone on the Board and for the full duration of World War I no coach was employed (MINUTES, BOARD OF TRUSTEES, Carson-Newman, April 5, 1917:66).

Since no coach was employed, a decision was necessary concerning continuation of athletics. It was thought that a strong team would advertise the college and help the program, but that a poor team would hurt the program. Under the leadership of John Kilpatrick an athletic fee was charged for each athletic team. This made it possible to equip all teams and also to have more games in all sports at home (ORANGE and BLUE, October 15, 1918:3).

Soon after this, President Burnett resigned and Dean William L. Gentry was selected as the new president. President Gentry was described as a man of courage, vision, and conviction. During the session of 1917-1918, student enrollment was 167 as compared to 284 the previous year. The college operated under great difficulty as there was no administration building in which to meet the classes and the country was involved in World War 1. Football was still played on the campus and was the number one sport even though there was no paid coach. Many of the boys were volunteering for the armed services and others were being drafted (MINUTES, BOARD OF TRUSTEES, Carson-Newman, April 15, 1917:66).

In his first report, President Gentry stated that there was a need for a gymnasium of some kind even if it was wooden. He mentioned that several colleges he knew of had gymnasiums of that type and found them satisfactory. He also mentioned that it would take money to maintain either athletics or a gymnasium and that the most common procedure was to charge the students a fee to cover the cost. The Building Committee was instructed to complete the new Administration Building in time for the opening of the college in September, 1918, if at all possible (MINUTES, BOARD OF TRUSTEES, Carson-Newman, April 5, 1917:78).

During this same time "the college conveyed title to all its property to the Educational Board of the Tennessee Baptist Convention." Though a rigid contract was involved, it was properly signed by both parties and recorded on April 19, 1919. Thus, President Gentry and the Board of Trustees had, by this arrangement, secured denominational control and also denominational financial support (Carr, 1959: 84- 85).

## STUDENT ARMY TRAINING CORPS

Carson-Newman College was included among the schools used by the government to train men for the military service during the war years. The program was called the Student Army

# *A History of Sports at Carson-Newman College 1851-1974*

Training Corps (S.A.T.C.) and its purpose was to take young men who were well prepared educationally and train them to be officers. The S.A.T.C. Units were located at Carson-Newman, Tusculum, King, and East Tennessee Normal. Each unit organized a football team and games were played against each other. This provided a team for the college and also provided the military unit with a part of its training program (ORANGE and BLUE, November 1, 1918:3).

## SUMMARY

Carson-Newman showed signs of growth in the area of athletics during her first sixty-eight years. Developments paralleled those of most other colleges in the United States by beginning the sports program with track and field. The first organized event held on the campus was a Field Day held on June 3, 1893.

The first intercollegiate athletic event was a baseball game played against The University of Tennessee on April 2, 1895. The "Invincibles," the 1912 baseball team, was an outstanding team and helped to increase the interest in the spring sport.

Organized football was the next intercollegiate sport played on the campus in the fall of 1895. The game was instituted by Luther M. Beeler of Jefferson City and James S. Floyd, who was a student at Carson-Newman at the time. The program continued until 1907 when a football player was killed and the sport was discontinued until 1913. During World War I, Students Army Training Corps units were located at Carson-Newman, Tusculum, King College, and East Tennessee Normal. In order to receive their training and continue the athletic program, a football team was organized using the S.A.T.C. members.

The basketball program was added to the athletic program around 1903 as some games were played informally with other schools but the 1908 team was the first recognized college team. By the 1911-1912 season, basketball was well established, with a men's team that was undefeated. Young women students in this early period participated in intercollegiate basketball during the administration of J.M. Burnett, L. Gentry, and C.E. Sams.

From the outset, intercollegiate athletics at Carson-Newman played an important role in the total college program.

# It Gets Foggy at Mossy Creek

**The First Intercollegiate Athletic Team at Carson-Newman 1895**

**Football Team 1903**

# A History of Sports at Carson-Newman College 1851-1974

Football Team 1903

Basketball Team 1913

**Baseball 1913**

---

**Track 1913**

# *A History of Sports at Carson-Newman College 1851-1974*

**1909 Carson-Newman Basketball Team**

*It Gets Foggy at Mossy Creek*

**Football Team 1913**

---

**Tennis 1912**

# *A History of Sports at Carson-Newman College 1851-1974*

1914

**Carson-Newman Spirit 1919**

# *It Gets Foggy at Mossy Creek*

**1915 Tennis Team**

# *A History of Sports at Carson-Newman College 1851-1974*

**Football Captains 1903**

*It Gets Foggy at Mossy Creek*

Spencer Tunnell

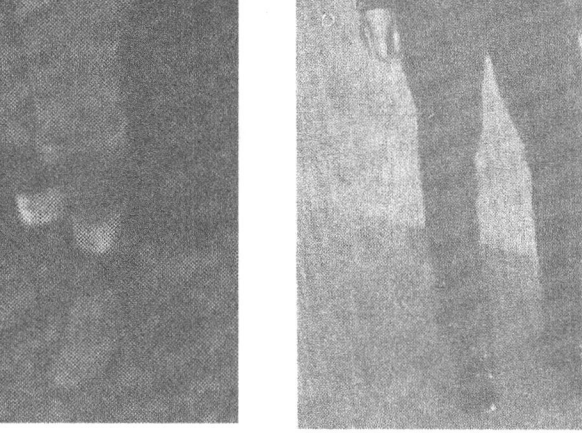
P. M. Utley

Paul Squibb

**Royal Order of Saintly Warts**

# *A History of Sports at Carson-Newman College 1851-1974*

Tennis 1913

---

Football 1913

*It Gets Foggy at Mossy Creek*

**Campus 1914**

**The First
Mossy Creek
College
Building**

**Administration
Building
1892-1916**

# A History of Sports at Carson-Newman College 1851-1974

**Raymond Fleener,
killed during a football game
1919**

**The Stew Bum Club 1917**

---

**Newman Dormitory**

**John Kilpattick
Athlete and Coach**

## It Gets Foggy at Mossy Creek

*A History of Sports at Carson-Newman College 1851-1974*

# THE FIGHTING PARSONS

# CHAPTER III

# THE TRANSITION PERIOD
# 1919 - 1939

The attitude toward athletics at Carson-Newman improved in the early 1920's. The community and college showed increasing interest in athletics and the athletic program began to grow. In addition, the news media showed more interest in the college, according to Coach Holt, since they were playing the best kind of football, basketball, and baseball--even better than the universities (Taped Interview with Coach "Frosty" Holt, March, 1972).

President O.E. Sams, who came to the college in 1920, was a great supporter of athletics. He believed that athletic contests should be not only wholesome activities for the students but could also provide an attractive advertisement for the college. This may have been the reason that he attached such extreme importance to athletics (Carr, 1959:271).

The year 1920 was the year that would reap the effects of the two previous years when no coach was employed and since practically all the material in football was "green, inexperienced, and unusually light," a rather disastrous season was experienced. Even though it was difficult from the standpoint of winning games, some of the men developed into good players for the future years (Carr, 1959: 271).

The first football game of 1919 brought with it a tragic accident and the effects were felt the remainder of the season. While playing a practice game with Central High School of Knox County on September 20, 1919, Raymond K Fleenor, a senior from Piney Flats, Tennessee, was severely injured.

> He lingered for several months, and much to the sorrow of the faculty and students the injury prayed fatal. He died on April 19) 1920. Fullback Fleenor had been relied upon for much of the heavy load of that season, and his injury and death were heavy blows to his teammates (THE GRENADE, Yearbook of 1920: 138).

The football team decided to continue the schedule in spite of the tragedy and the team improved with each game. They made their best showing of the year in their last game with The University of Chattanooga. Although the university had a much heavier and more experienced team, Carson-Newman held them to a 20-0 score (THE GRENADE, 1920:138).

A tribute was paid to Fleenor in the school newspaper, THE ORANGE and BLUE (May 1, 1920; I). The article recalled that Fleenor was a good student and a good athlete and that he was also interested in other phases of college life, especially the spiritual. It was said that he went about everything he undertook with earnestness and determination.

Even though there were many difficulties during the season, Carson-Newman produced one of its better basketball teams in 1920. The success was largely due to excellent team work and it was a well-balanced team with no particular star. Everyone had great plans for the future and felt that they would be realized if a new gymnasium could be completed in the immediate future (THE GRENADE, 1920: 139).

In addition to the intercollegiate schedule, class teams were provided for the boys who wanted to play basketball but who were not on the varsity team. The class teams had scheduled practices and played an intramural type of schedule. Some of these games were hotly contested, and much interest was shown by the class members (ORANGE and BLUE, February 15, 1920: I),

## SUCCESSFUL WOMEN'S COMPETITION

For the first time in several years, the girls of Carson-Newman College formed a basketball team. In fact, there were several teams sponsored by the societies, but the only one that played any games with out-of-town teams was the team composed of college girls who lived in town. The college did not support the local team, financially or otherwise. The team had a good record, winning three games (THE GRENADE, 1920:141).

The first girls' basketball game of the season was with a strong Knoxville High School team. The girls made a good showing in the game considering that it was their first game and the first game in which many of the girls had ever played. It was a hard fought game throughout but ended in a 9 to 9 tie which was never played off. The three victories were against The University of Tennessee girls, 14-13; Knoxville Y.W.C.A., 34-7; and Park City girls, 18-6 (THE GRENADE, 1920: 142).

Tennis was still one of the most popular sports for coeducational athletics. Before 1920, the only funds available for the upkeep of the courts were the dues paid by the members of the Tennis Club and the courts were open only to the members. When the college charged an athletic fee in 1920, tennis was included; thus it was possible to keep the courts in much better condition and they were opened to all college students (THE GRENADE, 1920:145). The Tennis Club was disbanded when the athletic fee was required of all students in 1920 (THE WANEHI, Yearbook of 1921: 132).

The adoption of the athletic fee improved the financial support of athletics. Prior to this time it had been the responsibility of the managers of the various teams to solicit money from interested students and townspeople in any way they could, The team usually ended the season in arrears (THE WANEHI 1921: 132). The managers of the team were no longer forced to solicit subscriptions and were able to spend more time helping the coaches by caring for team matters and players.

The Athletic Cabinet for the 1919-1920 session included Professor Roy L. McMurray, president; Professor Frank L, Haynes and John D. Everett, both coaches and members of the faculty Athletic Committee. Jesse Brown was manager of football, S, W. Holloway, manager of basketball, Robert Davis, manager of baseball, Maine Shoun, manager of tennis and J. G. Chapman, manager of track (THE WANE HI, 1921:132). The Athletic Cabinet selected the managers of the various sports on grounds of scholarship, athletic standing, and business ability (ORANGE and BLUE, February 15, 1920: 1).

## *It Gets Foggy at Mossy Creek*

All managers and players were required to abide by the Constitution and By-Laws of the Athletic Cabinet. A new rule was made in 1020 which stated "that members of the college association team could not play on any team not connected with the college, Violations of the rule would cause one to forfeit his place on the college team" (CARSON-NEWMAN CATALOGUE, 1919-1920:43). Also at that time there was no transfer rule; a student could begin playing the day he entered (Taped Interview with Coach Holt March 1972).

In the fall of 1920 Coach Kilpatrick, who had returned from World War I, again took up coaching duties. The football record of that year was very encouraging. Twenty-seven men were listed as being out for the team and they had a 3-3 record, losing the first three games and winning the last three (THE WANEHI, 1921: 117).

The basketball team of 1920 had only two lettermen returning from the previous year. Of the twelve basketball games played, six were staged on the local court, the remaining six being played away from home. Seven of the twelve games were won, and the team compiled 455 points against their opponents' 287. Carson-Newman lost by a small margin in three of the games; to Maryville by 5 points, to Milligan by 3 points, and to Johnson Bible College by only 1 point (THE WANEHI, 1921: 126).

Baseball and tennis were organized in the 1921 season, and the baseball team again had a good record. Tennis became a regular sport, sharing in funds received from the athletic fee. Under Manager Alex Chavis, schedules for the use of the tennis courts were established for all who wished to participate (THE WANEHI, 1921-: 132).

Dr. R.M. McCown became a volunteer coach that year. He practiced medicine during the day and coached the basketball team in the late afternoon and evening. Since there was no gymnasium in which to practice, basketball was played in commercial buildings located on Main Street.

> These improvised courts were inadequate and non-standard; but, nevertheless, they did serve to keep a sport going which college students greatly desired and needed for the maintenance of a wholesome student morale (Carr, 1959:271).

There had been a need for a gymnasium for more than forty years and President Sams knew that one had to be built if athletics were to be kept alive at Carson-Newman. Mr. Henry D. Blanc told President Sams he would donate $10,000 toward the building of a gymnasium if anyone would match his offer. Mr. D. L. Butler accepted the challenge and both men presented their money to Dr. Sams in chapel before the student body. President Sams formally accepted the money at a meeting of the Board of Trustees on May 18, 1921, and work was started immediately on the new gymnasium (Carr, 1959:208). Other gifts for the new structure then began to come in. Because of the attitude and support of many people, the gymnasium was made possible.

The 1921-1922 session marked a definite turning point in athletics at Carson-Newman. The people of Jefferson City locked arms with the college folk and the alumni in turn joined in. The strength of such unity manifested itself throughout the year (APPALACHIAN, name adopted for Yearbook, 1922:139).

# *A History of Sports at Carson-Newman College 1851-1974*

## "THE FIGHTING PARSONS"

The 1921 football season started off with excellent prospects. A number of players of experience and promise flocked to the gridiron, and the "thud of the pigskin was a song of optimism to the cheerful supporters of the orange and blue." The strength of the team attracted widespread attention, and the "ginger with which that strength was applied won for them the distinguishing pseudonym, "The Fighting Parsons." The cognomen followed on into basketball, track, and baseball; it looked like a permanent fixture to all Carson-Newman teams (APPALACHIAN, 1922:130).

Coach "Frosty" Holt, the quarterback of the team, related the following incident which gave the new name to the college team (Taped Interview with Coach Holt, March, 1972):

> The football team had journeyed by train to Athens College, which is known as Tennessee Wesleyan College today. The game during those days was more of a boxing match than anything else. One of our players, Ira Dance, a ministerial student, hit one of the Athens players during the course of the game and knocked him unconscious for several hours. The fans of Athens College were so mad that we had to take Ira up to our hotel room and keep him until things cooled off. The next morning in the Knoxville paper Carson-Newman was referred to as the 'Fighting Parsons' and that name stayed with us in all sports for many years.

Although Carson-Newman had a very successful year in football, it was believed that the next year would be even better. Tom Moran, an outstanding football player from Centre College, had been hired to come to Carson-Newman to coach the football team. Centre College at that time was one of the football powers of the South. Carson-Newman felt very fortunate to have such a man to head up their football program. He was the first full-time football coach hired at Carson-Newman, with no teaching duties included (Taped Interview with Coach Holt, March, 1972).

## BUTLER-BLANC GYMNASIUM COMPLETED

Although striving under many difficulties this season, one of the best basketball teams was turned out that we have had for several years. There is no doubt that if we had had a good gymnasium, a much better record would have been made by our team. The success of the team was largely due to the excellent team work shown by the fellows. There was no particular star, but everyone worked for the good of the whole team. They were a well balanced team. King, our lanky center, was good both at the tip-off and placing them in the basket. Davis and Gracey made a fine working pair of forwards. They were fast, hard-working fellows, both being good shots. In Kelley and Wiles we had two extra good guards. This team passed the ball almost perfectly. Wyatt, Hamilton, Garrison and others rendered good service at times during the season. Next year, with a good Gym., which we all are expecting to have by that time, we hope to have a string of unbroken victories at the close of the season. (TAKEN FROM 1920 ANNUAL)

## *It Gets Foggy at Mossy Creek*

In 1921, a long-time dream became a reality. The new gymnasium was finally completed and was the pride of the campus. It was named after the two men who contributed so much to make it possible--Henry D. Blanc and D. L. Butler. Butler-Blanc Gymnasium was referred to as the "showplace of the South."

It was one of the largest facilities in the area and other colleges would travel many miles to play in it. The main playing floor was 60 feet by 88 feet, with a running track above. The basement contained showers and a 21 x 60 foot swimming pool. On the main floor were also two suites of rooms which accommodated the athletic director (Carr, 1959:208). When Coach Holt returned to Carson-Newman in 1929 to be head coach, he lived in the gymnasium with his wife and two sons for ten years.

**Dr. R. M. McCown**
**Kept athletics alive in the 1920's**

# A History of Sports at Carson-Newman College 1851-1974

## ATHLETIC AID

In the 1921-1922 academic year, the college began to give limited athletic aid, a practice that contributed to the athletic program. Most of the money came from outside the college through the community and alumni, with the college making some appropriations. At that time it did not cost much to attend Carson-Newman--"a few hundred dollars went a long way" (Taped Interview with Coach Holt, March, 1972).

Coach McElveen took over the reins in basketball in 1921 and the development of the team was greatly facilitated by the new Butler-Blanc Gymnasium. Carson-Newman was blessed with a wealth of material that year; a number of new candidates, added to the returning veterans, gave the coach a complex problem in the selection of a team. An excellent combination was chosen, and' 'the quintet went forth, gloriously upholding the traditions of the 'Fighting Parsons.' Frosty Holt, a member of that team, recalled "what a thrill it was" to play in the new gymnasium. He also recalled that it was heated by a stove at each end of the floor (Taped Interview with Coach Holt, March, 1972).

The girls' team, under the leadership of Coach McElveen and Miss Izer Whiting, who was also a teacher of expression at the college, won four out of seven games played. The victories were against Johnson City High School, Newport High School, Tennessee Polytechnic, and The University of Chattanooga (APPALACHIAN, 1922: 145).

The baseball season opened with The University of Tennessee on March 25. With five lettermen back, Coach McElveen hoped to develop one of the fastest nines in the history of the school. The team ended the season in the winning column and a successful season was recorded (APPALACHIAN, 1922: 149).

Tennis was also offered during the year 1922. To those who felt that tennis was a game for delicate boys and girls, it was mentioned that one of the Parsons' best football players was also an excellent tennis player. "Tennis truly is a strenuous game and is guaranteed to develop muscle and at the same time to give the most valuable of exercise" (APPALACHIAN, 1922: 150).

In 1922, Carson-Newman advanced noticeably in its athletic program. There was more interest shown as the college began to play more difficult schedules in all sports and to bring in good coaches. Most of the players during the early 1920's were recruited from the immediate area but around 1924 the coaches recruited players from all over the country (Taped Interview with Coach Holt, March, 1972).

Tom Moran came to Carson-Newman in 1922. The college felt very fortunate to obtain him as a coach. "He was brought to Carson-Newman with one purpose in mind; to build a good football program, and build one he did" (Taped Interview with Coach Holt, March, 1972). The season ended with a 7-3 won-loss record. The team defeated Mars Hill, 45-0; Athens School, 45-0; Milligan College, 57-0: and Cumberland College, 86-0. The three losses were to The University of Tennessee, Washington and Lee, and Centre College; the score in the latter game was 73-0 (APPALACHIAN, 1923: 144).

*It Gets Foggy at Mossy Creek*

The Parsons were able to avenge their previous defeat by Centre College in 1923. With Centre again expected to run at will against Carson-Newman, the Parsons rose to the occasion and held Centre to a 7 to 0 victory. The game ended 13 to 0 in favor of Centre, but the rules committee later disqualified one of Centre's touchdowns because of an illegal play used in scoring the touchdown (Carson-Newman Athletic Office Records, 1923-1924). The 7 to 0 score was the lowest Centre had been held to on their own field in eight years (ORANGE and BLUE, October 1, 1923:3). The game played with Camp Banning on November 10, 1923, was historic in that Major Dwight D. Eisenhower, who was on duty at Camp Banning, was the assistant coach of that team (Carr, 1959:208). Carson-Newman defeated Camp Banning 16 to 6 (APPALACHIAN, 1924: 140).

In the 1923-1924 season, football games were scheduled well in advance under the direction of the head football coach, Tom Moran. He was regarded as the coach who made Carson-Newman famous in the football realm. "He would take a mediocre team and develop it into one of the South's outstanding small-college teams. Teammates appreciated his personal interest and could never forget how he cared for them" (APPALACHIAN, 1924: 141).

During the 1922-1924 season, Lake Russell, while still a student, coached the basketball team. The team won twelve of the fifteen games scheduled. The credit went to the excellent coaching of Coach Russell, and also the good team leadership of "Frosty" Holt. The team outscored its opposition 511 to 302. The record for the year included victories at all home games and only three defeats on the road--The University of Alabama, Virginia Polytechnic Institute, and Albany Y.M.C.A. (APPALACHIAN, 1923: 153).

The girls, coached by Tom Taylor, had a team for the season but played only three games, including two victories and one defeat. The Parsonettes put down The University of Chattanooga and Tennessee Polytechnic Institute, but were in turn beaten by the University of Tennessee. According to the yearbook, the defeat was registered against Carson-Newman because four members of the squad were unable to participate in the game (APPALACHIAN, 1923: 155).

Interest in baseball continued in 1923 and Lake Russell was also in charge of the baseball team. Thirty-one men came out for practice regularly. The season was a success as there were seven good pitchers and three good catchers (APPALACHIAN, 1923: 157).

The Athletic Cabinet during the mid-1920's remained in charge of the athletic program. The administration, however, reserved the right to limit the number of days which any team could spend a way from the college and to require that all athletic schedules be approved by the Dean. The schedules were made under the supervision of the Faculty Executive Committee, and the football schedule was made entirely by this committee through its secretary (BULLETIN OF CARSON-NEWMAN COLLEGE, 1923-1924:85).

The eligibility rules of the Appalachian Conference were enforced. There were also additional rules enforced by the college; one was that if a player had played as many as four years including his freshman year, he was not eligible to play. "A player must meet all admission requirements; must carry at least twelve hours 'of regular academic work;

successfully pass the same; and obtain promotion in his class" (BULLETIN OF CARSON-NEWMAN COLLEGE, 1923-1924:85).

At the annual meeting of the trustees on April 3. 1924, President Sams stated that with the dormitories literally overflowing with students it seemed that the time had come to eliminate the preparatory department of the college. During that session, it-had not been listed in the catalogue but some students had come anyway. He said that an announcement had already been made to the student body to the effect that each applicant for entrance the next fall must have fifteen high school entrance units, unless he was a ministerial student or was twenty-one years of age. He felt it very gratifying to realize that while high school attendance had already been reduced, the college had an increase of eighty-five in total attendance (MINUTES, BOARD OF TRUSTEES, President's Report, 1924: 149). During the period of eliminating the attendance of 150 in the preparatory department, college enrollment increased by approximately 550 (REPORT OF EXECUTIVE COMMITTEE attached to Trustees' Minutes, 1924:149).

The basketball schedule for the 1923-1924 year resulted in the winning of seventeen of the eighteen games scheduled. Carson-Newman outscored their opponents 677 to 281 points (APPALACHIAN, 1924:148).

The highlight of the basketball season was a 32 to 28 decision over Georgetown University of Washington, D. C. The first defeat in eight years for Georgetown (Carson-Newman Athletics Records, 1923-1924). "The story of the 1924 victory over Georgetown was one Carson-Newman would long remember" (ORANGE and BLUE, February 15, 1924: 1). The WASHINGTON HERALD (February 5, 1924) the following morning best presented the color behind the great upset. The headlines read thus:

*HILLTOPS DEFEATED BY CARSON-NEWMAN. SOUTHERNERS MAKE ATHLETIC HISTORY,*

*WINNING 32-28 FOR THE FIRST GEORGETOWN LOSS SINCE 1916 TO NEW YORK UNIVERSITY*

The account of the game read, in part, as follows:

> A bunch of raw-boned lads, wearing yellow jerseys and coming from what is familiarly known as 'the sticks' made athletic history last night by trouncing Georgetown University Racketeers 32 -28. These direct descendants of the late and honorable Daniel Boone left little to the imagination when it came to sticking the ball through the iron hoop. They were dead-eye dicks. Frosty Holt led the Carson-Newman victory with 11 of the 32 points scored.
> The 1924 basketball squad followed their great win over Georgetown by winning their remaining four road trip games (ORANGE and BLUE, February 15, 1924:3).

In the president's report of 1924, he stated that the year had been one of superlatives. "We had the greatest football team in the history of the college and a basketball team that would hold its own with any five In the South (MINUTES, BOARD OF TRUSTEES, President's Report, April 5, 1924:66).

## "RINGERS"

The following year, an incident occurred which greatly affected the athletic program at Carson-Newman. Unknown to the faculty, two football players who were registered under assumed names were playing on the Carson-Newman team. The football team had gone to Centre College in Danville to play a scheduled game. After several closed door meetings between the coaches and the administration, the game was canceled. It had been discovered that Carson-Newman had two ineligible players, so Centre College would not play the game. The two players were dropped from the team and later were dismissed from the college (Taped Interview with Coach Holt, March, 1972).

The private and church-related colleges were placing a new emphasis on intercollegiate athletics during the 1920's. Carson-Newman had a local citizens' group who promoted athletics at the college and, in their anxiety to win, they secured from other institutions two former players to whom they gave assumed names. The college also had other players taking below-normal academic loads. For these reasons Centre College refused to play a scheduled game. Acting Dean J. E. Everett, who signed the eligibility lists, stated later that he was not familiar with the conditions under which some of the athletes had entered college, and that he went to the president to discuss the situation. President Sams, an active member of the local organization, advised him to sign the eligibility lists, including the names of those later found to be disqualified. "I had no idea that I was approving irregular players. I had just been in the dean's office a short time and was not familiar with the records of those who had been accepted for admission before the opening of the semester" (Carr, 1959:273).

There was much talk concerning the "ringers" and some criticism was directed at the college during that period. In an interview with Coach Holt, who was a student at the college during that time, he stated that it was a practice that was carried on by all the schools in the area. Miss Mae Iddins, who was also a student at the time, related that many of the "ringers" would "hang out" down town and maybe take a class or two. Many of them had attended college previously and were playing again at Carson-Newman under assumed names. Miss Iddins recalled going to a banquet at the end of the year and sitting at a table with her escort and not knowing a single one of the football players seated at her table (Taped Interview with Miss Mae Iddins, April, 1972).

It was necessary for the Athletic Committee to enforce rules in order to prevent the recurrence of such an incident. In order to do this, two more rules were added to the ones already enforced. The first stated "that a student who had played upon the varsity team of any other university or college was ineligible to play in the same sport at Carson-Newman, until the athlete had completed one year's work in residence." This applied to intercollegiate games only. The other rule stated that no person would be permitted to take part in intercollegiate contests if he had played on any baseball teams operating under the supervision of the National Baseball Commission. This did not apply to a "tryout" (BULLETIN OF CARSON -NEWMAN COLLEGE, 1924-1925:24).

# A History of Sports at Carson-Newman College 1851-1974

Captain-elect Frosty Holt led the Fighting Parsons of 1924 to a great year in football. With fifteen of Carson-Newman's team missing because of eligibility rulings, Holt led a Carson-Newman team composed of second and third-string players against The University of Tennessee team, and helped hold it to a mere 13-0 decision (ORANGE and BLUE, October 15, .1924:3). Carson-Newman scored a 12 to 0 victory over a strong Sewanee team which had not lost a football game on their home field since 1913 (KNOXVILLE NEWS-SENTINEL, October 4, 1924).

## UNDEFEATED BASEBALL TEAM

Coach Lake Russell molded the team into one of the best group of baseball players to wear the orange and blue to that time. During the entire season, not a single game was lost. The Notre Dame Team came South on their annual tour and were seeking revenge as they had lost to Carson-Newman the previous year. "Big Red" Strange, All-American tackle for Notre Dame who was considered one of the best pitchers in the Big Ten Conference, had been saved to wreck revenge upon the Parsons. Notre Dame returned home with another revenge to seek as they were beaten 6 to 4. Also, Cumberland College, which had previously beaten The University of Tennessee went home with a defeat and a tie (APPALACHIAN, 1925:156).

During that time many of the athletic teams would come south to play because of the weather and also because of the new Butler-Blanc Gymnasium, the "show-place of the South." It was small, but it was one of the best facilities in the country. It also had the indoor running track which was one of the first of its kind in the East Tennessee area (Interview with Coach Holt, March, 1972).

In the yearbook of 1925, it was mentioned that the outlook for athletics at Carson-Newman was bright. "The 'clean up' took many of the best athletes out of school, but it left those with the proper morals, willing hearts, and those with the Carson-Newman spirit" (APPALACHIAN, 1925:140).

Basketball followed the "clean up" in football and the worst was feared. However, it was not as unfavorable as anticipated; the basketball team won 75 percent of its games, and this was thought to be a successful season (APPALACHIAN, 1925: 140).

Following the turbulent football season of 1924-1925, the young but able Coach Lake Russell wrote (APPALACHIAN, 1925: 140):

> I am happy that I can again say that the outlook for athletics at Carson-Newman is bright. We can look into the future with fond expectations and clear consciences. We can face the season to come without fear of shame, because irregularities which having heretofore caused us embarrassment have been abolished, and a possibility of a recurrence of any of these have been far removed. The clean-up has swept many of our best athletes out of school, but it left us with the proper morals, willing hearts, and those with the Carson-Newman spirit.

# It Gets Foggy at Mossy Creek

The Parsonettes for the 1925 season were coached by Wilton Abbott, who was a great punter on the football team. (It was not unusual for the girls' coach to be a student athlete at the college.) They outscored their opposition by an amazing 263 points to 125 points and their record was 14-2 (APPALACHIAN, 1925: 155).

After the violent shake-up in the team in 1924, the 1925 football results were not disheartening. The line average less than 170 pounds, and the backfield averaged about 136 pounds. The team was coached by Lake Russell as head coach and Frosty Holt, assistant coach and also a member of the junior class (APPALACHIAN. 1926: 162). Frosty Holt's eligibility ended in the spring of 1926, but because of the preparatory courses which he had taken at Carson-Newman to complete his high school work, he still lacked several hours of college work for graduation. Coach Lake Russell realized his coaching potential and since he could not use him as a player, he asked Frosty to be his assistant for the two remaining years he would be at Carson- Newman. Holt was also assistant coach in basketball and baseball and was coach of the girls' basketball team (Taped Interview with Coach Holt, March, 1972).

## OUTSTANDING BASKETBALL TEAMS

The basketball story for 1926 was favorable. In defeating every contender in East Tennessee, including The University of Tennessee, the Fighting Parsons' basketball team annexed the state crown of 1926 Coach Russell was in his fourth year as coach of the basketball team and each year was most successful: During those four years; he lost only eleven games and the team not only boasted a Championship team, but also boasted of having the tallest basketball player in the world, Milas Shoun (APPALACHIAN, 1926: 162). "Slim, as his teammates called him, was 7' 3 " tall and was not recruited to come to Carson-Newman but came on his own because his relatives had attended Carson-Newman. Coach Holt recalled that "Slim" played defense and would usually stay at one end of the court on defense, while the other four team members would play full court and press with the ball. During that time there was not a goal-tending rule and many times "Slim" would just reach up and knock the ball out of the basket, much to the opposing teams' disgust (Taped Interview with Coach Holt, March, 1972).

Mr. Abbott, who coached the tennis team in 1926, related that it was during that year that tennis became a major sport at the college (APPALACHIAN, 1926:167). Miss Mae Iddins, who was a student during the 1920's related that the girl's intercollegiate basketball team took trips as the boys did. The girls would play as many as six nights a week, with many of the trips on the road. The team traveled as the boys did, by train, and if the school was 'very far, spent the night and returned the next day (Taped Interview with Miss Mae Iddins, April, 1972).

## MAE IDDINS RETURNS

After graduating from Carson-Newman in the mid-1920's, Miss Mae Iddins took a position as physical education teacher at Jefferson City High School. Shortly after that, President James T. Warren felt the need for a full-time physical education teacher for women. Miss Iddins was approached about the position and after attending the American College of Physical Education for one year, she returned to her alma mater in 1928. She was in charge of the women's division of health and physical education (Taped Interview with Miss Mae Iddins, April, 1972).

During her first years at Carson-Newman, few girls participated in the physical education program. Coach Russell and Coach Holt were in charge of the boys' program, but they were so involved in coaching that Miss Iddins was given the responsibility for the physical education program (Taped Interview with Miss Mae Iddins, April, 1972).

In 1927, Coach Russell was assisted by Sam Kinsley as "Physical Director," but the football team had a losing season with a team of lightweights. According to the APPALACHIAN, Carson-Newman was no push-over as

> "they made Maryville and King fight for their oats. Milligan had no cinch, and Cumberland was thankful for their margin of one touchdown. Even the mighty Tennessee did not go into the game with a notion to make it a travesty."

Some of the other opponents were Emory and Henry, Georgetown, Lenoir Rhyne, East Tennessee State Teachers College, and Tusculum (APPALACHIAN, 1928: 101).
The basketball and baseball teams of 1927 also had losing seasons. In basketball, the varsity team played fifteen games, won five and lost ten, with a total of 483 points to the 539 points for the opposing teams (APPALACHIAN, 1928:108). Frank Mullendore, who participated in baseball from 1925-1928 and was captain of the 1928 team stated that not much emphasis was placed on baseball during this period (Questionnaire, April, 1972).

## PUBLIC RELATIONS POSITION ADDED

For many years there had been a need for publicity for the athletic teams. Some coverage was provided but as the interest grew and the teams improved more coverage was needed. Coach Russell also recognized that good publicity would help the overall sports program. Fletcher Sweet related his experience of becoming the first public relations employee of the college in 1927 (Questionnaire, April, 1972):

> I was out for the football team, taking my licks, and not hurting many people in return. Carson-Newman had some fair ball players and a freshman had very little chance of replacing one of them even though freshmen could play varsity ball then, if he could make it.
>
> Coach Lake Russell called me into his office one day and said, 'Sweet, why don't you turn in your uniform and cover our games for the press?'
>
> While my immediate goal was winning a letter, my long time goal was to become one of the world's outstanding journalists. So Coach Russell had me there. After all, I had been a stringer correspondent for a daily newspaper for a couple of years.
>
> 'We've never had much coverage in the papers," Coach Russell went on. 'And, right now I believe you can be of more value to us with a typewriter than with a uniform.

*It Gets Foggy at Mossy Creek*

Then came the clincher: 'I'll award you a letter as publicity manager.'

This was how I became Carson-Newman's first 'press agent.' This, too, explains one reason my attendance at every athletic event, along with my natural love for things athletic.

Well, it was a joy to cover the athletic news for daily papers, and, then something else bobbed up. Dr. O.E. Sams, Carson-Newman's president, came over to me at the football field one afternoon at spring practice and asked, 'Sweet, how would you like to be press representative for the college?'

'If I'm not here, I'll recommend that to my successor; Dr. Sams said. But, at that time, I didn't catch the significance in his 'not being there.' Had I been a little bit better newsman at the time, I should have pursued that angle, and could have broken the story on President Sams' going to Bluefield College. But, I was thinking of something else.

Then, from press agent to press representative to public information director came about in easy steps. Dr. Sams did go to Bluefield; and his successor Dr. James T. Warren did appoint me to the post, for the handsome salary of $15 per month. Oh boy! That 15 bucks per month just covered my dining hall bill ... and that was something. (I hear that good public relations directors command more kingly salaries now.) But, editorial work generally has improved its compensations, too. The things a fellow would do in 1927 to stay in college!

## "FROSTY" HOLT RETURNS

Toward the close of 1928-1929 academic session, Coach Russell was offered a position as head coach at Mercer University, Macon, Georgia, which he accepted. Before leaving, he strongly recommended Samuel B. "Frosty" Holt who since his graduation in 1927, had been coach at Virginia High School, Bristol, Virginia. His two years at Bristol had given him valuable experience and had been very successful. He, also, developed one of the all-time great football players--Beattie Feathers. In his years at Carson-Newman, Coach Holt was in charge of three major sports and the head of the Health and Physical Education Department of the college (Taped Interview with Coach Holt, March, 1972).

While Coach Holt was a student at Carson-Newman, he earned thirteen athletic letters in his four years of competition in football, basketball, baseball, and track. In 1922, Carson-Newman sponsored a track team and he earned his letter by participating in the 100 - and 220 - yard dashes (Billington, 1953:36).

During the early 1920's as Carson-Newman was growing, there was a big "push" for athletics. Toward the end of the decade, however, Carson-Newman was not placing as much emphasis on its sports program and the results were reflected. The facilities were only fair, the number of athletes were limited, and there were few scholarships. At that time the college had twelve $100 scholarships for all sports (Taped Interview with Coach Holt, March, 1972).

When Mr. Holt took over, he accepted a real challenge. His purpose was to bring all sports to the top and to build a good physical education program for the college.

The 1930 Carson-Newman yearbook (137) best described the situation that faced Coach Holt in football his first year as head of the Fighting Parsons:

> It is a difficult task for a coach with the ability possessed by Coach Holt ... with vain hopes of anything near an approaching success to receive the reins of a football team and find that his best horses have disappeared.

As Coach Holt himself expressed it, "I couldn't go in any direction but up." The squad was limited in size and number and lacked experience, but Coach Holt worked to develop speed to make up for the lack of size (Billington, 1953:47). Coach Holt led the 1929 Carson-Newman squad against such major schools as The University of Tennessee and the University of Kentucky; the squad won one, lost four, and tied one (KNOXVILLE NEWS-SENTINEL, September 29, 1929).

The 1930 football season was of special interest since Carson-Newman upset Mercer University by the score of 13 to 6. This "duel" was most interesting as a "pupil versus teacher" contest since Coach Lake Russell was head coach at Mercer University. The ORANGE and BLUE (November 22, 1930:2) had this to say about the game.

> The outstanding feature was the coaching of Coach Holt. 'He was a backfield man when he played for Carson-Newman and Coach Russell. He was the 'Fox' of Football in these parts and has more speed than a central office girl has wrong numbers.' It was a natural sequence that he drill his men for speed and endurance.

During his second season, Coach Holt's team won six games and lost three (APPALACHIAN, 1913: 130).

## "PARSONS" BECOME EAGLES

During the 1930-1931 school year at Carson-Newman, Coach Holt decided that a new name was needed for the athletic teams of Carson-Newman. He felt that people thought of Carson-Newman as a school for preachers and this made it a little harder for him to recruit athletes. Because of this, he conducted a contest, offering a $10 gold piece for the best nickname suggested for the college teams. The name chosen was "Fighting Eagles." The person submitting the winning name was Miss Tennessee Jenkins, professor of history at the college. Since that time all athletic teams representing the college have been known as the Fighting Eagles (Taped Interview with Coach Holt, March, 1972).

*It Gets Foggy at Mossy Creek*

Coach Holt said, however, that many times he wished he had not changed the name of the college teams. The name Fighting Parsons meant much because of its origin and since it was so unusual it had received national attention.

The college purchased two Eagle statues to stand guard over the portals of the Administration Building. It was felt the presence of the Eagles would inspire the team and student body each time they passed. The students were to show their appreciation by backing the teams. The students in an article written in the ORANGE and BLUE (September 29, 1931:1) were asked to, "Be a sport; cheer together, smile together and be together. The college expects it, the team expects it, and the students should not fall short of these expectations."

In January of 1931, Fred Noe, a former player at Furman University, was added to the coaching staff as an assistant. He and Coach Holt made an excellent coaching combination, and much of Carson-Newman's success during the 1930's was due to the coaching and scouting of Coach Noe (Billington, 1953:48).

The football teams had shown improvement from year to year and in 1931, when Coach Holt gave the practice call "some thirty candidates donned their pigskin togs and appeared for the first practice session." There were a number of new prospects available, along with seventeen lettermen reporting from the previous year, and Coaches Holt and Noe rapidly molded the candidates into a smooth-working machine. Everyone felt the year was a success because they ended the season with a record of six wins, two losses, and one tie game; but even more important they were runners-up for the championship in the Smoky Mountain Athletic Conference (SMAC) (APPALACHIAN, 1932: 132).

The 1932 football team had a record of five wins, two losses, and one tie and they were able to win the Smoky Mountain Athletic Conference title for the first time since the conference was organized in 1927 (APPALACHIAN, 1933: 109). The following year, the 1933 football team brought the conference championship to Carson-Newman [or the second straight year, with a season's record of seven wins and one loss (APPALACHIAN, J935: 118).

The record of the 1934 football team was average, with four games won, three lost and one tied (APPALACHIAN, (1935:111). It was the only Carson-Newman football team coached by Coach Holt to lose to Tusculum College when Tusculum won in the closing minutes of the game by kicking a field goal (Billington, 1953:49).

**UNDEFEATED FOOTBALL TEAM**

The 1936 football team, coached again by Coaches Holt and Noe was their best all-round team, according to the record book. The team won every contest of the season, consisting of ten games, making 219 points to 27 for their opponents and the Smoky Mountain Athletic Conference championship went to Carson-Newman once again. Only four touchdowns were scored against the Eagles during the season and no opponent scored more than once (APPALACHIAN, 1937: 124). Carson-Newman was beaten that year by East Tennessee State 2 to 0, hut because of an ineligible player, the game was declared a forfeit and Carson-Newman was given an undefeated season (ORANGE and BLUE, November 24, 1936:3). The learn was led by the All- Conference fullback Wendell "Yankee" Henderson who scored eleven touchdowns and fifteen extra points for eighty-one total points during the season. He scored the first eighteen points against Maryville in the last game of the season (ORANGE and BLUE, November 24, 1936: 1). From this team, Wendell Henderson (1937) and Oscar Monday (1940) both went on to play in the National Football League (Questionnaire by John C. Murray, April, 1972).

The record of that outstanding team was as follows (Billington, 1953: 164):

| | | | |
|---|---|---|---|
| Carson-Newman | 14 | 0 | Hiwassee |
| Carson-Newman | 26 | 8 | Western Carolina |
| Carson-Newman | 19 | 7 | Emory & Henry |
| Carson-Newman | 2 | 0 | E.T.S. Teachers |
| Carson-Newman | 54 | 6 | Tusculum |
| Carson-Newman | 32 | 0 | Milligan |
| Carson-Newman | 22 | 0 | Cumberland |
| Carson-Newman | 12 | 6 | King |
| Carson-Newman | 12 | 0 | Lenoir Rhyne |
| Carson-Newman | 26 | 0 | Maryville |

When Coach Holt called the 1933 basketeers, he was greeted by eight veteran players. The season proved to be highly successful as their record indicated. Eighteen games were played, thirteen in the conference, with nine victories and four defeats; five outside the conference, with three victories and two defeats (Appalachian, 1933: 116).

Coach Noe was in charge of the tennis team for the year 1933, which was to be the first tennis team to bear the Fighting Eagle name. The Eagle "clay court clouters" were unable to schedule as many meets as they desired because the spring semester closed in May, but they acquitted themselves well in the five meets in which they did participate (APPALACHIAN, 1933: 116).

## POINT SYSTEM

Women continued to play in inter-collegiate contests until 1931, when, in institutions throughout the land, participation by women in inter-collegiate basketball was largely discontinued. It was decided that inter-collegiate basketball was too strenuous. Carson-Newman accepted the trend and re-constructed its program to include intramural contests and other campus activities. Since Carson-Newman did not have inter-collegiate sports for girls, an extensive intramural athletic program was sponsored each year by Miss Mae Iddins, girls coach. All of the seasonal sports were included in the program and an opportunity was given to every girl in school to participate and to earn a letter. Miss Iddins developed a point system, giving credit in points to the girls entering the different sports. At the end of the year, the twelve girls having the highest number of points received a letter and a sweater. All making 500 points who did not receive a sweater were awarded the school emblem, an Eagle. In the fall, soccer, speedball, volleyball and tennis were offered to the girls. The winter and spring program included basketball, baseball, and track. The pool was open throughout the year and swimming was one of the most popular sports (APPALACHIAN, 1933: 119).

*It Gets Foggy at Mossy Creek*

The Eagle Club, which was organized in 1933, was made up of girls who had won an award in the college intramural program of sports. The award was based on winning 500 points. The Girls Letter Club was composed of those girls who won a second-year award in the intramural program, which was based on 600 points. A Girls Physical Education Club was made up of majors in the program. Miss Mae Iddins sponsored these organizations, which were related to the physical education for women, until her retirement in 1970 (Carr, 1959: 302).

An article written in the ORANGE and BLUE (September 10, 1935:3) reported concerning the point system, "Carson-Newman girls must participate in athletics to appreciate the real spirit of the way athletics should be carried on. In this, Coach Iddins excels any girls' coach that can be found. Acknowledgment should be given to her for her most attractive and systematic procedure."

Through the work of Coach Noe, an extensive tennis schedule was carried out. The teams improved and the participants took a greater interest each year (APPALACHIAN. 1934: 123).

In the 1935 -1936 session, scholarships increased from twelve $100 scholarships to twenty-four $100 scholarships. Mr. D. L. Butler, chairman of the Board of Trustees, was interested in athletics and helped out financially during that time. He was the same D. L. Butler who was co-builder of the Butler-Blanc Gymnasium (Taped Interview with Coach Holt, March, 1972). It was also during that year the school purchased a new bus in which to transport the athletic teams (APPALACHIAN, 1935:114).

The 1936-1937 basketball team followed in the footsteps of the football team by "taking the cup in basketball." The team met seventeen opponents and won sixteen victories, the only loss being to the powerful University of Tennessee cagers. They won all the fourteen conference games in which they participated and scored 730 points as compared with 509 scored by their opponents. Malcolm E. Brown scored a conference record of twenty-six points against Tusculum College. The "Eaglets" or freshmen, played a ten-game schedule, winning seven and losing three. With such a winning freshman team, the future looked favorable for the coming years (APPALACHIAN, 1937:129).

The 1937 football team brought the Smoky Mountain Conference Title to Carson-Newman for the second straight year. After getting off to a bad start by losing to Hiwassee, 18 to 12, the 1937 Eagles squad went undefeated for the remainder of the season, winning seven, losing one, and tying one (APPALACHIAN, 1938: 127).

Interest in all sports was rising, and the intramural program was advancing as a result of careful planning. Much credit was due to Coach Holt for fostering a spirit of friendly rivalry and competition and also for giving less talented athletes a chance to compete in the sport of their choice. No small credit was due the Athletic Committee of the two men's societies who carried out efficiently the well planned program of Coach Holt. The intramural program began each year in the fall and continued through the school term.

# *A History of Sports at Carson-Newman College 1851-1974*

The first event was the annual freshman cross country race, which was conducted on an intramural basis among the societies on campus. It was followed by speedball, volleyball, basketball and relays with the team having the most paints at the end of the school year being declared the winner (APPALACHIAN, 1938: 133).

## TRAGIC BUS WRECK

On February 1, 1938, the most tragic accident in the athletic history of Carson-Newman College occurred when two basketball players, Jimmie Grissom and Roy Roberts, were killed in a collision of the team bus enroute to an out-of-town game. The 1937-1938 Eagles' basketball squad was undefeated prior to the accident (Billington, 1953:50). The accident was a shock to everyone in the college and the community. After a period of time a decision had to be made whether or not Carson-Newman would carry on the basketball schedule or cancel for the remainder of the season. The ORANGE and BLUE (February 8, 1938:3) carried this story about the decision:

> After a very dramatic meeting with br. J. T. Warren (President) and Professor Alex Chavis (head of the Athletic Committee) Saturday morning, Coach "Frosty" Holt and his shattered basketball squad voted unanimously to carry the Eagles colors even onward in memory of their deceased teammates. Whatever the destiny of the new Eagle machine is, the Carson-Newman student body is behind them all the way.

The basketball season ended with only two losses (Taped Interview with Coach Holt, March, 1972).
Later, by vote of the student body, a metal plaque was placed on the entrance wall of Butler-Blanc Gymnasium which read as follows (Carr, 1959:276):

> To the Memory of Roy Roberts
> And
> James Grissom
> This Tablet is dedicated
> February, 1938
> By the Students of
> **CARSON-NEWMAN COLLEGE**

When the Holt Fieldhouse was built in 1959, the plaque was added to the trophy case.
The 1938 football schedule included larger schools in an attempt to upgrade the football program. Following is a write-up from the school paper (ORANGE and BLUE, September 13, 1938:3):

> *CARSON-NEWMAN LAUNCHES INTO BIG TIME FOOTBALL. EAGLES FACE UNDEFEATED MARSHALL OUTFIT, BUCKEYE CONFERENCE CHAMPS, THE BATTLE OF THE UNDEFEATED. CRAFTY VERSUS FROSTY.*
>
> Carson-Newman's gridiron stock is due for a bounce skyward around September 24 when Coach "Frosty" Holt and his pigskin protégés, for the first time in recent years,

launch into big time football competition at Huntington, West Virginia, engaging Marshall's "Big Green" Buckeye Conference Champions.

The contest will be a "natural" with Carson-Newman twice consecutive holder of the Smoky Mountain Athletic Conference crown, undefeated and unscored upon in the conference last year, locking horns with another team that swept through the season last year undefeated in the 8th ranking conference of the nation with a combined total of 274 points to lead the nation in scoring at the same time placing 10 men on the All-Buckeye Conference team. This year, losing only two men, Coach "Crafty" Cam Henderson, one time victor over Navy, Army, and Fordham, hopes to duplicate last year's great record by smashing Carson-Newman in their season's opener featuring High School Day in one of the seasons three feature games.

The Eagles fell to the mighty Buckeye Champions and lost three other games to end the season with a 5-4-1 record (Carr, 1959:140). The team was strong again in 1939 and won the Smoky Mountain Conference for the third time in four years. In a season that featured contests with very strong teams outside the conference. Coach Holt's 1939 squad won five, lost two, and tied two. The 1939 Carson-Newman - Milligan game (Which Carson-Newman won, 7-6) marked the first Carson-Newman football game to be broadcast from the local field (APPALACHIAN, 1940: 120).

In March of 1938, Coach Holt called spring basketball practice for the first time. The ORANGE and BLUE (March 15, 1938:3) had this to say:

With the exception of graduating seniors, the entire squad is now engaging in fast offensive drills that will place the Eagle basketball stocks at a definite above par value when the Smoky Mountain League hardwood season opens next January.

The 1939 season found Coach Holt losing player after player to the armed services, yet with only a small remnant of the conference championship team of the previous year, Coach Holt led his Eagles to second place in the conference, losing only one conference game (APPALACHIAN, 1941:51).

**SUMMARY**

The athletic program at Carson-Newman had been greatly reduced during World War I. Football was the only program sponsored by the college as a part of military training for the students. John Kilpatrick, returning from World War I, assumed coaching duties in 1920 and the team for that season broke even. The 1921-1922 season marked the turning point of the athletic program at Carson-Newman. This was the year that the college became known as the "Fighting Parsons" because of a football incident involving a Carson-Newman football player who was studying for the ministry.

The following year, Tom Moran was hired to coach football as the first full-time football coach with no teaching duties included. Even though he was only at Carson-Newman for two years, he was regarded at that time as the coach who made Carson-Newman famous in football.

# *A History of Sports at Carson-Newman College 1851-1974*

Under Coach Lake Russell and quarterback "Frosty" Holt, the early 1920's had some outstanding years in football as Carson-Newman was playing top schools and defeating them. Toward the close of the 1928-1929 academic session, Coach Russell was offered a position as head coach at Mercer University, Macon, Georgia, which he accepted. Before leaving, he strongly recommended Sam B. "Frosty" Holt as his replacement.

During the next few years, Carson-Newman had great success in football. The 1932 team won the Smoky Mountain Athletic Conference title for the first time and brought home the championship four out of the following seven years (1933-1939). According to the records, the 1936 team was the greatest of Coach Holt's teams and the greatest team at Carson-Newman.

In 1921, a long-time dream became a reality. The new Butler-Blanc Gymnasium was completed and was the pride of the campus. It was also during the 1921-1922 academic year that athletic scholarships were given to support the sports program. The 1926 basketball team defeated every contender in East Tennessee, including The University of Tennessee, and won the state crown. In a four-year period, only one game was lost to a Tennessee team coached by Russell; Carson-Newman lost a total of eleven games during his tenure.

The 1936 team won sixteen games and lost one to The University of Tennessee and was one of the most outstanding basketball teams in Carson-Newman's history.

After graduating from Carson-Newman in the mid-1920's, Miss Mae Iddins took a position as physical education teacher at the local high school and returned to her alma mater in 1928 after attending the American College of Physical Education for one year. She was in charge of the Women's Health and Physical Education Department and contributed greatly to the development of the program for the girls. Miss Iddins continued her program and the women continued to participate in intercollegiate contests until 1931, when, in colleges throughout America, intercollegiate basketball for women was largely discontinued.

Baseball was reorganized in 1921 and a good record was made. In 1924, Coach Russell had one of the best baseball teams to wear the orange and blue, and they were undefeated for the season,
The 1933 tennis team under Coach Noe was the first tennis team to bear the "Fighting Eagles" name. The team was unable to schedule as many meets as they desired because the spring semester closed in May, but they acquitted themselves well in the five meets in which they did participate.
The athletic program during this period of time withstood the depression and World War I to find the 1930's with a well-established and effective program.

*It Gets Foggy at Mossy Creek*

**Jellicorse**          **Lake Russell**          **Sharp**
                        **Football 1921**

---

**Basketball 1921**                    **Lake Russell**

# A History of Sports at Carson-Newman College 1851-1974

**McLain – Campbell – Kelly – Reece – McBee – King
Basketball Team 1920**

---

**The Jazz Baby Club**

# It Gets Foggy at Mossy Creek

**Ira Dance, the original "Fighting Parson" is pictured with teammates Moffett, Holt and Burnett.**

*A History of Sports at Carson-Newman College 1851-1974*

**Football Banquet – Hotel Farragut, Knoxville – 1923**

---

**Athletic Field - 1923**

# It Gets Foggy at Mossy Creek

Russell Bebb

John Hutchins

---

Letterman Club 1923

Athletic Field 1923

# *A History of Sports at Carson-Newman College 1851-1974*

# It Gets Foggy at Mossy Creek

**The Roaring Twenties**

---

**Injured "Frosty" Holt**

# *A History of Sports at Carson-Newman College 1851-1974*

**Gymnasium – 1925**

*It Gets Foggy at Mossy Creek*

**Velma Davis**        **Helen Patten**        **Vera King**

*A History of Sports at Carson-Newman College 1851-1974*

# FOOTBALL

*It Gets Foggy at Mossy Creek*

## A History of Sports at Carson-Newman College 1851-1974

ROBERTA SMITH — GUARD · MILDRED BOYD — CENTER · BETSY MARTIN — FORWARD · MILDRED SCARBOROUGH — GUARD

PARSONETTES

POLLY ROGERS — GUARD · LOIS HIXSON — FORWARD · VIOLA LINGERFELT — GUARD · BERTHA DAVIS — FORWARD

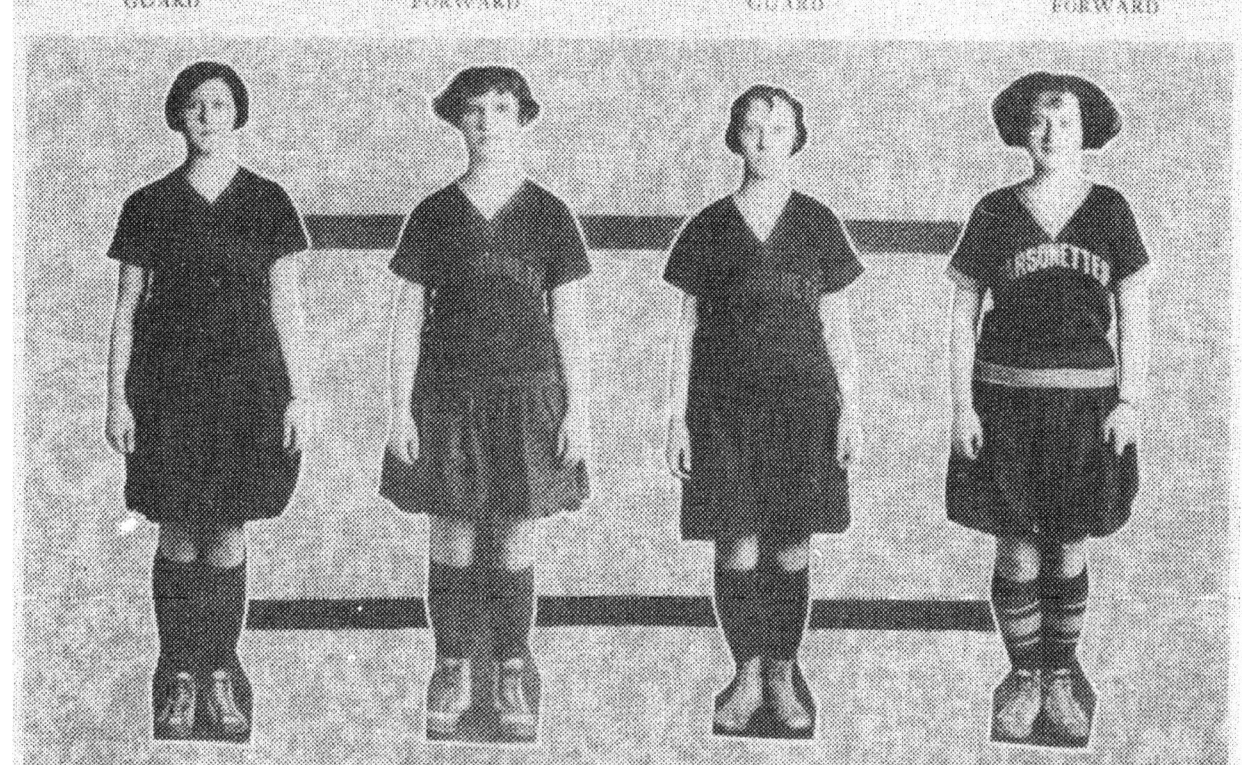

83

# It Gets Foggy at Mossy Creek

**Gymnasium Class 1925**

**Letterman Club 1924**

*A History of Sports at Carson-Newman College 1851-1974*

**Hypatian Basketball Team 1920's**

**1927 Offense**

# It Gets Foggy at Mossy Creek

**Bonita Sharp and Frosty Holt 1926**

# A History of Sports at Carson-Newman College 1851-1974

**J. Ferguson 1927**

**7' 3" Slim Shoun**

---

**Football Action 1927**

*It Gets Foggy at Mossy Creek*

      **Letter Men's Club**      **1929**      **Letter Girls' Club**

**Girls' Basketball Squad 1930**

# A History of Sports at Carson-Newman College 1851-1974

# *It Gets Foggy at Mossy Creek*

## A History of Sports at Carson-Newman College 1851-1974

*It Gets Foggy at Mossy Creek*

**Coach "Frosty" Holt
1931**

# A History of Sports at Carson-Newman College 1851-1974

**Cheerleaders 1930's**

---

**Girls' Gym Class 1932**

*It Gets Foggy at Mossy Creek*

**Football Stars 1931**

# A History of Sports at Carson-Newman College 1851-1974

**The 1936 Undefeated Football Team**

---

**Football 1935**

# *It Gets Foggy at Mossy Creek*

**Cheerleaders – Mosely, Wiggins, Rudder 1933**

---

**Girls Teams of 1936**

# A History of Sports at Carson-Newman College 1851-1974

*It Gets Foggy at Mossy Creek*

**Golf Club 1937**

**The basketball team of 1937-1938 was involved in a fatal bus accident which killed players Captain Roy Roberts and Jim Grissom.**

*A History of Sports at Carson-Newman College 1851-1974*

**Girls' Basketball 1932**

---

**Girls' Volleyball 1932**

*It Gets Foggy at Mossy Creek*

**Girls' Basketball 1937**

**Letter Men's Club 1932**

# A History of Sports at Carson-Newman College 1851-1974

**C. P. Wilson**

**Bill Catlett**

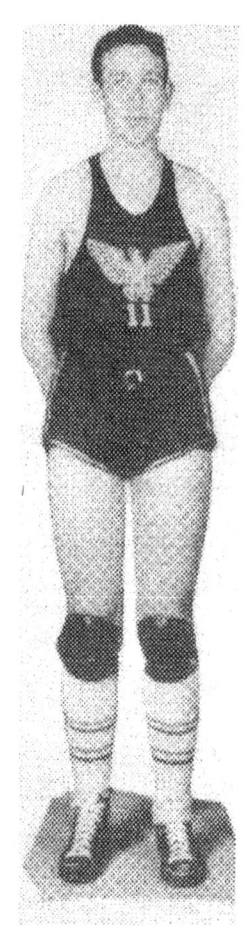

**Paul Layman**

**T. J. Stafford 1934**

**Coach Holt and Coach Fred Noe**

# *It Gets Foggy at Mossy Creek*

**Coach Mae Iddins**

**Women's Speedball Team**

**Coach Frosty Holt 1939**

# A History of Sports at Carson-Newman College 1851-1974

**Eagle Spirit 1939**

103

*It Gets Foggy at Mossy Creek*

# CHAPTER IV

# THE WAR YEARS AND A PERIOD OF GROWTH

## 1940 - 1959

The college, as did the nation, felt the effects of World War II. Carson-Newman had built up the athletic program and sports were on the upgrade when the war began. Naturally, most of the men, including the athletes, left college to serve their country.

Despite the loss of personnel, the "Fighting Eagles" continued their sports program and used the material at hand. The 1940 record showed Carson-Newman's football team with four wins and four losses. The game with Appalachian State Teachers College of Boone, North Carolina, was the first game played at night on McCown Field. Before that, home games had been played on Saturday afternoon (Billington, 1953: 51.) With still additional losses to the armed services, the team of 1941 had five losses, three wins and one tie. "This record did not truly show the fighting spirit the Eagles displayed all season despite lack of experience and size." Credit was given to the fine team play and spirit of the team members (APPALACHIAN, 1942: 115).

The 1940-1941 basketball team had "probably the worst record in the history of Carson-Newman." On the team, however, was Snead Nevils who broke the existing scoring record with thirty-six points. The squad also defeated Emory and Henry who had "the top scorer in the country" (Questionnaire by John C. Murray, April, 1972). The 1941-1942 basketball season "was one of the most successful in a student generation or so," winning twelve of eighteen games. By winning over Maryville, Johnson City Teachers, Milligan and Lincoln Memorial University, the Eagles established undisputed claim to the Smoky Mountain championship (APPALACHIAN, 1924:122).

## V-12 NAVY PROGRAM

In the spring of 1942, it became evident that having a football team at Carson-Newman during the coming school year would be impossible. When Sam Jones, Coach at Knoxville High School in Knoxville, Tennessee, was called into the service of his country in the middle of October, "Frosty" Holt was asked to replace him for the remainder of the season. Coach Holt would work in the physical education department at Carson- Newman in the morning and coach the Knoxville High School team in the afternoon (Billington, 1953:52-53).

When a V -12 Navy Unit made its training quarters at Carson-Newman, Coach Holt assembled a basketball team composed mainly of Navy men and enjoyed a winning season with a seventeen and three record (APPALACHIAN, 1943:119).

Coach Holt related that 275 men arrived on campus as part of the V-12 program. Other area schools which participated in this program were Emory and Henry, Milligan, Sewanee, and Howard College. Other schools participating in the V -12 program sponsored football teams as a part of the training program for the men. Coach Holt said he remembered how hard everyone at the college worked to get the commander to reconsider his decision not to allow the boys to participate in the football program at Carson-Newman.

Finally, the commander did reconsider and it was a "great day on the campus." It meant that Carson-Newman could once again have a football team and could compete with the other schools in the V-12 program (Taped Interview with Coach Holt, March, 1972).

Coach Holt was pleased because there were great players from all over the country involved in the V-12 program. Despite the obstacles that had to be overcome in order to field a football team during the war days, a schedule of five games was played in 1943. All games had to be played away from Carson-Newman, there being no football field, but this did not bother the players as they won four of the five games, losing only to Vanderbilt, another V-12 school (Taped Interview with Coach Holt, March, 1972), The second year of the V-12 football program at Carson-Newman, in 1944, Coach Holt's Navy men went through a four-game season undefeated (APPALACHIAN, 1945:53-54). This was the last year for the V12 program as the unit moved and football was not brought back until 1946.

The 1942-1943 basketball team with a record of 17-3 was the best team at Carson-Newman since the 1937 team with a record of 16-1. The basketball squad made a major contribution to the life of the college as it furnished them with many hours of fun and enjoyment. Basketball played an even more important role that year because there was no football program on campus. The college dedicated a special sports edition to the basketball team to show its pride, and in this issue was a comment about Coach Holt written by Dana X. Bible, an outstanding alumnus, "I congratulate Carson-Newman on having a man of his type heading up the athletic department" (ORANGE and BLUE, February, 17, 1943:1, 10).

## BASEBALL DISCONTINUED

In the following issue of the ORANGE and BLUE (March 30, 1943:3), this was said about baseball:

> Due to the existing circumstances, Carson-Newman will not have an intercollegiate baseball team this year. First, there are few baseball players left in the school. Second, there will be difficulty in securing equipment. Third, there would be only one or two teams in the vicinity to play. And fourth there would be little means of transportation.

Coach Holt, however, made arrangements for a softball team for the Reservists (about all the boys in the school), and four teams were organized to play a round-robin schedule within the school.

The 1943-1944 basketball squad had a record of 10-6, It was a year that was remembered by the civilian students because of the "fine spirit manifested by the Naval students, It was not long after the season started that they developed that fighting Carson-Newman spirit." Also in the yearbook, Roy Harmon, a student athlete who later became head football coach at Carson-Newman, had this to say about Coach Noe's leaving to go into the service (APPALACHIAN, 1944:84),

# A History of Sports at Carson-Newman College 1851-1974

> Coach Noe was one of the finest men that has ever been connected with this institution. He was a friend of the students and was always willing to help, As for his interest in athletics, others as well as I have expressed it this way: He was as interested in caring for a small scratch as he was for a broken bone, We're hoping that he will be back with "Frosty" soon,

After two great football seasons under Coach Holt, the V-12 program left the campus and there was not a football program in 1945, During the 1945-46 school year, Coach Holt took a leave of absence from Carson-Newman to coach at William and Mary College in Virginia (Billington, 1953:45).

## G. I.'S RETURN

When Coach Holt returned in 1946 he had a new assistant coach, T. J. Stafford, who graduated from Carson-Newman in 1937 after playing football under Holt. Coach Stafford remained as assistant for the 1946-1949 football seasons, took over as head coach in 1950 when Coach Holt retired from active football duty and in turn passed on the head coaching position to Roy Harmon, 1944 Carson-Newman graduate, after the 1951 season (Billington, 1953:55).

The final story of the 1946 Carson-Newman football team season read five victories, three losses, and one tie, The team was composed mostly of former G. I. 's "that seemed unable to completely hit its stride" until the last game when it trampled Cumberland, 41-0. The season not only brought Carson- Newman its first post-war football team, but it also introduced a new offensive system, The boys used the highly publicized "T" formation "with an occasional shift into the former Holt single-wing" (APPALACHIAN, 1947: 127).

The 1946-1947 Carson-Newman basketball team had a slow start but showed improvement by mid-season. The Carson-Newman five found Lincoln Memorial University to be the "class of East Tennessee" as they downed the Eagles 49-35 and 60-38. However, against other teams the Eagles more than held their own (APPALACHIAN, 1947:38).

## UNDEFEATED FOOTBALL TEAM

The close of the 1947 football season found the Eagles "with their most brilliant record in the past decade." After a rugged ten-game schedule, Coach Holt's gridiron unit finished without a defeat and with a record of eight wins and two ties. They won the Smoky Mountain Conference title with victories over Emory and Henry, Milligan, and Tusculum. Using the "T" formation, the team ran with "power and precision each time they took the field." Charles Moffett related his experience of how the "T" formation was installed at Carson-Newman (Questionnaire, Charles Moffett, April, 1972).

> Coach Holt, Bernie Moore, and I holed up in the Andrew Johnson Hotel in Knoxville upon my return from the Army in 1947. Coach Holt wanted to run the "T" formation for the first time and Bernie Moore had coached it at L. S. U. I was to be the "T"

## It Gets Foggy at Mossy Creek

quarterback. Using a shoe as a football--Coach Holt was center, Bernie and myself running backs--we learned in the room and went on to an undefeated season.

The keynote of the success of the 1947 Eagles was summed up in a statement from Coach Holt who "felt this team to be about the best he ever had." "Teamwork and cooperation were the leading factor in our victories" (APPALACHIAN, 1948: 127).

The record of the 1947 football team follows (APPALACHIAN, 1948: 129):

| | | | |
|---|---|---|---|
| Carson-Newman | 18 | 7 | Tennessee Tech |
| Carson-Newman | 13 | 7 | Western Carolina |
| Carson-Newman | 33 | 0 | Emory and Henry |
| Carson-Newman | 13 | 13 | Tennessee Wesleyan |
| Carson-Newman | 13 | 6 | Georgetown |
| Carson-Newman | 38 | 6 | East Tennessee State |
| Carson-Newman | 12 | 6 | Milligan |
| Carson-Newman | 48 | 6 | Tusculum |
| Carson-Newman | 7 | 7 | Maryville |
| Carson-Newman | 18 | 6 | Cumberland |
| Carson-Newman | 6 | 20 | West Chester State (Burley Bowl) |
| Carson-Newman | 219 | 84 | Opponents |

Glen Wade related that he was a member of the 1947 undefeated football squad and one of the things he remembered most was the defeat of Tennessee Tech, 18 to 7 (Questionnaire by Glen Wade, April, 1972). Also, Ernest Cosson remembered the 1947 season in which he played starting halfback on the team and the rivalry between Carson-Newman and Maryville in which the game ended in a 7 to 7 deadlock (Questionnaire by Ernest Cosson, April, 1972).

The 1947-48 basketball team had a mediocre season as they managed to capture winning decisions on only eight occasions while playing a twenty-one game schedule. This did not tell the whole story as they came through with some great performances and "gave the Carson-Newman fans untold thrills in chalking up seven victories out of ten appearances" on the home court (APPALACHIAN, 1948:137).

# *A History of Sports at Carson-Newman College 1851-1974*

Although Coach Holt fielded another good team in football the following year, the Eagles of 1948 could not seem to get started and ended the season with a record of four wins and six losses (APPALACHIAN, 1949:154).

With only four lettermen returning from the "ill-fated" squad of the year before, Coach Holt added some newcomers and built the basketball team into as "colorful a combination" as had worn the orange and blue in previous years (APPALACHIAN, 1949: 168).

### MAJOR PROGRAM FOR WOMEN INSTITUTED

During the war years, few girls attended Carson-Newman and the physical education program was limited. Miss Mae Iddins who was head of the girl's physical education department related that during that period she taught both mathematics and girl's physical education, After the war, the program expanded and in 1945 a physical education major program for the women was added, Miss Iddins had been planning this program before the war (Taped Interview with Miss Mae Iddins, March, 1972).

In addition to the major's program, physical education for all women students was offered. The freshman course introduced a wide variety of activities and after the freshman year, the students could choose the courses they wished to take. In 1968 a coeducational program was introduced.

The 1949 football season was a disappointing one of two wins, seven losses, and one tie. Despite their courage and determination, the Eagles of 1949 met with one bad break after another. The one bright spot of the season was a smashing 20-12 victory over their arch-rival, Maryville (APPALACHIAN, 1950: 172).

### "FROSTY" HOLT BECOMES BASEBALL COACH

Following an illness in 1950, Mr. Holt became director of physical education and baseball coach. During his nineteen football seasons as head coach at Carson-Newman College, Coach Holt produced six conference championship teams: 1932, 1933, 1936, 1937, 1939, and 1947. Of the nineteen seasons, only four were losing seasons. Coach Holt's total won and lost record while football coach at Carson-Newman totaled ninety-seven wins, fifty-one losses, and fourteen ties for a percentage of .655 (Billington, 1953:56).

### CHANGES IN COACHING STAFF

In 1950 Coach T. J. Stafford became the head football coach with George Watts as line coach. Many games were close, but the season record showed only three games won, one was tied, and five were lost. Coach Stafford had a successful basketball season, however, winning eleven games out of the twenty scheduled. The team journeyed to Lincoln Memorial University to meet East Tennessee State in the first round of the Smoky Mountain Tournament and lost a heartbreaker, 62-58, in an overtime (APPALACHIAN, 1951: 172). Coach Holt fielded a substantially new baseball team for the 1951 school year. The only returning lettermen were Joe Shipley, Hubert Ashe, and Tommy Northern. The season ended with a 6-5 overall record, a 5-2 conference record and the championship of the Smoky Mountain Conference (ORANGE and BLUE:, April 23, 1951:3). The tennis team under Coach Conwell had a winning season with an 8-5 record. Two juniors led the team in the number one and two position, Billy Beene and Bob Bates. The third position was filled by a freshman, Buddy Catlett (APPALACHIAN, 1951:147),

In the 1951 football season, Roy Harmon joined the staff and assisted Coach Stafford with the football program. Coaches Stafford, Harmon, and McBroon molded a "tough" determined aggregation of boys with only a few experienced lettermen sprinkled here and there, into a fast, hard-charging bunch of football players," Their won-lost record of 4-6 did not indicate their unbeatable spirit in one of the toughest schedules ever played by the college. Middle Tennessee State College, "boasting one of the finest small college teams in the South" and led by two "Little All-Americans" completely outclassed the Eagles in their opener at Murfreesboro and defeated the Eagles, 38-0. Carson-Newman next took on the Tennessee Tech Engineers and were again outclassed with a 42-6 defeat, Other colleges on the schedule were East Tennessee State and Western Carolina along with the regular conference schools, Some standouts were Hubert Ashe, David Smith, Sanford Gray, Bill Jennings, Jack Holt, Mac Lambert, and Harold Sorrells (APPALACHIAN, 1952:162-169). The following season, Coach Stafford left and Coach Roy Harmon was given the head position, He brought in as his assistant Jack Netcher. The story of the 1952 edition of the Eagles was one of "heartbreaking bad luck," Coaches Harmon and Netcher turned out a fine squad only to watch them lose seven games, six of which were by one touchdown or less (APPALACHIAN, 1953:96-103). The schedule again put the Eagles against some of the best college teams in the country, but they never gave up. Outstanding players were John Lambert, Jim Chesney, Tommy Dalton, Charlie King, Norman Wright, and Gene Burgin (APPALACHIAN, 1953:97-103). The 1953 season showed much improvement as Carson-Newman won five and lost two, each loss by a single touchdown. Coach Harmon changed his playing procedure from the "T" formation to the "single wing" (Carr, 1959:278). A spectacular win in this season was a victory over Austin Peay. The Eagles were considered a twenty-point underdog by sports writers, but when the final gun sounded, they were ahead 18-14 (APPALACHIAN, 1954:204).

The 1953 basketball squad under Coach Harmon had to fill every varsity position with new players except for one guard spot. Even though they did not have a winning season, the team showed improvement toward the end of the season (APPALACHIAN, 1953: 106). Baseball followed and again Coach Holt brought home the conference title with a 4-0 conference record. The team was headed by Hubert Ashe, Herky Payne, and Red Conner (ORANGE and BLUE, March 15; 1953:3).

The 1954 football season found Coach Netcher resigning for further graduate study and W. H. Roden, a candidate for the doctor's degree in physical education at Indiana University named to the athletic faculty (Carr, 1959:279). The record for that year under Coach Harmon and his new assistant showed five games won, two tied, and two losses. The basketball team won seven games and lost fifteen under Coach Roden. In tennis, the team under Coach Conwell was co-winner of the Smoky Mountain Conference championship and the baseball team under the leadership of Coach Holt was "runner-up" in the conference (APPALACHIAN, 1955: 152-158).

# *A History of Sports at Carson-Newman College 1851-1974*

In the 1956 football season, Carson-Newman won six games and lost three. After five games, the Eagles had a 2-3 record but this did not discourage them as they won the last four games giving them a 6-3 record APPALACHIAN, 1956:165). The basketball team under Coaches Holt and Roden ended their season with a 12-11 regular season record and a 6-4 conference record which placed them third in the conference. Coach Holt took the reins of the team in mid-season when Coach Roden left to complete work on his doctorate. "Perhaps the most thrilling part of the year was when the Eagles beat their tough rival Emory-Henry three times during the season," The Smoky Mountain Conference was held at Lincoln Memorial University and Arnold Mellinger, center, was placed on the All-Conference team; his game average for the season was twenty-one points (APPALACHIAN, 1956:165-170).

The 1957 football season found Carson-Newman with a 6-4 record. Going into their Homecoming game with a 4-3 record, the Eagles were not to be denied the victory as they rolled to a 35-7 victory over Georgetown. The Eagles then lost to Stetson before returning home to defeat Troy State by one point. In the last football game of the year, Carson-Newman defeated their arch-rival Maryville College 27-14 to complete a good season (APPALACHIAN, 1957:164-171).

The Eagles soared high above the basketball court to take the trophy as the 1956-1957 champions in the Smoky Mountain Athletic Conference. Two Carson-Newman players were named to the All-Conference team --Arnold Mellinger, who started every game during his four years at Carson-Newman and fouled out only once, received the honor for the fourth time; and Billy Henry who made it to the first time as a sophomore. The varsity team had a season record of 16-19 under Coach "Dusty" Roden and the "Baby Eagles" under freshman coach Bob Reagan had a season record of 17-3 (APPALACHIAN, 1957:172-176).

## BASEBALL ERA BEGINS

"With an all-conference catcher, first-string pitcher, second basemen and shortstop picked from one team, you could assume that a club had a pretty good year." Coach Holt had just that on his 1957 baseball club. It was the second year in a row that the baseballers had either won or split the Smoky Mountain Athletic Conference crown. The overall record was 12-5 and conference play was 8-2. "One of the wins Coach Holt and the whole team were very proud of was the 10-5 decision over The University of Tennessee." Other highlights of the season were wins over Lincoln Memorial University and two victories from East Tennessee State College (APPALACHIAN. 1957: 150).

## TENNIS HAS OUTSTANDING SEASON

The tennis team compiled a 16-1 record and won the Smoky Mountain Athletic Conference championship with a 9-0 record. "A win over Furman was probably the most striking jewel in the crown of J. O. Conwell's tennis team that year." The team was led by Otto Spangler, Kent Blazier, Leslie Peek, and Herb Childress. Professor Henry Dickenson, a biology teacher' at the college, assisted Coach Conwell and traveled with the team on several occasions (APPALACHIAN, 1959:151).

Fielding a football team that had nearly everything, the 1957 Eagles made an impressive record for themselves. Even with two close defeats on record, the team was rated very highly and was a colorful team to watch. The season ended with a 5-2-1 record, the only two defeats coming at the hands of Newberry College and Troy State. Coach Harmon had this to say about his club after the season ended, "One of the finest ball clubs I've had in recent years!' (APPALACHIAN, 1958:48).

The basketball season brought with it a new coach, Tom Bartlett, and a "banner year." The Eagles compiled a 17-7 overall record, with their 10-2 conference play gaining the Smoky Mountain Athletic Conference tournament was successful even though the Eagles were defeated in the finals by Lincoln Memorial University{APPALACHIAN,1958:'76-81).

The 1958 football squad encountered some "rough-going as well as winning some sweet victories." Coach Harmon had two new assistants, Ernest Cosson who had been an outstanding back in his Carson- Newman days and Jerry Morris, a University of Tennessee graduate who played on the line for the Volunteers during his four years at the university. The team felt they had a good season even though they fell short of a winning season by one game (APPALACHIAN, 1959:122-123).

## VOLUNTEER STATE ATHLETIC CONFERENCE FORMED

The 1958-1959 basketball season marked the first year in the Volunteer State Athletic Conference, made up of small colleges in the state of Tennessee. It was divided into the Eastern and Western Divisions--Carson-Newman being a member of the Eastern Division. The representatives of each division met at the end of the season to decide the Volunteer State Athletic Conference champion and the right to meet the Kentucky champion--the winner representing the district in the National Association of Intercollegiate Athletics.

The Eagles proved to be one of the strongest teams in the league. In the quarter finals of the tournament they beat Milligan only to lose a close game to Lincoln Memorial University in the semi-finals. In the consolation game they scored an impressive fifteen point victory over highly rated Austin Peay, Bill Henry was named to the season's All-Volunteer State Athletic Conference team. Leslie Peek and Billy Henry were also named to the All-Tournament team, Due to their fine showing in the tournament, the conference officials chose the Eagles as one of the three teams from the Volunteer State Athletic Conference to participate in the play-offs which led to competition in- the National Association of Intercollegiate Athletics tournament. After dominating the play for the first half, the Eagles fell behind and lost out in a thrilling game to the Union Bulldogs of Jackson, Tennessee, by a score of 66 to 65, the overall season record was fourteen wins and eleven losses (APPALACHIAN, 1959: 130-131).

With an overall 17-5 slate, the 1958 baseball team won both the Volunteer State Athletic Conference and the Smoky Mountain Athletic Conference crowns. Bill Henry and Pete Roach were named All-Conference along with the outfielder Ed Hicks. Frank Cate was one of the most effective pitchers in the league and he was given support by Jack Owenby, Jim Barr, and Bob Mann (APPALACHIAN. 1959: 136).

# *A History of Sports at Carson-Newman College 1851-1974*

## OUTSTANDING TENNIS TEAMS

The tennis team for that year had a great challenge as "a perfect record is hard to improve on in any league." The Smoky Mountain Athletic Conference title was won with a 13-0 record and in the Volunteer State Athletic Conference playoffs, visiting David Lipscomb bowed by a 6-3 score. Coaches J. O. Conwell and Tommy Bartlett guided the team to wins at Maryville and East Tennessee State, a 5-4 decision in each case. Entry in the Tennessee Intercollegiate Athletic Conference tournament in Chattanooga resulted in a third place position among all small colleges in Tennessee. Otto Spangler played the important games against all opponents and Captain Leslie Peek held the second position with only one conference loss and a win over The· University of Tennessee to his credit. Herb Childers at the number three position was "perhaps the steadiest performer" with T. S, Moore, Lloyd Parker, and Rill Foster playing fine tennis in the supporting positions (APPALACHIAN, 1959: 137).

## HOLT FIELDHOUSE BUILT

The 1959 version of the Eagles recorded "one of its most disastrous seasons in football history" with only one victory, that over Appalachian State. The highlight of the season was a last minute winning touchdown to topple five-touchdown-favored Appalachian State by a score of 26-22: At the conclusion of the season, guard Dalmouth Shealy and wing-back Ed Hicks were elected to the News-Sentinel's Small College All-Star Team (APPALACHIAN, 1960:116-127). In mid-September, the basketeers of Carson-Newman began their physical conditioning program and by the end of October they were in the newly built Holt Fieldhouse. They completed their twenty-seven game schedule with a won-lost record of 16-11; finishing second in the conference behind Tennessee Wesleyan with a record of 7-3. On opening night of the Volunteer State Athletic Conference tournament, Carson-Newman defeated David Lipscomb only to fall victim of Austin Peay and Belmont on successive nights to finish fourth in tournament play. Some of the outstanding players were Harry Sparks, Jack Owenby, Chris Jones, Howard Luttrell, and Gay Valentine (APPALACHIAN, 1960: 128-135).

Soccer was started as a non-varsity sport in the fall of 1958 and was highly regarded on the campus. Led by Brazilian captain Derrick Davis, the leader in scoring, the team ended the 1959 season in the loss column but showed improvement over the previous year. Some of the standouts were Danny Starnes, Charles Preston, Lamar Laing, Bill Bristow, Bob Rogers, and Captain Derrick Davis (APPALACHIAN, 1960: 139).

The tennis team was recognized as an outstanding small college team wherever they played. Year after year tennis at Carson-Newman continued to be a successful program. The netters of 1959 recorded a regular season record of thirteen wins and four losses. The Eagles, winning the Smoky Mountain Athletic Conference title and the Eastern division of the Volunteer State Athletic Conference, traveled to Nashville to play for the conference championship, Victory stood with the Eagles as they "smashed and lobbed their way to a 5-2 decision over the western division champions." The team also participated in the Tennessee Intercollegiate Athletic Conference tournament played at the University of the South in

# It Gets Foggy at Mossy Creek

Sewanee, Tennessee, and the Eagles established a fine record of ten wins and one loss (APPALACHIAN, 1960:p40).

## SUMMARY

Carson-Newman felt the effects of World War II as most of the men left the college to serve in the armed forces. Even though Carson-Newman lost many of their athletes, they continued their sports program and used the material available. In the 1940 and 1941 seasons, the football teams had average records but in the spring of 1942, it became evident that they would not be able to have a team the following fall. Coach Holt was therefore given other duties involving the physical education program.

It was during this time that one of the V-12 Navy Units was assigned for training at Carson-Newman. Coach Holt related that 275 men arrived on the campus as part of the program. Realizing the potential of these men, he persuaded the commander to allow them to play football for the college as part of their training program. Some of the other schools participating in the same program were Emory and Henry, Milligan, Sewanee, and Howard University.

The V-12 football team had a 4-1 record its first year and the following year, 1944, the team went through a four-game season undefeated. The V-12 program left the campus in 1945 and no football team was fielded that year. The following year, however, Coach Holt established a football program for the college again. He used the "T" formation with an occasional shift into the single wing. The success of his program was noted when the 1947 team had an 8-2 record, one of the best in a decade. In the following two years the teams did not make as good a showing.

Due to doctors' orders, Coach Holt was relieved of all coaching duties in 1950 with the exception of baseball. The head football position was turned over to T. J. Stafford and then to Roy Harmon in 1952. The football program remained about the same during the late 1950's with a record around the .500 mark or just below.

The basketball teams of the early 1940's were good, the 1942-1943 squad having a 17-3 record, one of the best since the 1937 team. The Navy students also played on the basketball team during their stay on campus and had two fine teams. The program continued with Mr. Holt as coach until 1950 when Roy Harmon became coach to be followed by W. H. "Dusty" Roden. The team's averages during this period were around the .500 mark. In 1957, Tommy Bartlett became head coach and had a 17-7 overall record with 10-2 in conference play. The following year, Dick Campbell became the new coach and with him came a new era in basketball as well as the new Holt Fieldhouse completed in 1959.

Mae Iddins continued to work with the girls' program both in intramurals and physical education. She was doing an excellent job with the department when the war years came. Miss Iddins related that during the war years she taught both mathematics and physical education. After the war, she expanded the program and in 1954 was able to introduce a women's major program for the department. She also introduced the "Freshman Program" which provided a variety of sports instruction for new students.

# *A History of Sports at Carson-Newman College 1851-1974*

Baseball was played on the campus until 1943. During the lapse of the sport on campus, Coach Holt organized softball teams which operated on an intramural basis. In 1950 when Mr. Holt was relieved of his coaching duties, he retained the baseball team and began the early 1950's by producing good clubs and in 1956 and 1957 won the Smoky Mountain Athletic Conference championships. Coach Holt also scheduled The University of Tennessee and defeated them. Tennis began the 1950's with good teams; the 1957 team had a 16-1 overall record and were 9-0 in the Smoky Mountain Athletic Conference under J. O. Conwell. The following season brought with it a 13-0 record and the Smoky Mountain Athletic Conference title.

The first soccer team was established on campus in 1958. Three games were scheduled and there was an unsuccessful effort to include soccer in the varsity program. The three matches were all against Maryville, and the Eagles won two out of the three encounters. The 1959 soccer team had a losing season but gained a great deal of valuable experience. Carson-Newman College met the challenge of many adversities during the 1940's and 1950's to strengthen the intercollegiate athletic program.

# It Gets Foggy at Mossy Creek

Tennis Action 1941

## A History of Sports at Carson-Newman College 1851-1974

**1943 Men's Letter Club**

**1942 Eagle Club**

# It Gets I

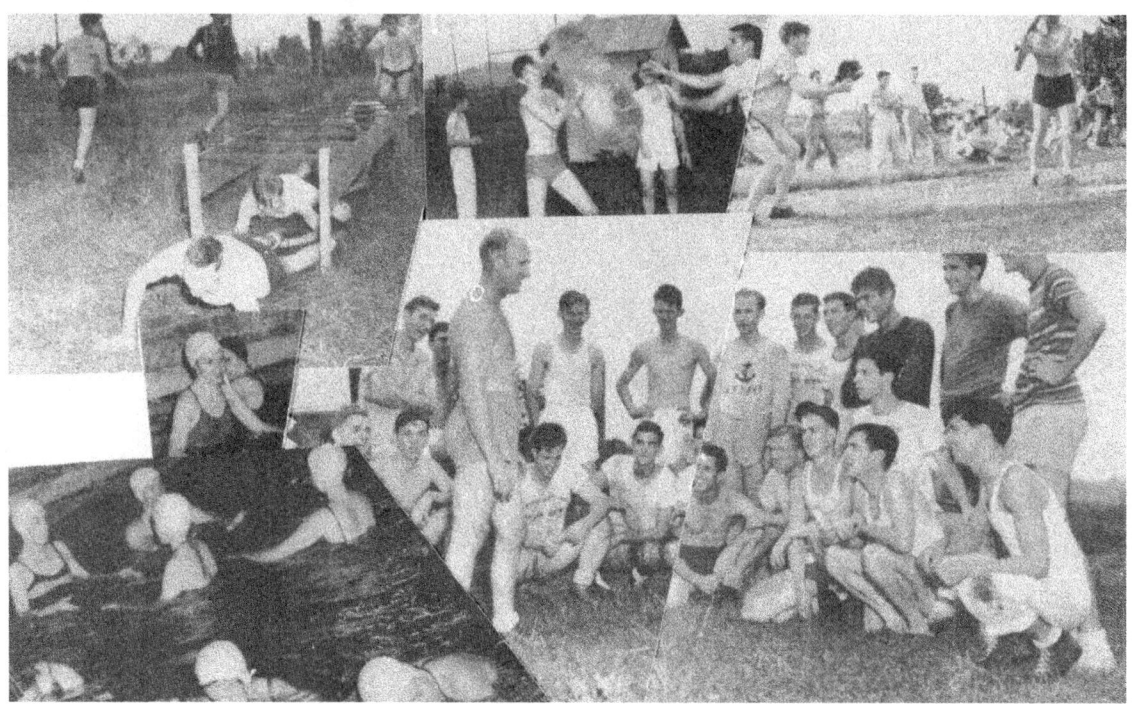

**Physical Education 1943**

**Buster Jennings 1947**

*A History of Sports at Carson-Newman College 1851-1974*

119

# *It Gets Foggy at Mossy Creek*

1946-47 Basketball Team

Action Shots in Butler Blanc Gym

# A History of Sports at Carson-Newman College 1851-1974

**1946 Football Action**

## *It Gets Foggy at Mossy Creek*

# *A History of Sports at Carson-Newman College 1851-1974*

Women's Sport in 1948

Glenn Wade – Captain

1949 Action Shot

# It Gets Foggy at Mossy Creek

# A History of Sports at Carson-Newman College 1851-1974

1949 Basketball Action

1950 Football Action

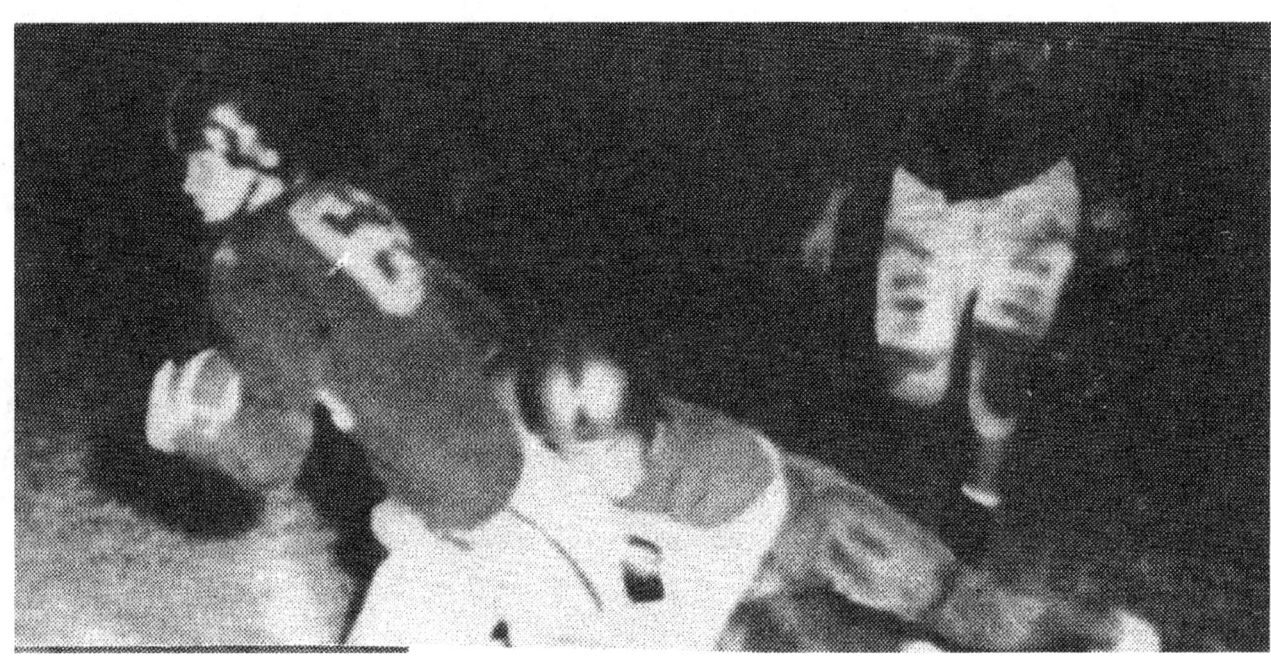

# It Gets Foggy at Mossy Creek

**Football Action - 1950**

**1952 Women's Letter Club**

# *A History of Sports at Carson-Newman College 1851-1974*

**Bud Bales 1959**

**Dusty Roden and Roy Harmon 1956**

# It Gets Foggy at Mossy Creek

**Carson College and Newman College**
**1951**
**100th Anniversary of Merge**

# A History of Sports at Carson-Newman College 1851-1974

**Holt Fieldhouse 1959**

# *It Gets Foggy at Mossy Creek*

**The Infamous Barn**

# *A History of Sports at Carson-Newman College 1851-1974*

Women's action in the early 1950's

**1951 SMAC Champions**

## *It Gets Foggy at Mossy Creek*

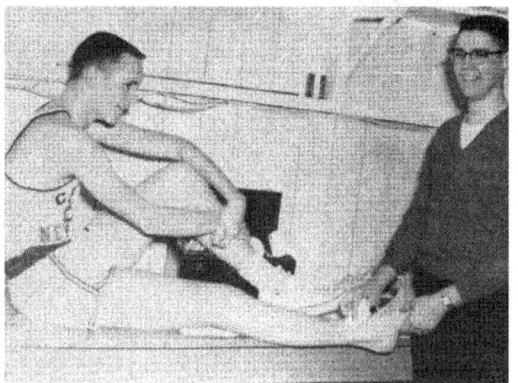

**Jack Holt 1952**

## A History of Sports at Carson-Newman College 1851-1974

**Baseball 1954**

# *It Gets Foggy at Mossy Creek*

**1956 Eagle Letter Club**
**Charlie King, President**

**Butler-Blanc 1921**

# A History of Sports at Carson-Newman College 1851-1974

**Women's Intramurals 1959**

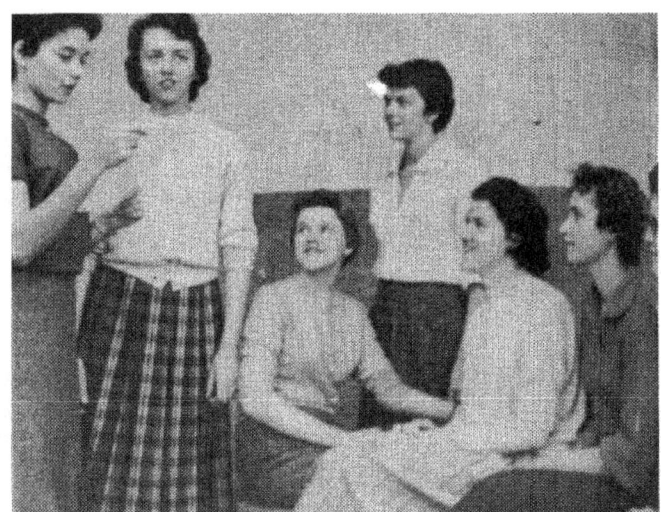

**The Eagle Club**

**The Majors Club**

# It Gets Foggy at Mossy Creek

**1957 Cheerleaders**

# CHAPTER V

# NATIONAL ACCLAIM IN ATHLETICS
# 1960 - 1969

The 1960's were good years for Carson-Newman College and a decade of success for all sports. Under the able guidance of President Harley Fite, Treasurer Albert Sloan, alumni, and Athletic Director "Frosty" Holt and his fine coaching staff, many sports reached their peak and many honors were bestowed upon Carson-Newman athletes and teams.

## BASEBALL ERA BEGINS

. The 1960 baseball Eagles were "another step forward in Coach Holt's lifelong dream and ambition" of a bid to the National Association of Intercollegiate Athletics tournament. After winning the Eastern Division of the Volunteer State Athletic Conference, the team went on to win the Volunteer State Athletic Conference championship and received a bid to the Regional playoffs. Carson-Newman lost to a highly rated Georgia Southern team which was runner-up in the nation. The Eagles completed their season with a 23-0 record (APPALACHIAN, 1961:68-71).
At the beginning of the season, Coach Holt had given the players three points to follow. "First, your books; second, baseball; and third, being a Christian gentleman." As summarized in the yearbook, "the record and attitude of the team speaks well for the ability of the men to carry out orders" (APPALACHIAN 1961:70).

## TENNIS ENTERS NATIONAL COMPETITION

The 1960 tennis team added new records and new trophies to the tennis program. "Since 1951, the tennis team at Carson-Newman had been one of the best in East Tennessee." The team record for regular season play was 14-2, with competition against such teams as The University of Tennessee, David Lipscomb College, East Tennessee State and Lincoln Memorial University; both losses were to a strong University of Tennessee team. The Eagles easily won the Smoky Mountain Athletic Conference crown without a loss and in the Eastern Division of the Volunteer State Athletic Conference they "smashed and lobbed their way to a 9-0 worksheet and a chance to meet the Western Division Champions." In a repeat performance of the previous year, they downed David Lipscomb College in the championship, "The tennis team was the first athletic team to represent Carson-Newman in a National Tournament of the National Association of Intercollegiate Athletics." Coach Henry Dickinson entered his number three and four singles players and the number two doubles team, but all were "eliminated in the second round of play" (APPALACHIAN, 1961: 74).

The 1960 football team was referred to as "an impressive team with an unimpressive 4-5 record," and was said to be one of the best defensive football teams in the history of the college. The highlight of the season was a defeat of Georgetown in a "pre-Homecoming warm-up" when the offense and defense "combined to offer a near-perfect game" in the 40-18 win. The team also provided upset victories over favored Austin Peay and Jacksonville

*It Gets Foggy at Mossy Creek*

State. Post season honors bestowed on Coach Harmon's squad came from the Volunteer State Athletic Conference and the KNOXVILLE NEWS-SENTINEL (daily newspaper). Coaches and sports writers selected Kenneth Bailey, Charlie McDonald, Don Newberry and John Frazier among the best in the Volunteer State Athletic Conference, Making the first team of the "much coveted" News-Sentinel All-Stars were Buddy Don Ramsey, Bob Baker and Don Newberry (APPALACHIAN, 1961: 50-59).

Under the direction of student coach, Cliff Malpass, the soccer team had a successful season with a 4-4 record. Outstanding players were Brazilian Derrick Davis and Bruce Threate on offense and Bill Bristow, Charles Preston, DeWayne Brooks and Lamar Laing on defense. Much interest was shown by the crowds and players and a squad of twenty-nine turned out for the team (APPALACHIAN, 1961:73).

### BASKETBALL TEAM QUALIFIES FOR NATIONAL TOURNAMENT

The basketball team made history for Carson-Newman College as they completed the regular season schedule with a 24-5 record. "From the Belmont game to the Chattanooga game the men on the hardwood were to taste defeat but once in the Eastern Division of the Volunteer State Athletic Conference--that being to the Tusculum Pioneers of Greeneville, Tennessee." This provided a league record of 9-1 and gained the Eastern Division crown for Carson-Newman. In the second game with Tusculum College for the league title, two records were set; the first was the Holt Fieldhouse record of 108 points scored by Carson-Newman and the other was the all-time individual scoring record of forty-four points set by Chris Jones (the record had been held by Snead Nevils who scored thirty-five points in 1941). The Eagles entered the Volunteer State Athletic Conference tournament in Nashville seeded number one but were defeated in the semi-finals by David Lipscomb. District 27 play-offs brought to Carson-Newman the four best National Association of Intercollegiate Athletics teams in Tennessee to vie for the right to represent District 24 in the National Tournament. In the finals Carson-Newman was pitted against Christian Brothers College of Memphis, Tennessee, who had represented the district the two previous years. It took an overtime for the Eagles to defeat Christian Brothers and earn the right to participate in the Nationals. Chris Jones, the leading scorer for two years, led the Eagle attack with fifty-nine points for two games. Clark Bryan and Jones were named to the All-Conference team with Bryan being selected as the Most Valuable Player of the Eastern Division. "The students this year witnessed the inauguration of a new era in the intercollegiate basketball program of Carson-Newman" as the Eagles finished with an overall record of twenty-eight wins and six losses (APPALACHIAN, 1961:60-64).

"The 1961 baseball Eagles were number nine in the nation in the final National Association of Intercollegiate Small College standings." They won the Eastern Division of the Volunteer State Athletic Conference, then the state Volunteer State Athletic Conference championship. Carson-Newman received a bid to the region playoffs, but lost in the finals to Eastern Carolina who won the national championship. Carson-Newman finished the season with 27-6 record (APPALACHIAN, 1962:72-73).

# *A History of Sports at Carson-Newman College 1851-1974*

## SOCCER HAS UNDEFEATED SEASON

The soccer team for 1961 was not to be outdone as they ended their season undefeated with a record of 4-0. The high point of the season was the trip to Blacksburg, Virginia to play Virginia Poly-technical Institute; Carson-Newman won by a score of 6-2. Derrick Davis, a four year stand-out for the soccer team signed a professional contract with the New York Americans of the International Soccer League. This was another first in the history of Carson-Newman sports (APPALACHIAN, 1962:76).

## TRACK REVIVED

Carson-Newman's modern track history began with Charlie Bryant in 1957 and primarily through his continuous efforts the 1960 team was produced. The first track team appeared on the campus in 1914, but the sport was discontinued in three years. It was revived in the mid-1920's for one year but interest was not shown again until 1957. Under Coach Harmon and Charlie Bryant, a student, the 1960 track team was undefeated. The cinder men were led by Martin Huckabee with 123 1/6 points (APPALACHIAN, 1961:77). The 1961 track team had another successful year losing only to East Tennessee State at Johnson City, Tennessee. The cinder men placed third in the Volunteer State Athletic Conference meet held at Austin Peay College (APPALACHIAN, 1962:71). The 1962 track team under Coach Harmon had another successful season and placed second in the Volunteer State Athletic Conference (APPALACHIAN, 1963: 185).

The 1961 football squad ended the year with a 3-6 record and were co-champions of the Volunteer State Athletic Conference with Austin Peay and University of Tennessee Martin Branch. "At one time during the season they had been ranked first in the nation in pass defense (small college)." Also in that same year the Carson-Newman football team made their first television appearance. Coach Harmon and his staff journeyed to Mississippi College for the debut but were defeated by the hard fighting Mississippi College team. Some of the standouts on the 1961 squad were Bob Baker, Fran Buhler, Danny Carter, Dale Rose, Bob Black, Kenneth Bailey, Meredith Gibson, Raymond Williams, and Eddie Collake. Coaches and sports writers selected Kenneth Bailey, Bobby Baker, Fran Buhler and Bobby Black to the All-Volunteer State Athletic Conference team. Kenneth Bailey was selected by the ORANGE and BLUE to receive its Outstanding Player Award. David Dale was selected to the Little All-American Academic football team at first team end position (APPALACHIAN, 1962:53-63),

## ALL-AMERICANS NAMED

The 1961-1962 basketball team produced an even better record than the previous year's team. They won the Eastern Division of the Volunteer State Athletic Conference with a 9-1 record, losing only to Tusculum by one point. They then entered the Volunteer State Athletic Conference tournament for the second straight year seeded number one and defeated Union University, Tennessee Wesleyan, and University of Tennessee Martin Branch to win the championship. "Carson -Newman carried everything back from the tournament but the gymnasium as they won the Eastern Division championship trophy, the Volunteer State Athletic Conference trophy for the championship, the sportsmanship trophy, Most Valuable Player of the conference trophy (Chris Jones), Most Valuable Player of the tournament trophy (Gilbert Luttrell), along with the game ball and nets from the basket." Three team members were placed on the All-Conference team and three members on the All-Tournament team. After this tournament Christian Brothers College of Memphis, Tennessee, came to Holt Fieldhouse for a best two out of three competition to determine the champions of District 27 and the right to represent the district in the National Association of Intercollegiate Athletics tournament in Kansas City. The Eagles won and were on their way to the National Tournament for the second year in a row. In the first round at Kansas City, Carson-Newman played second seeded Georgetown College of Kentucky. The final score was 75-51 with the Eagles moving into the second round of play. In the second round Carson-Newman defeated Peru State Teachers College of Nebraska in a close game, 67-65. In the quarter finals of play when the Eagles met Western Illinois, Western jumped off to a very quick lead and won easily, 91-65. "The Eagles played well and deserved the rating of the eighth top team in the nation in the National. Association of Intercollegiate Athletics." The basketeers ended their season with an impressive 29-7 record. "Coach Dick Campbell was nominated for the National Coach of the Year which in itself was a great honor" (APPALACHIAN, 1962:65-69), Chris Jones was also placed on the National Association of Intercollegiate Athletics All-American basketball team to become Carson-Newman's first All-American in any sport (KNOXVILLE NEWS-SENTINEL, April 21,1962).

The 1962 baseball team won the Volunteer State Athletic Conference championship for the third consecutive year and was tenth in the nation in the final small college standings. The team ranked in the top five of the National Association of Intercollegiate Athletics in runs scored. "This showed the offensive punch yet the great defensive ball club that the Eagles had." They made a clean sweep of the Volunteer State Athletic Conference by winning the Eastern Division and beating Union University, the Western Division leader by a score of 11-1 and 8-2, The Eagles then went to the regional National Association of Intercollegiate Athletics tournament in Statesboro, Georgia. Carson-Newman defeated Salem College and met St. Bernard in a game which was tied after the fourteenth inning, postponed on account of darkness, and resumed the next morning with the Eagles winning in the fifteenth inning. In the championship game for the losers bracket, Carson-Newman was defeated by Georgia Southern who went on to win the National championship. Carson-Newman ended their season with a 27-7 record (APPALACHIAN, 1963: 176-177).

The 1961 tennis team was hurt when three of the six lettermen did not return. However, the season record was 6-7 (APPALACHIAN, 1962:180). The 1962 tennis team also under Coaches Dickenson and Conwell had what could be called another "rebuilding year" since the team lacked experience. The team centered on the playing of Lloyd Parker and J, W. Overbay. The regular season was ended with a 9-5 record and the team had a successful year but lost in the Volunteer State Athletic Conference play-offs (APPALACHIAN, 1963: 182).

# *A History of Sports at Carson-Newman College 1851-1974*

## CROSS COUNTRY AND WRESTLING ADDED

A new fall sport of cross country was added to the athletic program in 1961. The new team coached by "Frosty" Holt "gained much in school competition but lacked support of the student body." The team was led by Jerry Turley and met many of the teams in the Volunteer State Athletic Conference and the Ohio Valley Conference. Some standouts on this first cross country team were Jerry Hyatt, Bob Hall, Jim Asher, and Jamie Brietton (APPALACHIAN, 1963: 180).

Cross country was not the only new sport on campus as wrestling was also added with Bob Davis as coach. The team had to be satisfied with experience since their only two wins were over the Knoxville YMCA and the Birmingham YMCA (APPALACHIAN, 1963: 180).

The 1962 football season brought a second television appearance when the Eagles journeyed to Alabama to play the Howard Bulldogs on local television, "This team gave Coach Harmon and his staff their first winning season in three years with a 5 -4 -1 record." The Volunteer State Athletic Conference representatives for the football squad that year were Bob Baker, Nick Bratcher, Bob Black and Roy Bayless. Bob Baker was also named to the Little All-American football team and was the second All-American at Carson-Newman and the first to make it in football (APPALACHIAN, 1963:156-157). The following year "life on the gridiron was not an easy one for the ball players." The 1963 record of 3-7 "did not portray a true picture of the effort put forth by both coaches and team" It was a season of close games and although the team did not have a great season, several honors were bestowed on the team, one being the naming of a second All-American in football--Bob Black (APPALACHIAN, 1964:156-157; 167).

## BASKETBALL TEAM HAS A FIVE OVERTIME GAME

The 1962-1963 basketball season brought with it another outstanding team and another winning season. The opening game against King College marked the one hundredth win for Coach Campbell in a four-year period. The longest game in the history of basketball at Carson-Newman took place when the Catamounts from Western Carolina invaded the Holt Fieldhouse before a large crowd. The Eagles won, 53-49, after the fifth overtime period (APPALACHIAN, 1963:169-170). The most talked-about game of the season was between Carson-Newman and Oglethorpe College of Atlanta. At that time, Oglethorpe was ranked second in the nation in defense under Coach Pinholster and Carson-Newman was ranked third. Carson-Newman defeated Oglethorpe 49-10 for their thirty-ninth home victory. The Eagles ended their regular season with a forty-game home winning streak and won their third consecutive District 27 National Association of Intercollegiate Athletics tournament at the expense of host, Tennessee Wesleyan, 48-45.

Carson-Newman was ranked second nationally among National Association of Intercollegiate Athletics teams in defense allowing an average of 50.8 points per game. In the national tournament in Kansas City, the Eagles were seeded ninth and defeated their first two opponents--Rider College of Trenton, New Jersey and Indiana State: 'The third game found Carson-Newman facing Grambling University led by All- American Willis Reed. (Reed later

## It Gets Foggy at Mossy Creek

became a National Basketball Association Most Valuable Player). Grambling edged the Eagles in quarter-final play and went on to win the National Association of Intercollegiate Athletics championship (APPALACHIAN, 1963: 170,173-174).

As Volunteer State Athletic Conference champions for the fourth consecutive year, the Carson-Newman baseball Eagles posted an excellent 24-8 season record in 1963. Led by Carson-Newman's "grand old man of baseball, Coach Holt, the Eagles were considered to be one of the finest small college baseball teams in the nation." From 1959 through 1963 the Eagles were ranked among the top twenty small colleges. In the Volunteer State Athletic Conference, Carson-Newman beat Tennessee Wesleyan 16-4, and also beat Lincoln Memorial University, Milligan, and Tusculum and moved into championship play without losing a conference game. Coach Holt and his Eagles invaded Belmont College to battle for a fourth Volunteer State Athletic Conference championship in as many years. "True to form they dropped their first game 3-2, but Coach Holt said for three years he had had to win a doubleheader to take that trophy home. So Coach and his men hitched their pants, came back and walloped Belmont 14-3, and then copped the second, 4-2; put the trophy in their pocket and went home." The Eagles then traveled to Statesboro, Georgia, for the District 27 National Association of Intercollegiate Athletic playoffs. They were ready for Kansas City, but East Carolina had the same idea and defeated the Eagles, 6-5. Carson-Newman controlled the losers' bracket by defeating Troy State and West Liberty, but Georgia Southern scored three runs in the ninth inning of the final game to put the Eagles out of the playoffs (APPALACHIAN, 1964: 189; 191).

Wrestling, under Coach Bob Davis, was officially added to the sports program during the 1963-1964 school term. Coach Davis "had to recruit and shift a majority of inexperienced wrestlers who had never seen a wrestling match." With the help of David Rathersdale, and the experience of Roger Hooker, Wilbur Taylor, Jerry Loveday, Dale Chrisman, Bob Crowland and Benny Collins, Carson-Newman was represented by a fine team. The interest of the student body increased as such big-name schools as Auburn, Emory University, and the University of Chattanooga were on the schedule. Carson-Newman was represented in the Southeastern Conference tournament (APPALACHIAN, 1964:193).

Although inexperienced, the 1963 netmen completed a winning season, achieving third place in the Volunteer State Athletic Conference tournament, and compiled an 8-3 record. They lost once to Howard and twice to Milligan College, both of which had strong scholarship-supported programs (APPALACHIAN, 1964; 194).

After a 3-5 record in dual meets, the Carson-Newman track team wound up their 1963 season in a joint meet with The University of Tennessee freshmen, Knoxville Track Club, East Tennessee State, and Tennessee Polytechnical Institute. Several new school records were set--Ron Holt increased the shot put record from 43 feet, 1 1/2 inches to 44 feet and 7 inches; and the javelin from 153 feet to 177 feet 6 inches. Jim Collins set a new record for the discus 14 feet, 9 inches. Coach Roy Harmon was again in charge of the track team (APPALACHIAN, 1964; 196-197).

# *A History of Sports at Carson-Newman College 1851-1974*

## BASKETBALL TEAM HAS WINNING STREAK SNAPPED

In 1963-1964, Coach Campbell was assisted in basketball by Jim Collins, a player sidelined with a knee injury and who was also in charge of the freshman squad. The varsity saw their forty-four game home court winning streak snapped when they were beaten by Union College of Barboursville, Kentucky, in their own Invitational Tournament by a score of 55 to 54. This did not seem to dampen their spirits as they finished the regular season with a perfect 10-0 conference record and the Eastern Division championship. Carson-Newman defended its title successfully and again won the championship. The team was voted unanimously by the District 27 coaches to represent Tennessee in the National Tournament at Kansas City for the fourth consecutive year where they won the third place in the national tournament trophy. Mr. Campbell was runner-up for the national coach-of-the-year title (APPALACHIAN, 1964: 180-187).

The following year, 1964-1965, the Eagles came back again to win the Volunteer State Athletic Conference and tried for their fifth consecutive trip to Kansas City. Transylvania shattered the Eagle's hopes of being the only small college team ever to go to the national tournament five consecutive years by downing them 59-57 in an overtime. They had another outstanding year, however, as they ended the season with a 24-5 record. The team participated in the Quincy Invitational Tournament in Quincy, Illinois, where they won the championship. In so doing, they defeated Western Illinois 88-71, slipped by national champion Rock Hurst 72-71, and beat host Quincy, 67-61. The Eagles had national ratings in the top ten throughout the year with their highest rating coming after the Christmas break when they were rated second in small college standings (APPALACHIAN, 1965:134-135),

The 1964 baseball team had an impressive record as they posted "a more than respectable 27-8-1 record, won the Volunteer State Athletic Conference and were also representatives to the District 27 playoffs." In the game in Statesboro, Carson-Newman defeated District 27 rival William-Carey, 11-4. They lost to perennial rival Georgia Southern 6-3, and then lost the next game to William-Carey, 8-4, thus ending hopes for a bid to the national tournament. Some of the major schools on the Eagles schedule were the University of Kentucky, University of South Carolina, Bowling Green University, Eastern Kentucky, and East Tennessee State University--"all falling before the Eagles." "It was perhaps with an added relish, however, that the Mossy Creek nine demolished the neighboring University of Tennessee on two occasions, 6-2 and 6-0." The Eagles conference record was 6-2 (APPALACHAIAN, 1965: 128-131).

The tennis team had eight courts for varsity play in the fall of 19M, and began the 1064 season "in splendid fashion" by defeating East Tennessee State University, 8-1. After that performance they won nine straight matches but were finally beaten by Sewanee, 7-2. This proved to be the only regular season loss and the netters came back and won the next two matches. In the Volunteer State Athletic Conference tournament play, the Eagles "took second place with 23 of 36 possible points." In the national tournament, the Eagles finished thirteenth among the twenty-eight schools represented. The doubles team bowed, 6-4 and 6-4, to the team which won second place in the tournament (APPALACHIAN, 1965: 134-135).

# *It Gets Foggy at Mossy Creek*

"'Improvement seemed to be the key word in the vocabulary of Coach Harmon's tricksters." They came back in 1964 to win six meets while losing only three. Roy Seville and Clifford Crews set new records in the 330 intermediate hurdles and the-two mile run, respectively (APPALACHIAN, 1965:136-137). Under new head football coach Bob Davis, "a rebuilt 1964 Eagle squad braved bad breaks, bad luck, and injury to surprise the 'experts' by winning six games while losing only three, and by frosting the cake with a splendid 24-14 victory over previously unbeaten Maryville." The most disappointing game of the season was the homecoming game with Appalachian State in which the Eagles "dropped a heart stopper." With seconds left to play, they had a first-and-goal on the Appalachian 6 and a chance to leave the game victorious. "Three plays netted four yards and with a fourth-and-two an attempted pass was made only to have it intercepted in the end zone thus ending the threat" (APPALACHIAN, 19G5:114-121).

## BASEBALL WINS NATIONAL TOURNAMENT

The 1965 Eagle baseball squad followed "in the tradition of Coach Holt" by posting one of the finest records in the history of baseball at Carson-Newman. They ended the season with a 36-3 mark and the national baseball championship. Due to illness, Coach Holt was forced to give up the baseball team which was coached by Bobby Wilson, already on the staff at Carson-Newman. The Eagles captured the Eastern Division of the Volunteer State Athletic Conference and then defeated the Western Division champions. From Nashville tile Eagles went to Statesboro, Georgia, and this time won the National Association of Intercollegiate Athletics District 27 tournament with victories over Pembroke State, 1-0, and Georgia Southern, 1-0 and 4-1. The "Fighting Eagles" from Carson-Newman College went through the ninth annual National Championship Tournament undefeated, "displaying brilliant pitching along the route." The pitchers were Clyde Wright. .John Manner and Mike Levi (APPALACHIAN, 1966:214-219). Coach Bobby Wilson was name the National Area 7 Coach-of-the-Year for 1965. The team felt that the honor was shared by both coaches, Holt and Wilson. Clyde Wright was drafted by the Los Angeles Angels and has played for the Angels since 1965.

The 1965 tennis team posted an impressive ll-0 record in regular season play. The Tennessee Intercollegiate Athletic Conference tournament held at the University of the South saw the netmen under Coach Henry Dickenson place fifth. The Eagles were again Eastern Division champions in the Volunteer State Athletic Conference but were defeated by Western Division champions, David Lipscomb in the tournament (Athletic Records, 1965). The track team was "hampered by a shortage of participants," and fared rather poorly. They won two meets and lost five over a period of three weeks (APPALACHIAN, 1966:222,225). In his second year as head football coach of the Eagles, Bob Davis and his 1965 team posted a 5-4 record. The victories came over Emory-Henry, Missouri School of Mines, Mars Hill, Maryville and Elon in the homecoming game. Special recognition was given to middle guard Dale Chrisman as he was named Player-of-the-Year on the KNOXVILLE NEWS SENTINEL Area Small College All-Star Team. Named to the same team on offense were Larry Hester, Bobby DE Lozier, Sam Cox, and Lowell Haggy; and on defense Tommy Pair, Paul Glover, and Dale Chrisman (APPALACHIAN, 1966: 198-204).

# *A History of Sports at Carson-Newman College 1851-1974*

In reference to his 1965-1966 Eagle basketball squad, Coach Dick Campbell felt "it was the best road team we have ever had, When any other team would quit, this one played like they didn't know they were supposed to lose," He felt the regular season record of 20-4 was achieved by team work and spirit. The team that was said to be rebuilding after the graduation of two outstanding players, held the number four position in the national ratings of the National Association of Intercollegiate Athletics during the season. Despite an upset loss in the semi-final round of the Volunteer State Athletic Conference tournament, the Eagles received a bid to the District 27 play-offs in Barbourville Kentucky, where they won the championship trophy. Once again the Eagles were ranked number one and went to Kansas City with a number two seeding in the national tournament. The first game found them facing an unseeded but determined Indiana Central team, with a 23-5 record, "With a five point lead in the closing seconds, Central was allowed to score two baskets only to lose 88-67." The second night brought Morris-Harvey from Charleston, West Virginia, "who were completely outclassed as they became the victims of the first Carson -Newman team to break the hundred mark in a national tournament, 103-74." In the following game, Oklahoma Baptist University "caught Carson-Newman flatfooted and rode the 32 point performance of All-American Tucker to a 25 point victory." Jim Shuler from Carson-Newman was named All-American and also made the All- Tournament team (APPALACHIAN, 1966:206-212). The following year found Coach Campbell in a "rebounding year." Four of his first five players graduated and he was working with a new team (APPALACHIAN, 1967:108). The season ended with a 19-10 record and a second place in the Volunteer State Athletic Conference tournament (BASKETBALL PRESS GUIDE, 1972). As the fall of 1966-1967 began, new coaches were employed for both football and wrestling. Coach Davis returned to his alma mater, The University of Tennessee, in a coaching position and Coach Richie Gaskell was given the head position at Carson-Newman, The "spirited pig-skinners fought battles on the grid" and turned in a record of seven wins, three losses, and one tie, The Eagles were invited to the Exchange Bowl which was played in a downpour but "made it a successful venture" as they defeated Georgetown, 9-0 (APPALACHIAN, 1966:221), Wrestling began its regular season in 1965 without the leadership of a regular coach, Operating under the leadership of captain Bob Crawl and student coach Harold Taylor, the team compiled a 2-4 won-loss record "before the loss of Taylor forced the squad to cancel its remaining matches" (APPALACHIAN, 1966:110). The following year Coach Richie Gaskell and the Eagle wrestlers stood 2-2 with wins over Furman and Knoxville Y.M.C.A. and losses to Maryville College (APPALACHIAN, 1967:120).

The next two years for football brought winning seasons. The 1967 squad started off the season with a loss to Western Carolina by four points but "snapped back brilliantly with four straight wins." The season closed with a good 6-4 record "despite the loss of three valuable players to injury." The passing offensive proved to be one of the strongest factors in the Eagles performance for that year (APPALACHIAN, 1968:94). The 1968 season brought with it "one of the best records in over a decade," It began with "their first opening game victory in at least four years." The only two defeats were to Emory and Henry, 35-27 and Lenoir-Rhyne, 37-26, while victories were against such strong opponents as Catawba, Western Carolina, Georgetown, Elon, Appalachian State, Maryville, Presbyterian, and Wofford. Following the 8-2 season, Tom Jones, "C-N's ace receiver, 'I was named to the National Association of Intercollegiate Athletics first team; Dale Rutherford, quarterback, and Harold

*It Gets Foggy at Mossy Creek*

Denton, tackle, were named to the National Association of Intercollegiate Athletics third team (APPALACHIAN, 1969:89-95),

**FIRST VOLUNTEER STATE ATHLETIC CONFERENCE TITLE WON BY CROSS COUNTRY TEAM**

Carson-Newman's 1966 cross country team compiled a 2-4 dual meet record and placed third in the Volunteer State Athletic Conference tournament in Nashville. Lenard Markham, a freshman, took individual honors with a second place finish in the meet (APPALACHIAN, 1967: 124). One of the highlights for the 1967 cross country team was the running of the game ball from Carson-Newman to Maryville for the annual football game (APPALACHIAN, 1968:97). The 1968 team was "short on manpower but long on desire" (APPALACHIAN, 1969:102), but the following year was improved for Troy Haydon and his cross country team as they had a 15-4 record and captured the Volunteer State Athletic Conference championship for the first time in the history of the college (ORANGE and BLUE, November 1969:7). In taking over the Volunteer State Athletic Conference crown, the Eagles unseated the seven-year defending champion, Milligan College. They also saw action in the Tennessee Intercollegiate Athletic Conference in Cookeville, Tennessee, over a four-mile expanse of golf course. Over eighty runners participated in the "cold and rainy meet" and Carson-Newman placed its top five men in the first twenty-one positions. For their effort, the team won the runner-up trophy with McPherson and Doane pacing the squad by finishing eighth and ninth (ORANGE and BLUE, November 13, 1970:8).

With Coach Dick Campbell leaving Carson-Newman to become head basketball coach at The Citadel, Dr. Gene Mehaffey was given the position of basketball coach and Jerald Ellington was named as his assistant. With Coach Mehaffey came a "running, fast breaking offense" which provided many hours of excitement for the team's followers. Captain W. A. Wright closed out a brilliant career as the Most Valuable Player of the Volunteer State Athletic Conference tournament. A team composed mainly of rapidly improving underclassmen, the Eagles finished their 1967-1968 season with a record of 22-8. After a "brilliantly played, but heart-breaking" loss to Union University in the final game of the Volunteer State Athletic Conference tournament, this team left the students eagerly anticipating the next season (APPALACHIAN, 1968:82). The 1968-1969 season started disastrously but ended with the Volunteer State Athletic Conference championship in Nashville. The team lost four of their first six games, but then only lost five of their remaining twenty-four contests. In posting a record of 21-9, the Eagles played "one of the toughest schedules ever faced by a Carson -Newman quintet." The home floor proved to be a welcome sight to the Eagles as they lost only one game in Holt Fieldhouse to Union University by a close 92-87 score. Carson-Newman lost only a single game in the Eastern Division of the Volunteer State Athletic Conference to tie with King College for the season championship of the division. The Eagles were also winners of the Union Invitational Tournament, placed third in the High Point Classic and climaxed their season by winning the Volunteer State Athletic Conference championship. Carson-Newman placed three men on the All-Tournament Team--Tony Mills, Les Spitzer, and Tommy Everett. Everett was also selected as the Most Valuable Player in the Volunteer State Athletic Conference tournament (APPALACHIAN, 1969:98-101).

# *A History of Sports at Carson-Newman College 1851-1974*

The 1969 football squad ended its season with a 5-2-1 season record and a victory over Presbyterian College in the final home game. The CHATTANOOGA TIMES selected an All-State Football team which included five Carson-Newman gridders: Don Gray, Sam Morrison, Tom Jones, Billy Wilson, and Larry Lay. Tom Jones was also recognized as the Most Valuable Player on the 1969 squad and selected to the second team All-American squad. Dal Shealy, a 1960 graduate of Carson-Newman and an outstanding football player, was selected as the 1970 football coach. Coach Shealy brought with him Fred Sorrells and Sam Green as assistant coaches. Charlie King, another former football standout at Carson-Newman, was retained on the staff to work with Coach Shealy (ORANGE and BLUE, December 5, 1969:3).

The baseball teams for the next three years, 1967, 1968, and 1969, had winning seasons. The 1967 team had a record of 27-11, were Volunteer State Athletic Conference champions, District champions, and runner-up in the Area VII play-offs. Lowell Hagy, Mike Levi, John Maury, and W. A. Wright were among the team leaders. The 1968 season record was 28-11; the team was Volunteer State Athletic Conference runner-up, District 24 champions, and runner-up in the Area V play-offs. Frank Fillman and Tom Jones were valuable as pitchers for this team. The following year, 1969, the Eagles were again led by Frank Fillman and Tom Jones at the pitching position and ended the season with a 23-10 record. Despite injuries to key players, they were again Volunteer State Athletic Conference runner-up, District 24 champions and Area V runner-up (Athletic Records, 1967, 1968, 1969).

The 1967 soccer squad had a 4-1 record and was led by Valentine Mbong, Mike Atherton, Pedro Gomez, Khalid Raviah and John Mein. The "talent-toed" Valentine Mbong scored sixteen goals for the season, two-thirds of the twenty-four goals scored by the Eagles. Defensively, goalie Mike Atherton was the mainstay for the team (TRIBUNE, November 16, 1967). The following season, Erich Dietz took over as a volunteer coach for the Soccer Club. Dietz, a native of Germany, came to the United States in 1956 and was employed by Magnavox Corporation of Jefferson City, "Though he received no pay, Erich Dietz coaches because of a genuine love for a game and--more importantly--his interest in the men who play under his guidance." With a 3-0 record; the club had "teamwork" as their key. Although he pointed out individual efforts on the part of Valentine Mbong, Jim Hunsicker, and Sidney McGee, Coach Dietz emphasized the work of the team as a unit {ORANGE and BLUE, October 27, 1968:7). The Carson-Newman Soccer Club finished fourth in the Southeastern tournament held, at The University of Tennessee in Knoxville. Other schools in the competition were Louisiana State University, Vanderbilt, The University of Tennessee and Georgia (APPALACHIAN, 1970:102)

The 1969 club was again coached by Dietz, and many of the players had learned the game overseas -- Valentine Mbong from Cameroon and Pedro Gomez from Colombia; Sidney-McGee, who played in Nigeria; Joseph Weah from Liberia; and from Turks Island, Lee Ingram, Other team members were Jan Hudspeth, George Howell, John Cady, Steve Morris, Steve Rutherford, David Goodroe, Sheldon Livesay, Gary McCool and Khalid Rabbiah (ORANGE and BLUE, September, 1969:6). The season record was 4-5 with defeats by Vanderbilt, George Peabody, The University of Tennessee and King College (ORANGE and BLUE, October 1969:7). The team was led by Pedro Gomez and Valentine Mbong, who were selected to the All-Star Team at the Southeastern tournament (APPALACHIAN, 1969: 112).

The 1967 wrestling team was led by David Guinn, Reed Dixon, and Danny McMullins. Wrestling became a popular sport under the leadership of Coach Richard May and it was a good season despite the 4-5 record (ORANGE and BLUE, February 18, 1967:7). The next year the wrestling team competed against some of the strongest teams in the South and failed to win a match. "Four points proved to be the greatest margin of victory over them as they were defeated by LSU, 22-18." Carson-Newman was also beaten by the University of Chattanooga, 23-22 and 22-18. The Eagles were represented in the Georgia Invitational and the Southeastern championships, where Dave Guinn won four matches, three on pins. Much recognition came to the wrestlers through the efforts of Dave Guinn and Larry Crisafulli as both were undefeated during the 1968 season. (Larry's overall record was 11-3 while Dave had a 25-3 record during his years at Carson-Newman.) In recognition of their efforts the two were invited to the National Association of Intercollegiate Athletics Finals at Omaha, Nebraska. In addition to that honor, Dave was featured in Sports Illustrated for his fine record in collegiate wrestling (APPALACHIAN, 1969:110-111). The 1967 track team had an 11-0 regular season record and won the Volunteer State Athletic Conference championship for the first time in Carson-Newman's history. The team was led by Jim Frost in the triple jump; Larry Campbell in the discus and shot put; Mike Lovett in the broad jump and hurdles; Ray Maynard in the one-half mile run; Leonard Markham in the two-mile run and also the one-mile run; and Larry Smith in the high jump (APPALACHIAN, 1968:99), The following year the team compiled an 8-0 meet record under Coach Dal Shealy and went on to set a conference meet record with 93 points, winning the Volunteer State Athletic Conference crown for the second straight year. Jim Frost was the high point man of the year both at Carson-Newman and in the conference where he gathered fourteen and one-half paints (Athletic Records, 1967: 1968). Coach Shealy was voted the National Association of Intercollegiate Athletics District 25 Track Coach-of-the-Year and National Association of Intercollegiate Athletics Area V Track Coach-of-the-Year (ORANGE and BLUE, February 8, 1969:7-8). The team participated in the Tennessee Intercollegiate Athletic Conference and finished fourth out of eleven schools in the college division, with a twenty-six point total. Field strength was the strong point for Carson-Newman in the meet. The first night meet in the history of the school was a dual meet against Bryan College; the final score tallied up to Carson-Newman 115 and Bryan College 30. Good performances in the meet were by pole vaulter Hendrix with a new school record-- 13' 9" and John McPherson's two-mile time of 9:54.6. The 1969 track team also had a good season under Troy Haydon with a 14-8 regular season record. They set a point scoring record by amassing a total of 105 points to again bring home the Volunteer State Athletic Conference crown for the third consecutive year (Athletic Records, 1969). Jim Raines held the VSAC record in the 440 intermediate hurdles and John McPherson won the conference two-mile run and set a Carson-Newman record for the three-mile run (ORANGE and BLUE, May 12, 1970: 10).

## A DECADE FOR GOLF

The golf team completed its first decade in the 1970's. The team had its beginning in 1961 under Coach Dick Campbell and did not fair very well during its early years. The 1961 team was led by Eugene "Pottsy" Wright, Jim Crutchfield, and Roger Grimsley with a record of 3-4. The 1962 team had the same players with the addition of Bobby Graves. Bobby was the number one man followed by "Pottsy" in the number two position. This team participated in the Volunteer State Athletic Conference for the first time. The 1963 team had the same team members and ended the season with a 6-5 record. They participated in the Volunteer state Athletic Conference and the Tennessee Intercollegiate Athletic Conference. Golf was discontinued for three years but was started again in 1967 and has continued to improve each year (Interview, "Pottsy" Wright, 1972). The 1967 golf team placed second in the Volunteer State Athletic Conference held in Elizabethton, Tennessee (ORANGE and BLUE, May 13, 1967:11). The 1969 golf team had a 9-0-1 conference record and a 10-2-1 overall record, the two losses being to Cumberland College, a perennial champion of their Kentucky conference, and to East Tennessee State University which had university status and was "most likely the best team in the state." The team was organized by the Physical Education Department, included in their budget and coached by Richard May (ORANGE and BLUE, May 12, 1969:6).

## SUMMARY

The 1960's were good years and a decade of success for all sports at Carson-Newman. New sports were added to the varsity program, established teams competed in national meets and outstanding athletes brought honor to the college. The first All-American was named during this era.

The spring sports of baseball and tennis began the 1960's with championship performances and set a hard pace for the other sports to follow. The tennis team, since 1951, had been considered one of the best in the East Tennessee area and the 1960's were to be no exception. The 1960 tennis team was the first athletic team to represent Carson-Newman in a national tournament in the National Association of Intercollegiate Athletics. It was during the fall of 1964 that the tennis team had access to four new courts making eight courts for varsity play on campus.

The baseball program continued under Coach "Frosty" Holt with each year bringing a better team until the climax in 1965 with the national championship. The 1965 season again under Coach Holt was to be the "team of his dreams" but due to doctor's orders, he was asked to turn the team over to Coach Bobby Wilson who carried the "Holt men" through the Volunteer State Athletic Conference, District playoffs, to the National Tournament crowd.

Football ushered in the fall sports program for the 1960's. Three head football coaches guided the Eagles during this period. They were Roy Harmon, 1952-1963; Bob Davis, 1964-1965; and Richie Gaskell, 1966- 1969. The best team was the 1965 squad with an 8-2 record.

The 1960's provided a new era in basketball. Coach Dick Campbell had started his program in "the late 1950's and it was beginning to reach its peak during the 1960's. Beginning with the 1962 ball club, the team won the Volunteer State Athletic Conference every year Campbell was head coach at Carson-Newman with the exception of the 1960 season when they placed second. He took his Eagles to six NAIA National Championship Tournaments during this period. The 1967-1968 season brought with it a new basketball coach; Dr. Gene Mehaffey replaced Coach Campbell who went to the Citadel.

Under student coach Cliff Malpass, the soccer team began the 1960 season with much interest shown by the crowds and players as the team had a 4-4 record. The 1961 season brought an undefeated season with a 4-0 record. Soccer then had a lapse on campus until it was revived again in 1967 and in 1968 Erich Dietz became a volunteer coach for the Soccer Club. Under his guidance, the Club had two good seasons and increased their schedule to include the larger schools.

Cross country was added to the athletic program at Carson-Newman in 1962 by Coach Holt. The program lasted only one season, but was reinstated in 1966. Again in 1968 the schedule was cancelled due to the lack of manpower, but the 1969 team under Coach Troy Haydon had an outstanding year with a 15-4 record including the Volunteer State Athletic Conference championship for the first time in the history of the college.

After a lapse on campus of many years, interest was again shown in track in 1957 and because of this interest, the 1960 track team was fielded. Under Roy Harmon and Charlie Bryant, a student, the 1960 track team was undefeated.

The golf team at Carson-Newman had its beginning in 1961 under Coach Dick Campbell and did not compete very successfully during the early years. In 1964, the team was discontinued for three years for lack of funds. Golf was again introduced as a team sport in 1967 and has continued to improve each year since then.

Wrestling was officially added to the sports program at Carson-Newman in 1963-1964 with Bob Davis as coach. Coach Richard May took over the team in 1967 and it was a good season even though the record was not outstanding. The following year the team competed against Louisiana State University, University of Chattanooga and other outstanding teams in the Georgia Invitational and Southeastern tournament.

National acclaim was brought to Carson-Newman during the 1960's through the athletic program.

## WHAT MY LETTER MEANS TO ME

Every normal person has at some time in life taken an active part in or been a follower of some form of athletics. The foremost prize that every athlete desires to win is his monogram. The idea of giving a monogram or better known as a 'letter' by a school to members of its student body originated in the realm of athletics. Today, unfortunately, we have in some instances drifted far from the original idea of the monogram. However, no matter how far we have deviated, if we know anything of what a letter represents we admire, almost with reverence the young athlete who bears on his chest the stamp of achievement, the monogram of his school.

Almost anything that we possess is valued by what it cost 'us.' That is the reason that we should prize our letter very highly. Before we are eligible to receive a letter we first must have taken part in a specific amount of competitive athletics. Which ultimately means that we have paid almost with a price of blood, for the letter that is ours.

To me, a letter should represent first of all, the personalities that we have contacted during our athletic career. Each individual boy with whom you have fought, shoulder to shoulder, both on the field of practice and in the game. It should represent the long hard days of practice and the grueling contest, many times at the risk of our own lives. It also represents the loyalty, the faithfulness and the unselfishness of each boy as he sacrificed all personal interest in the pursuit of a definite goal.
It also brings cherished memories of both pleasant and unpleasant experiences with the coaches, the men who have worked, drilled and planned day after day to develop whatever athletic ability that you possessed.

It represents each individual game, specific opponents, strategic moments and specific instances in every contest that you took part in. It reminds you of the trips that you made, the jokes that were cracked, scenes in the dressing room, groans from sore muscles, the odor of sweat from well used uniforms, the dirty, sweaty, blood smeared face, as a result of the contest ; the hand clasp of loyalty, the symbol of a task well done. All of these should be represented in your letter.

Last and far from the least, your letter is the stamp of approval or seal of recognition of your Alma
Mater for your athletic achievement. That letter represents the purposes and ideals for which your college stands. You are the proud possessor of something that every student and every follower of athletics envies and admires. Are you willing to live up to the high ideals and purposes of the institution that has publicly stamped you as their representative? If not you are not worthy of a letter. That letter is yours to wear whenever and wherever you choose. You have justly earned it. Never wear it anywhere or so conduct yourself as to bring disgrace and ill favor upon yourself or your school.

Your letter should be sacred to you. It should be a perpetual spring of inspiration and a constant welling forth of pleasant memories. So keep it as such.

Be such a good sport in the athletic contest or in the greater contest of life that 'when the scorer comes to write against your name, he will write not whether you won or lost, but how you played the game.'

Frank Grubb
Captain Football Team
Season 1936

## *It Gets Foggy at Mossy Creek*

Carson-Newman's tough defense holds tight - 1960

Dan Wade – 1960

Coach Holt watering field

## *A History of Sports at Carson-Newman College 1851-1974*

**Line Coach Bob Davis**     **Head Coach Roy Harmon**     **End Coach Paul Brewer**

**Men's Letter Club 1961**

*It Gets Foggy at Mossy Creek*

**Tom Meigs – 1961**

**Rugged Dal Shealy goes after the enemy - 1960**

# A History of Sports at Carson-Newman College 1851-1974

# It Gets Foggy at Mossy Creek

**Bob Baird**

**Bill Kinser**

**Gay Valentine - 1961**

# A History of Sports at Carson-Newman College 1851-1974

"Chico" Wright 1963

Football Managers 1961

Running Back, Bobby Baker 1962

# It Gets Foggy at Mossy Creek

**Cheerleaders 1962**

**Jim Barr 1961**

# A History of Sports at Carson-Newman College 1851-1974

**Safe!! Ernie Hill**

**Intramural Director Charles Wright and Assistant Carroll Helton-1962**

*It Gets Foggy at Mossy Creek*

**President Truman great Chris Jones and the 1962 basketball team at the National Basketball Tournament.**

# A History of Sports at Carson-Newman College 1851-1974

**The Truman Team 1962**

# It Gets Foggy at Mossy Creek

**Jimmy "Chief" Carter**

**Jim Collins 1964**

**Clyde Wright and W. A. Wright with Coach Wilson**

# *A History of Sports at Carson-Newman College 1851-1974*

**NAIA Baseball 1965**

Vic Arwood 1965

Diane Hodge – 1963 Miss Appalachian contestant

## It Gets Foggy at Mossy Creek

**Bob Davis**
**Wrestling Coach**

**Wrestling 1965**

**No team wins without good managers**

**John Evans (l)**

**Jerry King (r)**

**1962**

# A History of Sports at Carson-Newman College 1851-1974

**Larry Conner 1965**

**Bill Dawson 1965**

**Wilbur Taylor 1965**

**Joe Bill Sloan 1965**

# It Gets Foggy at Mossy Creek

**Men's Letter Club 1966**

**Cheerleaders 1965**

# A History of Sports at Carson-Newman College 1851-1974

**VSAC and District Champs**

**"Leaper" Tony Mills**

*It Gets Foggy at Mossy Creek*

**Football Team Action Shots 1968**

**Tom Jones**

**Fellowship of Christian Athletes 1966**

# A History of Sports at Carson-Newman College 1851-1974

**Track Team 1969**

# *It Gets Foggy at Mossy Creek*

**Softball Champions
1969**

# A History of Sports at Carson-Newman College 1851-1974

**Soccer Team 1969**

---

**Eagle Baseball 1969**

*It Gets Foggy at Mossy Creek*

**Basketball in the early 1960's
4 out of 5 - 5 elected MVP in conference**

**Eagle Hardware Display 1962**

# A History of Sports at Carson-Newman College 1851-1974

**Geno is first to the tape - 1962**

**Coach Harmon Instruct - 1962**

**Martin Huckabee Record Sprinter**

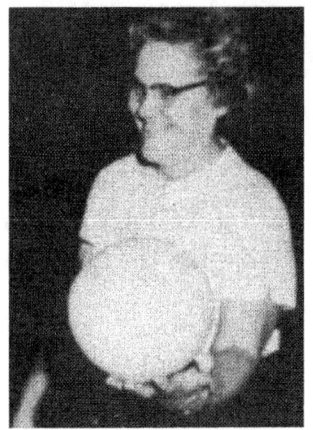

**Miss Iddins**

---

**Libby Hudson shows 'em how it's done**

**Luttrell, Coach Campbell, and Ellington**

*It Gets Foggy at Mossy Creek*

Eddie Collake carries the ball.   1964

The fog lifted after another victory 1965

---

**Two National Champions in one year.  Dr. Harley Fite and Coach Bobby Wilson proudly display the National Debate and Baseball Championship trophies in 1965**

# A History of Sports at Carson-Newman College 1851-1974

**Volleyball 1966 and 1967**

## It Gets Foggy at Mossy Creek

# A History of Sports at Carson-Newman College 1851-1974

**Henry Dickinson**
**Tennis Coach**

**Larry Ware 1965**

**Volleyball 1965**

*It Gets Foggy at Mossy Creek*

**Volleyball 1965**

**Baseball Team 1968**

# *A History of Sports at Carson-Newman College 1851-1974*

**Pitcher Mike Levi**
**1966**

**Hitter Gene Lively**
**1966**

# It Gets Foggy at Mossy Creek

**Les Spitzer**

**Fielder Randy Marsh 1969**

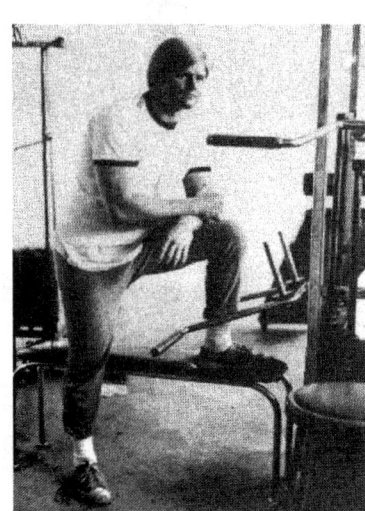
**Danny Mason 1968**

**Harold Denton 1968**

**Tom Jones 1969**

**Larry Lay 1969**

# A History of Sports at Carson-Newman College 1851-1974

**Soccer 1968**

---

**Men's Letter Club 1969**

Roy Hill, winner of Most Valuable Player award in VSAC 1968

Bud Seviles 1968

# *It Gets Foggy at Mossy Creek*

**Women Sports**

**1960s**

# A History of Sports at Carson-Newman College 1851-1974

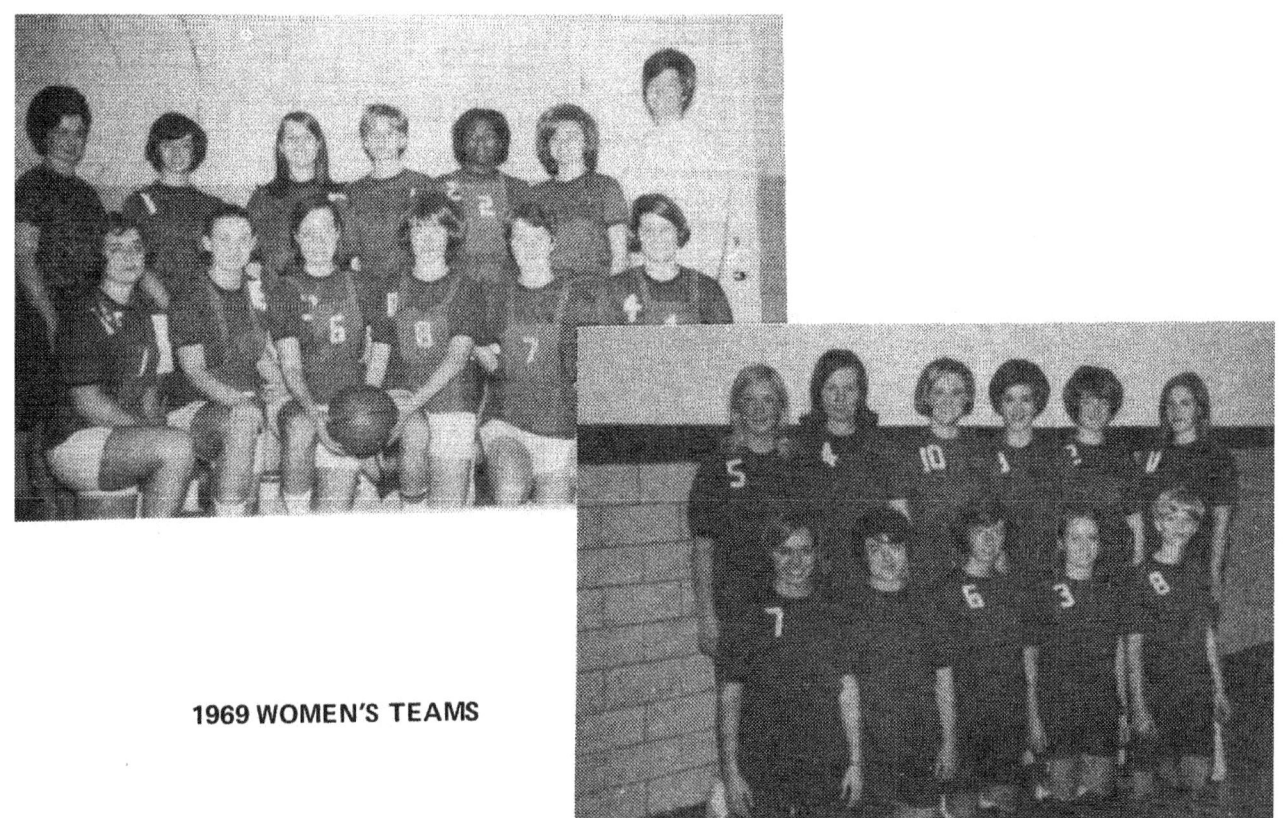

**1969 WOMEN'S TEAMS**

# *It Gets Foggy at Mossy Creek*

**Hypatian Society vs. Calliopean Society Annual Football Game 1969**

**Hypatian Society vs. Calliopean Society Annual Football Game 1970**

# CHAPTER 5

# OUTSTANDING ATHLETES AND COACHES IN CARSON-NEWMAN SPORTS HISTORY

Since 1895 Carson-Newman College has received valuable publicity through its athletic program and through the efforts of many outstanding athletes, coaches and teams assembled at Carson-Newman. Little did these men and women realize that the goals they shot, balls they hit, races they won, men they pinned, goals they kicked and touchdowns they scored would be remembered as establishing the pride and winning tradition that placed Carson-Newman high on the list in athletics and that their efforts would help to keep open the doors of a small private Baptist liberal arts college.

Following is a list of some of the outstanding athletes, coaches and individuals who gave impetus to Carson-Newman College through their efforts and their accomplishments:

1. Roy A. Henderson--First physical education director at Carson-Newman in 1892. He was an early leader in sports and physical education before intercollegiate athletics were initiated. He often played games with the young men of the college and was noted as being an outstanding sportsman of that day (CARSON-NEWMAN CATALOGUE, 1892-1893: 32-33),

2. Luther B. DeArmond--President of the Athletic Association in 1893-1909 (CARSON-NEWMAN CATALOGUE, 1903-1904:430). While he was very instrumental in bringing intercollegiate sports to Carson- Newman, he also organized many physical activities for the school in the 1890's before intercollegiate athletics began. One of his first activities was a Field Day held in the spring of 1893 (ALUMNI BULLETIN, October, 1948:12). In 1895, he helped organize the first baseball team and in 1903 reintroduced football to Carson-Newman following a lapse of several years (Carr, 1959:260-261).

3. W. S. Wilson--An early sprinter. In 1893 he won the 50-yeard dash, the 100-yard dash and the 200-yard dash in the first Field Day (CARSON-NEWMAN CATALOGUE, 1892-1893:32-33),

4. J. B. Bundren--A jumper who won most of the jumping events in the Field Days and track events held in the early 1890's, He won the high jump, high kick event and the running jump (CARSON-NEWMAN CATALOGUE, 1892-1893:32-33).

5. James Floyd--An outstanding athlete in both baseball and football. He played shortstop on the first Carson-Newman baseball team and led Carson-Newman over The University of Tennessee, 4 to 3, in the first intercollegiate athletic event in which Car son-Newman participated. This was in 1895. In addition to being a fine baseball player, he was also captain and quarterback of the first Carson-Newman football team in the fall of 1895. Along with his quarterback duties, he

was assistant coach of the first football team for Carson-Newman College (ALUMNI BULLETIN, 1948:12),

6. Luther M. Beller--Played second base on the first baseball team in 1895. He studied football at Yale during that summer and in the fall was Carson-Newman's first football coach, Under his leadership, football became an intercollegiate sport at Carson-Newman (Carr, 1959:260-261)

7. Ed "Tip" Lawrence--Captain and leading scorer of the first Carson-Newman basketball team (CARSON-NEWMAN CATALOGUE, 1903-1904:43).

8. Clarence A. Bales--A leading touchdown runner and captain of the 1903 football team. A hard running back, he brought glory to Carson-Newman in the early years (Carr, 1959).

9. Dana X. Bible--One of Carson-Newman's most celebrated early athletes. He was president of the Tennis Club in 1911-1912, captain of the 1909, 1910, 1912 basketball teams, president of the Columbian Literary Society in 1912, Athletic Editor of the COLLEGIAN (the annual of 1911-1912) and led the 1912 baseball and basketball teams to undefeated seasons, He later became one of the country's all-time leading football coaches (THE SWANN, 1912:7, 12, 13).

10. John Kilpatrick--One of Carson-Newman's finest three sport athletes in the years of 1913-1914. He excelled in baseball and was a member of the 1914 team which only lost one game. His strong points were hitting and fielding (CARSON-NEWMAN COLLEGIAN, 1913-1914:75-77). In the autumn of 1915, he took over full duties as a coach in the athletic department at Carson-Newman (Carr, 1959:268).

11. Spencer M. Tunnell--Credited with bringing football back to the campus when there was much opposition from the faculty. His keen business ability helped him to carry out a successful football program. As the president of the Athletic Cabinet, he caused the standards of athletics to be raised to a remarkable degree. At the close of the season the faculty and students presented him with a beautiful silver loving cup in appreciation of his work (CARSON-NEWMAN COMMENCEMENT, 1914-1915:62). Tunnell was a fine track man and captain of the first organized track team in 1914 (CARSON -NEWMAN COLLEGIAN, 1914:43).

12. Paul J. Squibb--He was an outstanding track star on the first recognized Carson-Newman track team in 1914 who led in the dashes and jumping events. He was also a fullback on the football team at 5'11" and 200 pounds. Paul was quoted in the 1915 APPALACHIAN (school annual) as saying, "If I cannot find a gap that suits me, I will make one" (APPALACHIAN, 1915).

13. Phil M. Utley--A fine quarterback for Carson-Newman in 1914, noted for his drop kicking skills. He was responsible for the victory over Maryville in 1915 with a

# A History of Sports at Carson-Newman College 1851-1974

55-yard drop kick from a 45 degree angle (CARSON-NEWMAN COMMENCEMENT, 1915:40), He coached at Carson-Newman and his 1913 team had a 7-2-1 record which was the best football record a Carson-Newman team had ever had up to that time. An interesting point about Utley was that he coached the team to a great season in 1913 and played quarterback in 1914 (at that time the coach could also play on the team) (CARSON-NEWMAN COMMENCEMENT, 1914-1915:64-69).

**Luther M. Beeler**
**First Football Coach**

**James S. Floyd**
**First Football Team, Captain**

## Two Great Coaches

Dana X. Bible

Bernie Moore
(inset)

14. P.M. "Lee" McElveen--A fine two sport athlete--football and basketball--who later became a great Carson-Newman basketball coach. His 1913 team won fourteen games and lost only one (that to The University of Tennessee). "The basketball fever was at an all-time high with overflow crowds, a good schedule and an orchestra to play music at the home games. Everyone left the game feeling that they had had a great treat," Also, a big factor in Coach McElveen's favor was that basketball was not in debt and was paying for its existence (CARSON - NEWMAN COMMENCEMENT, 1914-1915:73).

15. C. N. Wheeler--He was the leading hitter for Carson-Newman's fine baseball teams of 1914-1915-1916. He led the 1914 team to a 12-1 season and in one game against Tusculum he batted 7 times hitting a home run, 2 triples, 3 doubles, and a Single. He was captain of the 1916 baseball team (CARSON- NEWMAN COLLEGE COLLEGIAN, 1914).

16. R. "Bo" Bohannon--He was an outstanding pitcher who helped to bring success to the 1915-1916 baseball team as he pitched numerous shut-outs. He was also a fine football tackle during those same years (COMMENCEMENT, 1915-1916).

17. R. H. Humphreys--An outstanding tennis player in1914.::r916 winning most of the singles tournaments held on campus; He played on the 1914 team against Tusculurn, believed to be the first intercollegiate tennis match for Carson-Newman(CARSON-NEWMAN COLLEGIAN. 1916:43).

18. Bernie "Grits" Moore--Athletic Editor of the ORANGE and BLUE (the school newspaper) in 1917. He played tackle on the football team in 1915 at Carson-Newman and was one of the South's outstanding coaches at Louisiana State University from 1935 to the early 1950's. He then became Commissioner of Athletics of the Southeastern Conference and served for a number of years. Sports in the Southeast should be greatly indebted to this outstanding graduate of Carson-Newman College (Interview with Coach Holt, June, 1972).

19. C. Paul Plemmons--He was an outstanding baseball pitcher who was a member of the famous 1917 baseball team at Carson-Newman (19-4 record). He played first base and shortstop and was the leading hitter. He was considered one of Carson-Newman's all-time leading fielders (ORANGE and BLUE, May, 1917).

20. Pat Wells--He was the leading pitcher of the 1916 and 1917 baseball teams (APPALACHIAN, 1917). He won 11 games in 1917 on 1 hitters, 2 hitters, and 3 hitters; also pitching quite a few shut-outs.

21. J. R. West--He was the number one tennis player at Carson-Newman during World War I. He played and won many tournaments in 1917, 1918, and 1919 (ORANGE and BLUE, May, 1919).

## *A History of Sports at Carson-Newman College 1851-1974*

C.N. Wheeler
E. H. Humphries
J. P. Philips
1915

Bernie "Grist" Moore
Top Right

Football 1916

*It Gets Foggy at Mossy Creek*

**John Hutchins**     **Clay "Wild Bull" Kyker**     **Harold "Red" Higgins**

**Walt Abbott and Teammates**     **Walter Haas 1927**     **Tip Smith 1931**

## *A History of Sports at Carson-Newman College 1851-1974*

**Wendell Henderson**  **John Hudson**  **Sneed Nevils**

**Grant Jones 1940**  **Flex Knight 1942**

*It Gets Foggy at Mossy Creek*

**William "Dusty" Roden 1946**

**Fred Woolwine**

**Charles Moffett**

**Fred Keller 1949**

# *A History of Sports at Carson-Newman College 1851-1974*

22. John and Brice Bittinger--Famous brother combination on the tennis team who played doubles and won numerous matches and tournaments in 1917-1919 (ORANGE and BLUE, May, 1919).

23. Dr. R, M. McCowan--A volunteer coach in the early 1920's practiced medicine during the day and coached the football team in the afternoon. He supported Carson -Newman athletics with his time, money and interest in the early 1920's and continued this support through the years. McCowan Field was named in his honor (Carr, 1959:219, 271).

24. Raymond K. Fleenor--A great fullback who gave his life on the football field. He was injured in a game with Knoxville Central on September 20, 1919 and died April 19, 1920. He was president of the Columbian Literary Society in 1918 and 1919 (THE GRENADE, 1920).

25. Don "Lark" King--A 6' 3 " center who was the leading scorer on the basketball team in the early 1920's. He was also a valuable first baseman in baseball (APPALACHIAN, 1922).

26. Frank Hayes--He was a coach in the early 1920's who did much to help get athletics going during that period; especially football (THE WANEHI, 1921).

27. Russ Bibb--A 6' 4" All-Star center on the basketball team who led the Eagles in scoring during the early 1920's He also played football and baseball excelling in both of these sports (APPALACHIAN, 1924)

28. William "Powder River" or "Rabbit" Abbott--He was one of Carson-Newman's fastest and most versatile halfbacks who played in the middle 1920'S. The 1924 APPALACHIAN stated:

"Rabbit" the speediest man on our squad or any other squad in the South. In "Rabbit" we have a "sheik" indeed. He could pass with either hand, punt with either foot, and was a wonderful side stepping, elusive, broken field runner who broke many a game open with his length of the field run. In the Carson-Newman versus Mercer game, he booted the wet, muddy pigskin 75 yards out of danger (APPALACHIAN, 1924).

29. Henry D. Blanc and D. L.Butler--Donated most of the money to build a much needed gymnasium. The building, named in their honor, Butler-Blanc Gymnasium, was completed in 1921 (Carr, 1959:208- 209).

30. Lake "Boom Boom" Russell--Given his nickname because of the way he tackled on the gridiron. As captain of the 1922 football team, which had a 7 -3 record, he played tackle both on offense and defense (APPALACHIAN, 1922: 136-140). Coach Russell will always be remembered as one of Carson-Newman's finest all-round coaches. He made his best coaching record in basketball, losing only seven games in four years, and coached the undefeated team in 1927 which won 17-0,

## It Gets Foggy at Mossy Creek

He compiled a four-year record in basketball of eighty-three wins and seven losses. In addition to his great basketball teams, he also had a 7-2 football team in 1924 and an undefeated baseball club in 1924 which was 12-0 (Carr, 1959:272-275).

# A History of Sports at Carson-Newman College 1851-1974

Football Team 1922
7 wins - 3 Loses

Henry Blanc 1922

Frank Haynes

# It Gets Foggy at Mossy Creek

**Terry "Sunshine" Mudford**

**"Tommy Gun" Taylor**

**"Frosty" Holt**

**Frosty Holt**

**Slim Shoun**

**Harold McNabb**

# *A History of Sports at Carson-Newman College 1851-1974*

**Malory Phillips 1927**

**Hugh Ladd 1932**

**Frank Grubb 1935**

**Roy Roberts 1937**

*It Gets Foggy at Mossy Creek*

Vance Davis

Clif Meredith

Mac "Bull" Biddle

Roy Schubert

# A History of Sports at Carson-Newman College 1851-1974

Earl Ogle and Sanford Gray

"Baldy" Cosson

Loy Bowman and Lynn "Puddles" Murdock

Cleve Compton

*It Gets Foggy at Mossy Creek*

Hyder  	Norman Wright and Bill Bacon 1955

Herbert Ashe  	Charlie Lowery

# A History of Sports at Carson-Newman College 1851-1974

**James Middleton 1941**

**Joe Wiggington 1941**

**Roy Harmon 1942**

**Joe Shipley 1951**

*It Gets Foggy at Mossy Creek*

**Arnold Mellinger and Max Bevins**

**Max Lambert**

**John Lambert**

**Folk Lambert**

# A History of Sports at Carson-Newman College 1851-1974

31. Terry "Sunshine" Midfard and Tommy Taylor--Both were around 230 pounds of bone and muscle and were unmerciful to all opponents on the gridiron. They formed what is thought to be one of Carson-Newman's greatest guard combinations in the school's history (APPALACHIAN, 1924). Tommy Taylor was also an outstanding boxer.

32. Walter Hass--He was captain of the undefeated 1927 basketball team and a fine leader on and off the court. Walter was also a hard running 180 pound fullback on the Parson's football team (APPALACHIAN, 1927).

33. Malory Phillips--He led the Parson's at quarterback in the late 1920's as a fine passer and runner (APPALACHIAN, 1928).

34. Fletcher Sweet--First Public Relations man at Carson-Newman hired in 1927, he was responsible for reporting information concerning athletics and he did an outstanding job (Questionnaire from Fletcher Sweet, April, 1972).

35. John "Hutch" Hutchins--Described in later years by Coach Holt as Carson-Newman's greatest all-time running back. The annual of 1923 (145) stated, "Hutch is the biggest and fastest man on the team. His fast end runs, hard line plunges, and his forward passes and catches were responsible for most of our touchdowns." He was captain of the 1923 football team, selected on the All-Southern team from all colleges and universities in the South three years and named All-State first team for three years (APPALACHIAN, 1924: 141). In 1925, his senior year, he was selected as the best college football player in the state of Tennessee, an honor awarded by the KNOXVILLE JOURNAL (APPALACHIAN, 1925:142, 156). Hutchins played first string guard on some of Carson-Newman's finest basketball teams in the early 1920's and was a good baseball player on the teams fielded by Carson-Newman (Carr, 1959:273).

36. Sam B. "Frosty" Holt--Earned thirteen letters at Carson-Newman--four in football, four in basketball four in baseball and one in track (the only year Carson-Newman had a team in his four years). He was captain of the football, baseball, and basketball teams. In football he was first string quarterback for four years. The 1924 APPALACHIAN (140) stated, "Frosty is the pep and life of our team, proved to be classed among the best field generals in Dixie. He directs the team with the guiding hand of the master tactician. He is an excellent runner, passer and interference. His hard tackling and offensive plays have led Carson-Newman to many victories." In basketball, "Frosty" played on three consecutive outstanding teams. His play-making, passing and scoring led Carson-Newman to great basketball heights. In those three years, 1923-1926, he captained the team his sophomore and senior years and was the leading scorer two out of the three years from his forward position; he was second leading scorer his sophomore year. In baseball, "Frosty" played every position. Though mostly an infielder, he led the Carson-Newman hitters. He was captain of the great undefeated 1924 baseball team. The one year they had a track team, he led in the scoring (Billington, 1953:27-36).

Although Carson-Newman's greatest all-round athlete, "Frosty" brought even more fame to Carson-Newman athletics as a coach and athletic director. He described his early career as a coach at Carson-Newman (Interview with Coach Holt. March. 1972):

My family and I lived in Butler-Blanc Gymnasium for the first 10 years of my career (when the gymnasium was built, rooms were made available for the athletic director to live). I was "The" coach-- football coach, basketball coach, baseball coach, track coach, tennis coach, athletic director, Head of the Physical Education Department, taught six physical education classes a day, the intramural director, the manager, janitor, doctor and whatever else I needed to be. But I didn't complain and got the job done. A typical late fall day went like this..... Teach 6 classes of physical education, make sure my intramurals were operating, coach the football team in the afternoons, walk off the football field and exchange my cleats for some tennis shoes and prepare my basketball boys for the on-coming season plus fixing schedules for all sports and trying to keep my boys in line.

"Frosty" Holt has given fifty years of his life to better Carson-Newman athletics. The "old man" as he is reverently called by many, can still be seen each day at Holt Fieldhouse, on the baseball field, football field or talking to "his" boys about their athletic skills. White hair parted in the middle, darting eyes, shoes shined, tie, weather beaten and tanned from many years of coaching, this is the living legend of Carson-Newman athletics who has been an inspiration to thousands of athletes.

37. Ira Dance--The original "Fighting Parson." He was studying for the ministry while at Carson-Newman. In the Athens College (now Tennessee Wesleyan) football game of 1921, he became angry and knocked out one of the Athens players during the game. This started a fight and Ira had to be locked up in a hotel room for his safety. The next day the KNOXVILLE NEWS-SENTINEL carried the headlines, THE FIGHTING PARSONS DOWN ATHENS COLLEGE. The name stayed for many years thereafter until it was changed in 1930 by Coach Holt (Taped Interview with Coach Holt, March, 1972).

38. Harold "Red" Higgins--Helped Coach Holt and Russ Bibb from a nucleus to lead Carson-Newman to great heights in athletics in the early 1920's. "Red" made the All-Southern team in football at an end position. The 1924 APPALACHIAN (142) had this to say:

Red is one of the fastest and best ends that has hit this section of the country. He knows the game and can play it to perfection. On offense, he can spear a pass out of the air like a magician; while on defense, it was customary to spill the man with the ball yards behind the line. He is down under punts before the ball arrives, waiting to tackle as soon as the oval is caught.

# *A History of Sports at Carson-Newman College 1851-1974*

39. Milas "Slim" Shoun--A 7' 3" center described in the 1926 APPALACHIAN (162) as being "the tallest college basketball player in the world" at that time. Coach Holt, who played with "Slim" and later coached him, said that Slim stayed on the defensive end of the court and knocked the ball out of the basket--at that time there was no goal tending rule (Taped Interview with Coach Holt, March, 1972).

**Basketball 1953-54**

**Football 1955**

# *It Gets Foggy at Mossy Creek*

**Arnold Mellinger 1957**

**Jack Owenby 1959**  **Bill Henry 1959**  **Harry Sparks 1959**

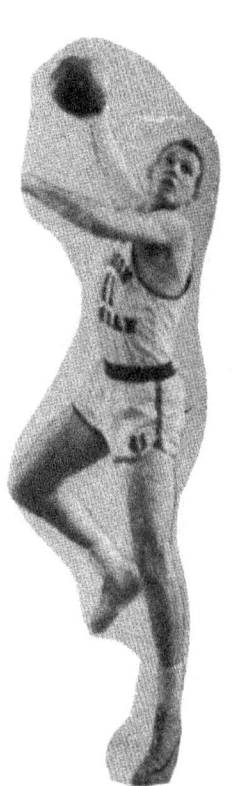  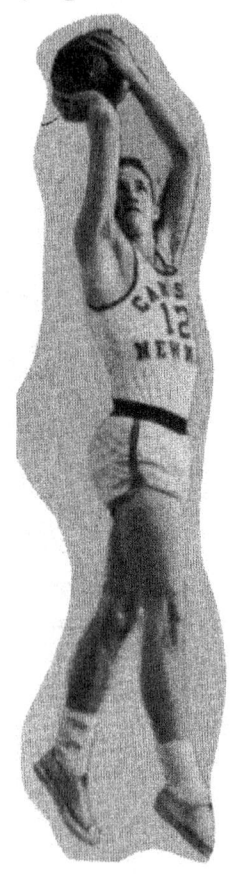

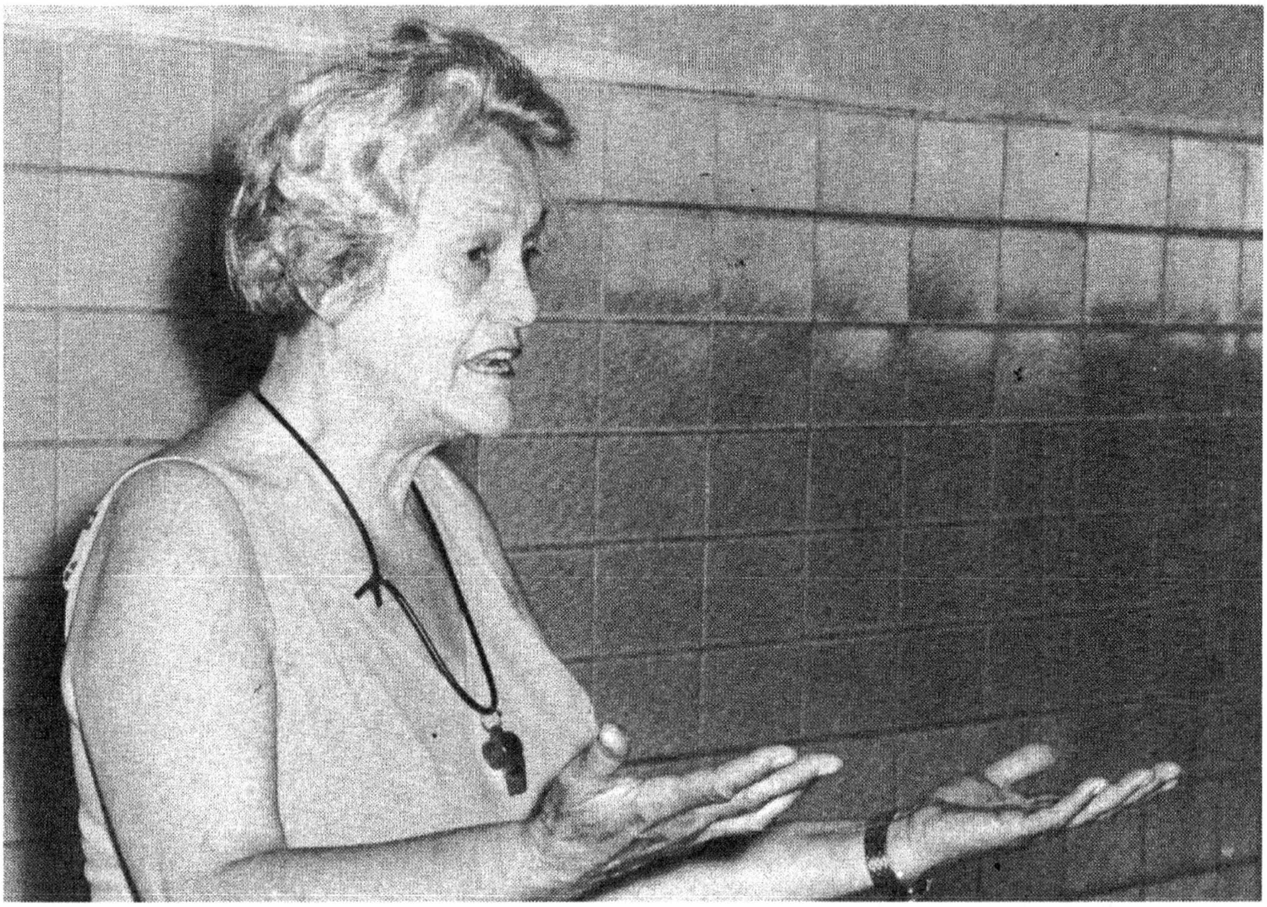

# A History of Sports at Carson-Newman College 1851-1974

Mae Iddins

Coach "Frosty" Holt

## *It Gets Foggy at Mossy Creek*

**Fred Sorrells**   **Dalmuth Shealy**

**Ed Hicks**   **Charlie Bryant**

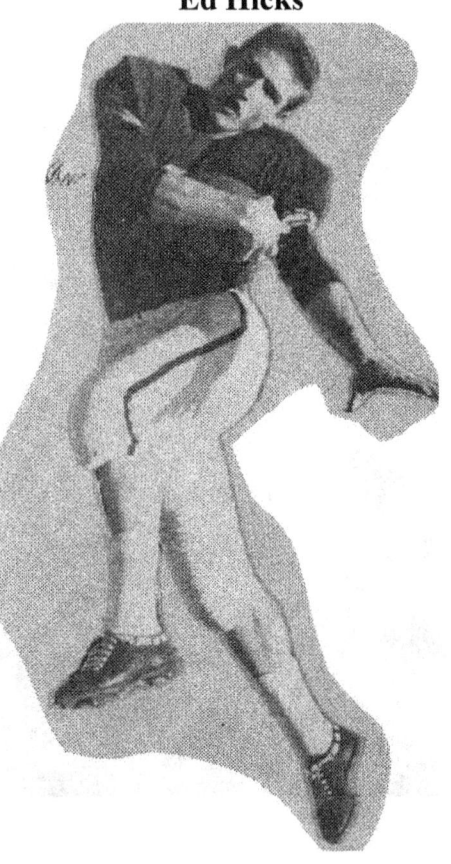

# A History of Sports at Carson-Newman College 1851-1974

**Ed Hicks**

**Les Peek 1958**

**Smiley Oliver 1956**

# It Gets Foggy at Mossy Creek

**Bobby Black**

**Cliff Malpass**

**Betty Roden**

**Bobby Baker 1963**

# *A History of Sports at Carson-Newman College 1851-1974*

Gil Luttrell

Danny "Mac" Pierce 1966

John McPherson

Tom Jones

# *It Gets Foggy at Mossy Creek*

**Clyde Wright**

**Dewayne**

**Valentine Mbong**

**Bruce**

# A History of Sports at Carson-Newman College 1851-1974

Pedro Gomez

Jim Shuler 1965

Jerry Cannon

213

# *It Gets Foggy at Mossy Creek*

Tommy Everette

Larry Ware

# *A History of Sports at Carson-Newman College 1851-1974*

**Lib Julian 1957**

**Al Mashburn 1962**

**Chris Jones 1962**

**Clark Bryan**

# It Gets Foggy at Mossy Creek

Jerald Ellington 1963

Vic Arwood

Al Mashburn

Clyde Wright and Tom Jones

# A History of Sports at Carson-Newman College 1851-1974

Mike Levi

W. A. Wright

Clyde Wright

Jim Shuler

40. Tip Smith--Captain of the 1931 basketball team which had a 16-4 record and were runners-up in the Smoky Mountain Athletic Conference (SMAC). Captain Smith was selected as the Most Valuable Player in the Smoky Mountain Athletic Conference in 1931 (APPALACHIAN, 1932). He later coached and was Athletic Director at Tennessee Wesleyan College in Athens, Tennessee. He did much to keep athletics going in that small church-related college.

41. Kenneth Wood--A 6' 6" center in basketball who helped spring the Eagles to the top in the Smoky Mountain Athletic Conference in the early 1930'S, Kenneth was also a fine pass-catching end for the Eagles in football (ORANGE and BLUE, 1932).

42. Horace "Warhorse" Lawson--He was like a "brick wall draped with o range and blue color." He was a huge tackle known for stopping all opponents (APPALACHIAN, 1932).

43. John Carbon, Wibb Combs, Clyde Childers-All three were quarterbacks in the early 1930'S who led their teams to many victories (APPALACHIAN, 1931-1933).

44. Johnny Roberts --He was an outstanding runner halfback who broke loose for numerous long exciting touchdown runs. He was also a fine tennis player who played the number one position and won many tournaments (ORANGE and BLUE, September, 1932).

45. Hugh Ladd--Captain and play-making guard of the 1933 and 1934 teams, he was also the leading scorer and a good defensive player (ORANGE and BLUE, November, 1933).

46. Paul Layman--He was a 6' 4" leading scorer for three years. He was All-Smoky Mountain Athletic Conference selection and won the Most Valuable Player award for the Eagles basketball team. Paul was a Jefferson City product (APPALACHIAN, 1934).

47. T. J. Stafford--Excelled in both football and basketball in 1934. He returned in 1946 to coach with "Frosty" Holt and became head football coach in 1950 when Coach Holt stepped down (Billington, 1953:277). He did much for Carson-Newman athletics as a player, coach and alumnus.

48. Wayne "Yankee" Henderson--One of the greatest running halfbacks Carson-Newman ever had and one who could score from anywhere on the field. Records show that "Yankee" is still one of Carson-Newman's all-time leading scorers in football. Selected the Most Valuable Player of the Smoky Mountain Athletic Conference two years in a row, "Yankee" was outstanding in every game. He was selected on numerous All-Star teams during his career at Carson-Newman, was All-Smoky Mountain Athletic Conference for four years (APPALACHIAN,

# A History of Sports at Carson-Newman College 1851-1974

1938:123-127) and helped lead the 1936 football team to their undefeated season, the greatest in Carson-Newman's history (APPALACHIAN, 1937: 124, 128).

49. Frank Grubb--Captain and tackle on the 1936 undefeated football team which had a 10-0 record. He was one of Carson-Newman's greatest linemen, winning honors as All-Srnoky Mountain Athletic Conference three years in football and the Most Valuable Player of the Smoky Mountain Athletic Conference (APPALACHIAN, 1936: 73).

50. John Hudson--Center and leading scorer of the great 1936-1937 basketball team which had an 18-1 record and was winner of the All-Smoky Mountain Athletic Conference (APPALACHIAN, 1937:129-131).

51. Hubert Ramsey--Led Carson-Newman to a Smoky Mountain Athletic Conference football championship in 1937. He was quarterback and captain of this team and was named to the All-Smoky Mountain Athletic Conference team (APPALACHIAN, 1938:124, 128).

52. Roy Roberts--Outstanding athlete who died in the bus wreck of 1938. He was a guard on the basketball team and a leader on and off the court. In addition, he was Carson-Newman's leading baseball catcher, president of the Booster Club and a top student (APPALACHIAN, 1937: 128-131; 1938: 132).

53. Vance Davis--All-Smoky Mountain Athletic Conference back and co-captain of the 1939 football team (APPALACHIAN, 1939:131-134).

54. Cas P. Wilson--A fine all-round athlete who helped the Eagles have a winning tradition in the late 30's. He played first team back in football, first team guard in basketball, baseball and tennis (APPALACHIAN, 1937).

55. Jimmie Grissom--He was a fine substitute guard on the basketball team who died in the bus wreck of 1938 (ORANGE and BLUE, February, 1938).

56. Charlie Meredly--Co-captain and All-Smoky Mountain Athletic Conference tackle on the 1938 football squad. He was "a feared tackle and blocker who was proved to be capable in all phases of the game- a fighting spirited football man" (APPALACHIAN, 1939:131-134).

57. Ed "Cutaw" Brown--Lettered in baseball and basketball for four years--1937 through 1940. He was a great defensive guard and floor general and captain of the 1940 basketball team. In his junior year he scored twenty-six points to break the Smoky Mountain Athletic Conference one-game scoring record. (APPALACHIAN, 1940:126)

58. Bill Catlett--He was a hard running All-Smoky Mountain Athletic Conference back in 1940 who played varsity football for three years (APPALACHIAN, 1940).

59. Snead Nevils--Football tackle and outstanding 6' 4" basketball center scoring thirty-five points for an all-time single game record which stood for twenty years. He was an All-Smoky Mountain Athletic Conference performer in both sports (APPALACHIAN, 1941:122).

60. Roy Shubert--A "hard-nosed running back" in football and an All-Srnoky Mountain Athletic Conference performer for two years. He was also the captain of the team in 1941 (APPALACHIAN, 1942).

61. Joe Wiggington--An All-Smoky Mountain Athletic Conference end in football in 1941 (APPALACHIAN, 1942).

62. James Middleton--He was All-Smoky Mountain Athletic Conference in football in 1941 and felt by many to be one of Carson-Newman's finest centers of the 40's (APPALACHIAN, 1942).

63. Flex Knight--The leading hitter and All-Smoky Mountain Athletic Conference player in baseball in 1941 (ORANGE and BLUE, May, 1941).

64. Grant "Casey" Jones--Leading scorer on the basketball team and an All-Smoky Mountain Athletic Conference selection for three years. He scored 350 points in one season (1943) which was a record at that time and led the team in rebounding from his forward position (APPALACHIAN, 1942: 125; 1934: 119).

65. Mac "Bull" Biddle--One of the hardest running fullbacks in the late 1930's and early 1940'S. He was an All-Smoky Mountain Athletic Conference first team selection for two years (ORANGE: and BLUE, November 15, 1941:6).

66. Charlie Moffett--Quarterback of the 1947 football team which had an undefeated season. He led the scoring in basketball that season. He was an All-Smoky Mountain Athletic Conference performer in three sports--basketball; baseball and football (APPALACHIAN, 1948: 130-1-38).

67. William "Dusty" Roden--A strong halfback during the war years (APPALACHIAN, 1947: 128, 133) who returned to Carson-Newman as head basketball coach and assistant football coach. After completing his Doctor's degree he served as Dean of Students at Carson-Newman (APPALACHIAN, 1957: 16).

68. Fred Woolwine--A good football place kicker and hard running halfback of the late 1940's (APPALACHIAN, HJ49).

69. Fred Keller (guard) and Vernon Kyker (tackle)--Both were stonewalls in the Eagle line in the late 1940's (APPALACHIAN, 1948).

# A History of Sports at Carson-Newman College 1851-1974

70. Eugene Cullum--He was the number one tennis player in 1949 (ORANGE and BLUE, May, 1949).

71. Coach Fred Noe--Coach Noe was one of the finest men that has ever been connected with this institution. He was a friend of the students and was always willing to help. As for his interest in athletics, he was as interested in caring for a small scratch as he was a broken bone." He served as coach of tennis, baseball, basketball and assistant football coach under Coach Holt (APPALACHIAN, 1944:84).

72. Roy Harmon--A fine athlete (football and basketball) during the war years who returned to his alma mater in 1951 as assistant football coach under Coach Stafford. The following year he was given the head position when Coach Stafford left (Carr, 1959:278). Coach Harmon did much to upgrade the physical education program and was instrumental in bringing track back to the campus in the early 1960's (APPALACHIAN, 1961:77).

73. Bob "Dog" Watts--A famous barefoot tennis player in the late 1940's who always drew a crowd not only for his performance on the courts but for his shoeless antics (ORANGE and BLUE, May 16, 1949:3).

74. Joe Shipley--Center and captain of the 1931 basketball squad. He was the leading scorer and rebounder for that team and was selected All-Smoky Mountain Athletic Conference performer for two years. He was also a fine baseball pitcher (APPALACHIAN, 1951:202).

75. Max Bevins--Graduated in 1954 holding many of Carson-Newman's basketball scoring records. He was an All-Conference performer for two years and during his senior year he was captain of the team and Most Valuable Player of the conference (APPALACHIAN, 1954: 208-209).

76. Earnest "Baldy" Cosson--A Morristown, Tennessee, product who ran many touchdowns for the Eagles at halfback in the early 1950's. He was selected the Most Valuable Player in the Smoky Mountain Athletic Conference in 1950, his senior year (APPALACHIAN, 1951).

77. J. O. Conwell--The Tennis coach during the late 1940's and 1950's. He meant much to Carson-Newman through his coaching of many championship teams and individuals (ATHLETIC RECORDS).

78. John, Mac and Folk Lambert-- John and Mac played the tackle positions for the football team in the middle 1950's. Both were All-Smoky Mountain Athletic Conference and captains of the team. Another brother, Folk.-was-an outstanding tackle on the undefeated football team of 1936 (APPALACHIAN, 1937: 1954).

# It Gets Foggy at Mossy Creek

**Ed Bodin   1966**

**Richie Gaskell**

**Troy Haydn**

**Dal Shealy**

# A History of Sports at Carson-Newman College 1851-1974

Ray Maynard 1968

Bill Stover 1971

Carl Torbush

Scotty Powers 1971

# It Gets Foggy at Mossy Creek

Tommy Ducey

Johnny Orr

"Papa" John Fox

David Johnson

# *A History of Sports at Carson-Newman College 1851-1974*

**Chris Jones with Cross Country Team**

**Buzzy Stokes and Billy Wilson**

**Gary Prater and Mike Hooker 1974**

**Jim Sullivan**

# *It Gets Foggy at Mossy Creek*

**Rodney Wampler**

**Richie Gaskell**

**Soccer action with Prince and Pius**

# *A History of Sports at Carson-Newman College 1851-1974*

**Gary Chesney 1972**

**Frank Fillman 1971**

**Tim George**

**Mike Ogan 1973**

# It Gets Foggy at Mossy Creek

Mike Bales and Tommy Dickerson

**Football Defense 1971**

**Sanders Shiver 1973**

# *A History of Sports at Carson-Newman College 1851-1974*

# It Gets Foggy at Mossy Creek

Libby Hudson

Carl Torbush and Dal Shealy

Al Canty 1972

Edra Cureton - 1974
Secretaries take care of Eagle coaches

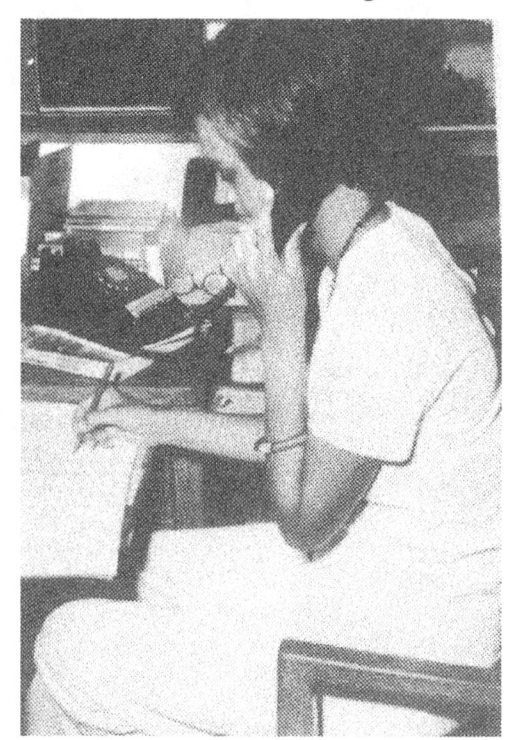

# A History of Sports at Carson-Newman College 1851-1974

David Guinn

Two of Carson-Newman's all-time great wrestlers

1969

Larry Crisafulli

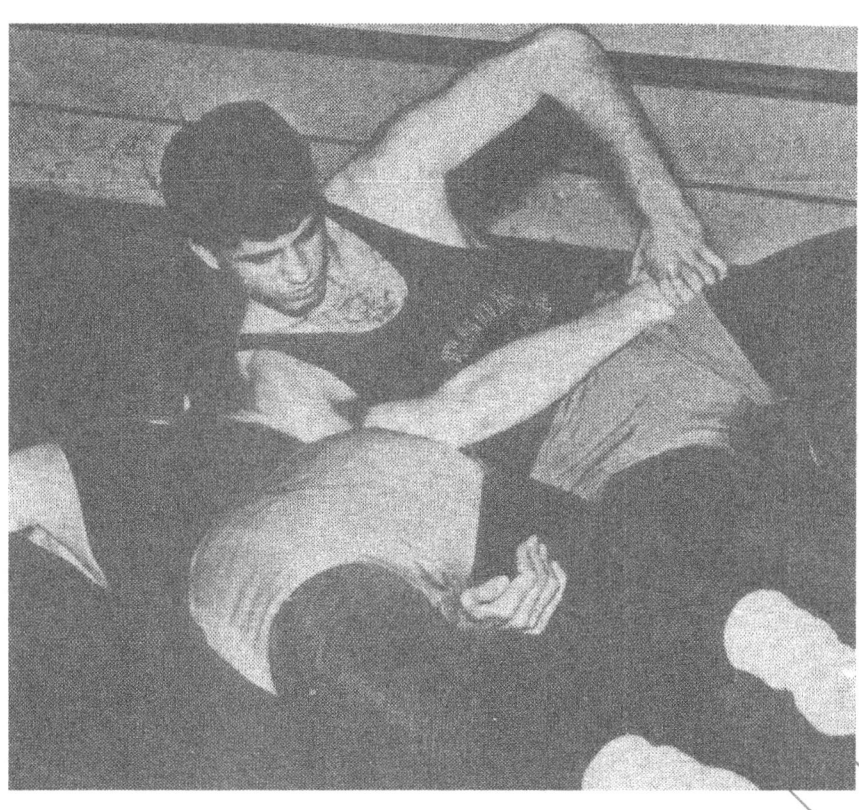

## *It Gets Foggy at Mossy Creek*

79. Hubert Ashe--One of Carson-Newman's finest two-sport athletes of the 1950's leading the nation in punts for small colleges; scoring on many long runs and earning Honorable Mention All-American his junior year. He was All Smoky Mountain Athletic Conference for two years in both football and baseball. In baseball, he excelled as a great hitter--leading the team to the conference championship in 1951 (APPALACHIAN, 1952:163-171).

80. Buddy Catlett--One of the finest tennis players of the 1950's if not the best in the history of the college. He played the number one position for three years, winning many individual conference champion- ships and playing on one of Carson-Newman's greatest teams in 1954 (APPALACHIAN, 1955:164).

81. Kendell Morgan and Norman Wright--Both were fine ball carriers in football during the middle 1950's (APPALACHIAN, 1956).

82. Randall Jones--Wingback and fullback on the football team, he was All-Smoky Mountain Athletic Conference performer in football. He was a break-away threat from anywhere on the field and led Carson-Newman to many victories in the middle 1950's (APPALACHIAN, 1956).

83. Charlie Lowery--A left-handed pitching ace of the middle 1950's who brought Carson-Newman many conference championships. He was an All-Conference performer (ORANGE and BLUE, April, 1955),

84. Arnold Mellinger--Considered by many to be the finest all-round performer in Carson-Newman's basketball history. He was in the starting line-up of every game (99) during his four years and led the Eagles in scoring and rebounding. He was voted All-Conference in each of those years by the coaches. In recognition of his tremendous performance, his jersey was retired after his graduation in 1957. He is the only Eagle basketball player to have received this honor (C-N Basketball Brochure, 1972).

85. Charlie Bryant--An outstanding triple threat halfback in the late 1950's as well as an excellent track man. He later helped bring back track to the Carson-Newman campus in the late 1950's (APPALACHIAN, 1959: 123)

86. Billy Henry-- "The Little General" at 5' 7" tall, he was an outstanding basketball player, making all-Conference three years in a row. He was also an AD-Conference baseball player for two years and a favorite of the fans (APPALACHIAN, 1959: 130-131).

87. Otto Spangler--Number one tennis player for three years. He led the Eagles to the Smoky Mountain Athletic Conference championship three years in a row and in 1958 led the team to a perfect 13-0 record (APPALACHIAN, 1959: 137).

88. Harry Sparks--A three year All-Conference basketball player who played at the guard position and "could do it all--defense, rebound and score." Harry was noted

for his tremendous leading ability as he was able to dunk the ball while standing under the goal. He was the captain of the 1960 team (APPALACHIAN, 1961).

89. Leslie Peek--An All-Conference basketball forward in 1959. Les was the leading scorer noted for his one hand jump shot from anywhere on the floor. He also led the Eagles tennis team to many Smoky Mountain Athletic Conference championships from his number 1 position on the team (APPALACHIAN, 1959).

90. Albert "Chief" Graves--A fine triple threat tailback in football during the late 1950's and early 1960's (APPALACHIAN, 1961).

91. Hank Dickerson--A biology professor at the college who worked with the tennis team during the late 1950's with Coach J. O. Conwell and then took over as head when Coach Conwell retired. Under the leadership of these two men, tennis was brought to the top of Carson-Newman's athletic world (ATHLETIC RECORDS).

92. Bud Bales--An All-Conference catcher on the baseball team who was known for his powerful arm and booming bat. He led the team to three straight conference championships during the early 1960's (APPALACHIAN, 1961).

93. Ed Hicks--An All-Conference performer in football and baseball during the early 1960's. Ed was responsible for many long 'touchdown runs in football and many home runs in baseball (APPALACHIAN, 1966).

94. Cliff Malpass--A leading hitter and shortstop on some of Carson-Newman's best baseball teams of the early 1960's, An All-Conference performer, Cliff is currently the assistant basketball coach at Clemson University (KNOXVILLE NEWS-SENTINEL, June 18, 1970).

95. Tom Meigs--The number 1 tennis player in the early 1960's for the Eagles. The "fiery red-head" from Florida won many individual conference championships while leading his team to victory (APPALACHIAN, 1961).

96. Vic Arwood and Albert Mashburn--Both were steady basketball performers who might have been over-shadowed by others but yet helped through their rebounding, defense and scoring efforts to build Carson-Newman basketball to great heights. Vic started all four years at it forward position while Al started three years at center. Both were All-Conference players (ATHLETIC RECORDS).

97. Jimmy Ray Carter--A track star of the 1960's. He was a very fast dash man and also started as a ball carrier on the football team (APPALACHIAN, 1963).

98. Eugene Wright and Bobby Graves--Both played number 1 and 2 positions on the first golf team of 1961 (APPALACHIAN, 1961).

99. Derrick Davis--Helped form the first soccer team on the campus. Upon graduation, he was selected to play in a professional International Soccer League with the New York Americans (APPALACHIAN, 1962:76).

100. Coach Dick Campbell-- Turned Carson-Newman College into a national basketball power during more national tournaments during his career. His teams won six straight Volunteer State Athletic Conference Eastern Division titles and four straight Volunteer State Athletic Conference tournament championships. He also coached six All-Americans during his years at Carson-Newman, was named conference Coach-of-the-Year and National Association of Intercollegiate Athletics Coach-of-the-Year (Athletic Records, 1959-1966).

101. Chris Jones--Recognized as Carson-Newman's first All-American in any sport, making the National Association of Intercollegiate Athletics All-American team of 1962. He was the leading scorer for three years in basketball at Carson-Newman, for two years in the Volunteer State Athletic Conference, and left Carson-Newman as the all-time leading scorer. He was named to the All-Conference team for three years and earned the Most Valuable Player of the Conference award. Many of the records he established still stand. Chris participated in the first two National basketball tournaments into which Carson-Newman went, in four National Amateur Athletic Union tournaments and in the World Cup tournament, an international event, He was the first Carson-Newman basketball player to be drafted into professional basketball (Cincinnati Royals) (C-N Basketball Brochure, 1972).

102. Bobby Baker--First football player to make All-American at Carson-Newman. Bobby led the Eagles to many victories as he averaged five yards each time he carried the football, one of C-N's best running backs. (APPALACHIAN, 1963: 167).

103. Clark Bryan--Elected the Most Valuable Player in the Volunteer State Athletic Conference during his sophomore year, 1961. He received many honors before he graduated: All-Conference, All-Tournaments of numerous tournaments and Most Valuable Player awards (APPALACHIAN, 1962:66-69) (APPALACHIAN, 1963: 173). He has been a part of Carson-Newman since his graduation, first as Student Activities Director and presently as Dr. Clark Bryan, Dean of Students.

104. Bobby Black--Center and linebacker in football earning All-American honors in 1964 (APPALACHIAN, 1964:179).

105. Gilbert Luttrell--Twice All-American basketball guard of the early 1960's. Besides being named All-American, Gilbert was an All-Conference performer, being named to the Most Valuable Player of the Volunteer State Athletic Conference for two straight years, one of Carson-Newman's all-time leading scorers and participant in four consecutive National tournaments. Gilbert was also an outstanding third baseman in baseball (APPALACHIAN, 1964: 186-191).

106. Jerald "Mule" Ellington--One of Carson-Newman's most outstanding basketball forwards of the early 1960's, he was named All-Conference for three years and one of the all-time leading scorers at Carson-Newman. He played in four straight National tournaments (APPALACHIAN, 1964:186-191).

107. Martin Huckabee--Outstanding track man in dash and broad jump. Records he set in 1961 still stand (APPALACHIAN, 1963:184).

108. Clyde Wright--Called by many as Carson-Newman's greatest baseball player, he led them to the National Association of Intercollegiate Athletics baseball championship in 1965 and won the Most Valuable Player award. His senior year he hit .453--13doubles, 13 home runs, and 54 runs batted in and was selected for the All-American team. He is now a star pitcher for the Los Angeles Angels where he has been a twenty-game winner and has been selected for baseball's All-Star game (APPALACHIAN. 1966:219).

109. Jerry Cannon--An All-American guard in basketball in 1967. Jerry's great jump shot led the Eagles to many victories. He was a great offensive player but could also "do it all." He played good defense, handled the ball, rebounded and was a good assist man. Jerry was All-Conference and also Most Valuable Player of the Conference (APPALACHIAN, 1967).

110. Larry Ware--An outstanding tennis player who won many championships while an Eagle. He led the team to the Volunteer State Athletic Conference and also participated in a national tournament. Larry also excelled in basketball, starting at guard-he was a good floor general and defensive specialist (APPALACHIAN, 1967)

111. Mike Lewis--An All-American baseball player in 1966. (APPALACHIAN, 1966). He was a great pitcher who won many victories with his blazing fast ball.

112. Dale Rutherford--A great passing quarterback of the late 1960's who brought the passing game and many thrilling touchdowns to the Carson-Newman gridiron. Dale was one of the leading small college passers in the nation (APPALACHIAN, 1969).

113. Harold Denton--A standout football tackle who helped Carson-Newman to an 8-2 record in 1968 (APPALACHIAN, 1968).

114. Larry Crisafulli--An undefeated wrestler in his senior year at Carson-Newman. He made it to the national tournament in 1969 (APPALACHIAN, 1970).

115. David Johnson--A track star of the late 1960's and early 1970's. David still holds records for the low and high hurdles and the pole vault. He aided Carson-Newman in bringing home numerous conference championships (APPALACHIAN, 1971).

## *It Gets Foggy at Mossy Creek*

116. Billy Wilson and Jim Sullivan--They were responsible for much of the Eagles football success in the early 1970's. Billy was a linebacker who probably made more individual tackles than anyone who ever wore the orange and blue. Jimmy was a great passing quarter-back who always finished high in the national statistics (ATHLETIC RECORDS. 1971; 1972).

117. Bob Davis--Head football coach and wrestling coach who brought wrestling to the top as an inter-collegiate sport at Carson-Newman (APPALACHIAN, 1966:200).

118. Roy Hill--Came to Carson-Newman without an athletic scholarship having been told by many college coaches that he was too small and too slow for college sports. However, he left Carson-Newman the first two-sport All-American in the history of the college. In baseball he played on the national championship team of 1965. In basketball, he led the team in scoring and was elected the Most Valuable Player of the conference. For his accomplishments, he was named to the All-American teams both in baseball and basketball (APPALACHIAN, 1965: 127).

119. Jim Shuler--A 6'7" All-American forward' in basketball who was considered one of Carson-Newman's finest big men to play the game. Jim led the scoring and the team to many championships (APPALACHIAN, 1966:211).

120. Danny Mac Pierce--An All-American baseball player in 1967 who helped to lead Carson-Newman to many championships including a national championship in 1965. He was also an outstanding basketball guard (APPALACHIAN, 1967: 117).

121. Pedro Gomez and Valentine Mbong--Two foreign students who were valuable to Carson-Newman's soccer program and who were selected to the All-Southern All-Star Soccer team. Valentine was also an outstanding soccer-style kicker on the football team (ORANGE and BLUE, October 11, 1968:7).

122. Coach Bob Wilson--Coached the 1965 baseball team to the national championship. He has been elected Coach-of-the-Year on numerous occasions. He is currently the assistant Athletic Director and head baseball coach at Carson-Newman (ATHLETIC RECORDS, 1965-1972).

123. David Guinn--Carson-Newman's finest wrestler with a record during his four years at Carson-Newman of 25-3 in the heavyweight division. He represented Carson-Newman in the National Association of Intercollegiate Athletic Wrestling tournament in Omaha, Nebraska (APPALACHIAN, 1969; 111).

124. W. A. Wright--An All-American catcher whose direction behind the plate helped Carson-Newman win the 1965 National championship. He was a basketball star, too, and was voted the Most Valuable Player of the 1968 basketball squad for the conference tournament (APPALACHIAN, 1967: 108; 1968:82).

## A History of Sports at Carson-Newman College 1851-1974

125. Tommy Everett--An All-American basketball center for the Eagles. He left Carson-Newman with numerous scoring and rebounding records--one being the all-time leading scorer for four years with 2,365 points. Consistently named to the All-Tournament teams and three years All-Conference, he was selected the Most Valuable Player of the Conference (C-N BASKETBALL BROCHURE, 1970).

126. Tony Mills--One of Carson-Newman's first outstanding black athletes. He was co-captain of the basketball team and an All-Conference player (APPALACHIAN, 1970:38).

127. Tom Jones --Named All-American both in football and baseball his sophomore and junior years. He was a split receiver in football catching numerous touchdown passes. In baseball he was one of Carson-Newman's greatest left handed pitchers. He made All-American four times (a Carson-Newman record), twice in baseball and twice in football. Following this most unusual achievement, he signed a major league baseball contract, thus giving up his eligibility for college sports (APPALACHIAN, 1969:90, 95, 104).

128. Coach Troy' Haydon--Helped to build Carson-Newman's track team to full potential and coached the Eagles to numerous conference championships in cross country and track (APPALACHIAN, 1969: 108).

129. Bill Stover--An All-American baseball player in 1970, led the team in hitting for two straight years, and was also an All-Conference selection (Athletic' Records, 1970).

130. Dr. Gene Mehaffey--Has served as head basketball coach, Athletic Director and Physical Education Department chairman since 1968. His organization has kept both the physical education department and athletics at the top of the Volunteer State Athletic Conference. He was voted National Association of Intercollegiate Athletics Coach-of-the-Year for District 27. He is chairman of the District National Association of Intercollegiate Athletics Basketball Coaches Association (C-N BASKETBALL BROCHURE, 1972).

131. Scotty Powers--An outstanding cross country runner who won the Volunteer State Athletic Conference and many Invitational Tournaments and who helped lead the Eagles to the National Cross Country Meet held in Kansas City, Missouri, in 1971 ( Athletic Records, 1972).

132. Tommy Dicey, Bobby Vann, David Whaley and Peggy Blackman--Participated in Carson-Newman's first appearance at a national golf tournament. They were Carson-Newman's leading players (Athletic Records, 1972).

133. Coach Falmouth Shealy--Coached the Fighting Eagles to one of their best records in football in the 1971 season. The following year his team placed second in the National Association of Intercollegiate Athletics playoffs in Commerce, Texas. This was the first Carson-Newman football team ever to participate in a national

tournament. He has been selected National Association of Intercollegiate Athletics District Coach-of-the-Year in two sports--football and track. He was also an outstanding lineman at Carson-Newman in his playing days (Athletic Records, 1971; 1972).

134. Carl Torbush--He was All-American catcher in baseball his sophomore year, 1972, and was also an outstanding linebacker in football. He has and will bring home many victories and will reap many individual honors on the diamond and the gridiron of the Eagles in the future (Athletic Records, 1972).

135. Rodney Ampler--A bone-crushing fullback who made his own holes in the line if he didn't have one. He led Carson-Newman to a great season in 1971. He was an All-American and elected the Most Valuable player of the Share Bowl.

136. Mark Mason--One of Carson-Newman's finest shooting guards in basketball. He was All-VSAC selection in his junior year and helped Carson-Newman to win 31 games in the 1972-1973 season. He was selected on numerous All-tourney teams and honorable mention All-American.

137. Fred Sorrells--Captain of the football Eagles in playing days of the late 1950's and early 1960's (APPALACHIAN, 1959: 123). He coached the track team to a conference championship in 1972 (Athletic Records, 1972).

138. Charlie King--A standout tackle on the Eagles football team in the middle 1950's (APPALACHIAN. 1956: 160). He was chosen District Golf Coach-of-the- Year for 1972 (Athletic Records, 1972).

139. Sam Green--Led the Carson-Newman tennis team to an eighth place ranking in the national tournament in Kansas City. For his efforts he was chosen District Coach-of-the-Year (Athletic Records, 1972).

140. Johnny Orr--Number one tennis player at Carson-Newman for three years, He won the Volunteer State Athletic Conference singles three years, the Volunteer State Athletic Conference doubles three years, the District singles two years and participated in the national tournament in Kansas City during his senior year where he was beaten in the fourth round (Athletic Records, 1971: 1972)

141. Tim George--An All-American football player his senior year and holder of many school records including touchdown passes caught, yardage receiving and passes received (Athletic Records, 1971; 1972; 1973).

142. Al Canty--Led the nation in pass interceptions for the fabulous 1972 Eagle football squad which finished number two in the nation in small college competition. He was selected to the All-American team thus becoming the first black athlete in Carson-Newman's sports history to be so honored (Athletic Records, 1972; 1973).

# *A History of Sports at Carson-Newman College 1851-1974*

143. Steve Williams--Stands 5'2" tall, was written up in BASKETBALL NEWS (1973:7) as the smallest college basketball player in the world and was known as "The Mighty Mite." He was co-captain of the team in 1973. Steve set a national NAIA assist record and was voted the Most Valuable Player of the Eastern Division of the Volunteer State Athletic Conference (Athletic Records, 1973). His career. His teams won six straight Volunteer State Athletic Conference Eastern Division titles and four straight Volunteer State Athletic Conference tournament championships. He also coached six All-Americans during his years at Carson-Newman, was named Conference Coach of the Year and National Association of Intercollegiate Athletics Coach of the Year (Athletic Records, 1959-1966).

144. Mike Ogan--A basketball All-American who is Carson-Newman's all-time leading scorer. He rewrote many of Carson-Newman's rebounding and scoring records. Mike was elected the Most Valuable Player of the Volunteer State Athletic Conference tournament two consecutive years, All-Conference, leading scorer in the Volunteer State Athletic Conference, and elected to the All-District 24 team. He started every game at C-N his first 3 years.

Dedicated women who have played a very important role in the women's program at Carson-Newman are mentioned below:

145. Mae Iddins--Has done for the women of Carson-Newman College what "Frosty" Holt did for the men. She worked very hard to establish a complete sports program for the women of the college. Awards were given such as pins, sweaters, and letters to girls who reached established point totals through the women's sports program. She also established a Women's Letter Club and other organizations related to women's athletics. Through her efforts for more than thirty years she brought Carson-Newman to the top in women's athletics, intramurals, Play-Days, and Physical Education. "Miss Mae" was also an outstanding woman athlete in her student days during the mid-1920's being captain of the fine Parsonette basketball teams (Carr, 1959:278). For her efforts, Miss Iddins was the recipient of the coveted Distinguished Alumni Award.

146. Frances Roden--An outstanding physical education teacher. She worked hard to present a challenging program for the women athletes. Mrs. Roden was a fine athlete in her student days at Carson- Newman under "Miss Mae" (APPALACHIAN, 1963:193-194).

147. Martha Wilson--Brought to the college outstanding teaching skills and enthusiasm for her physical education classes. She has taken up where Miss Iddins left off-- trying to keep the women's athletic program established, She sponsors such organizations as the Women's Letter Club and Women's Physical Education Major's Club. She has been a member of the Carson-Newman Physical Education staff since 1964.

148. Libby Hudson--One of Carson-Newman's most skillful all-round women athletes, She led the Carson-Newman's Women's basketball, volleyball and other athletic

teams during her student days to many victories and was selected to numerous All-Tournament teams and voted the Most Valuable player on many occasions. She is currently on the physical education staff at Carson-Newman using her many skills to better establish the women's sports program.

# *A History of Sports at Carson-Newman College 1851-1974*

## 1960's All-Americans

Chris Jones

Bobby Black

Bobby Baker

Gil Luttrell

# It Gets Foggy at Mossy Creek

Roy Hill

Clyde Wright

Roy Hill

Danny Mack

# A History of Sports at Carson-Newman College 1851-1974

Jim Shuler

Mike Levi

W. A. Wright

Jerry Canon

# It Gets Foggy at Mossy Creek

Tom Jones

Tom Jones

# *A History of Sports at Carson-Newman College 1851-1974*

## TRIBUTE TO PUBLIC RELATIONS MAN, MANAGER AND ATHLETIC ADMINISTRATION

Athletic Committee Chairman - Since intercollegiate athletics began in 1895 at Carson-Newman, there has been a faculty member behind the scene doing his part to see that the athletic program continues. This paragraph is dedicated to those men too numerous to mention that have given of their time and talent to assure the Eagles success in athletics. For example, Mr. Albert Sloan for the past thirty years has been such a man. Serving as Conference Committee chairman, Eligibility Chairman of the National Association of Intercollegiate Athletics and in charge of finances for the Eagles, he has done much to assure the athletic success of sports at Carson-Newman College.

The Managers - From the first intercollegiate team in 1895, the manager has played an, important part in the success of the athletic program at Carson-Newman. Various duties have been bestowed upon these hard-working students. In early times, he helped "manage" the team in such ways as scheduling, financial arrangements, and even helping coach the team on occasion. Down through the years he has taken on such duties as custodian janitor, statistician, scorebook keeper, laundry man, bus loader, trunk packer, Gym sweeper, cheerleader and trainer. For example, Jerry "The Buff" King, who was the manager of the basketball team and my roommate in the early 1960's, when going to the national tournament was an every year event, spent many hours of his college career dedicating himself to keeping all the players and coaches happy. No publicity, few thank yous or appreciation was given to the hard working managers but they are definitely the men behind the scenes.

The Publicity Director or Public Relations Man - These are the men who put the Eagles in the head-lines and make the star athletes known to the public. The Fletcher Sweets (first P. R. man). The Warren Weirmans, the John Foxes, and the Carl Tiptons - they are the men behind the scenes. Without the dedicated Public Relations Man the public would not know of the accomplishments of the many athletes and teams of the Eagles. This paragraph is dedicated to those men who took time to go to the ball games, attend practice sessions, and sit in on conference meetings and just for being a friend to the coaches and athletes of the college.

**Albert Sloan, Jr.**

# It Gets Foggy at Mossy Creek

Chris Jones
Cincinnati Royals

Clyde Wright
California Angels

## Gone Pro!!

Tim George
Cincinnati Bengals

# A History of Sports at Carson-Newman College 1851-1974

**Larry Ledford**

**Eddie Roberts 1974**

**Troy Hayden**

**Bill Herron**

# It Gets Foggy at Mossy Creek

**Ken Sparks**

**Gene Meheffey**

**John Wike**

# *A History of Sports at Carson-Newman College 1851-1974*

**Libby Hudson**
**One of Carson-Newman's all-time great women athletes.**
**Shown here with her Most Valuable Player Award in Basketball - 1966**

**A 1985 Eagle?**

# *It Gets Foggy at Mossy Creek*

## INFORMATION INVOLVING THE WOMEN OF C-N COLLEGE

### 1921 BASKETBALL TEAM

Players:
Pauline Disney
Grace Disney
Latchie Allison
Sophie Tindell
Alice Waite Moser
George Blalock

Schedule:
Newport High School
Martha-Washington College
Maryville College
Cumberland College
Martha-Washington College

Record: 2-3

### 1923 BASKETBALL TEAM

Players:
Olive Brown
Inez Higgins
Velma Davis
Alice Waite Moser
Margaret Sizer
Lois Hixon
Jessie Sams
Martha Sherwood
Coach Taylor

Schedule: Record 2-1

| | | | |
|---|---|---|---|
| Carson-Newman | 18 | University of Chattanooga | 13 |
| Carson-Newman | 10 | University of Tennessee | 20 |
| Carson-Newman | 17 | T.P.I. | 10 |

### 1924 BASKETBALL TEAM

Players:
Sams
Thomas
Iddins
Rosie
Davis
Cable
Rhymer

# A History of Sports at Carson-Newman College 1851-1974

**Schedule: Record 4-7**

| | | | |
|---|---|---|---|
| Maryville | 16 | Carson-Newman | 12 |
| Maryville | 13 | Carson-Newman | 18 |
| Knoxville-YWCA | 15 | Carson-Newman | 14 |
| Martha-Washington | 18 | Carson-Newman | 16 |
| E.T.S. Normal | 17 | Carson-Newman | 12 |
| T.P.I. | 17 | Carson-Newman | 26 |
| T.P.I. | 13 | Carson-Newman | 25 |
| Cumberland | 20 | Carson-Newman | 22 |
| Peabody | 26 | Carson-Newman | 17 |
| Peabody | 25 | Carson-Newman | 18 |
| Chattanooga | 19 | Carson-Newman | 17 |

## 1925 BASKETBALL TEAM

Players:  Velma Davis (Captain)
Inez Higgins
Geneva Thomas
Mae Iddins
Ada Roberts
Ruth Rose
Margaret Sizer
Ruby Purkey
M.E. Martin
Lula Shipe
Roberta Smith

**Schedule: Record 6-2**

| | | | |
|---|---|---|---|
| University of Tennessee | 38 | Carson-Newman | 30 |
| Grace Avenue | 4 | Carson-Newman | 56 |
| E.T. Normal | 17 | Carson-Newman | 15 |
| Erwin | 7 | Carson-Newman | 27 |
| Martha-Washington | 12 | Carson-Newman | 36 |
| University of Tennessee | 16 | Carson-Newman | 36 |
| Erwin | 12 | Carson-Newman | 36 |
| E.T. Normal | 19 | Carson-Newman | 27 |

## 1926 BASKETBALL TEAM

Players:  Mae Iddins (Captain) Coach Abbott
Frank Roberts
Martha Taylor
Polly Brummit
Inez Higgins
Margaret Livesay

# *It Gets Foggy at Mossy Creek*

Rachael Rose
Roberta Smith
Mildred Boyd
Betsy Martin
Mildred Scarbough
Polly Rogers
Lois Hixsor
Viola Lingerfelt
Bertha Davis

Schedule: Record 12-2

| | | | |
|---|---|---|---|
| University of Chattanooga | 8 | Carson-Newman | 40 |
| Cumberland College | 14 | Carson-Newman | 39 |
| Tusculum College | 19 | Carson-Newman | 35 |
| E. T. Teachers College | 15 | Carson-Newman | 41 |
| Milligan College | 10 | Carson-Newman | 44 |
| T'usculum College | 19 | Carson-Newman | 26 |
| T. P. I. | 21 | Carson-Newman | 39 |
| Centenary | 4 | Carson-Newman | 15 |
| Maryville College | 32 | Carson-Newman | 12 |
| University of Chattanooga | 21 | Carson-Newman | 30 |
| M. T. Teachers College | 34 | Carson-Newman | 21 |
| Cumberland College | 24 | Carson-Newman | 36 |
| T.P.I. | 19 | Carson-Newman | 20 |
| Maryville College | 12 | Carson-Newman | 34 |

## 1929 BASKETBALL TEAM

Players: Margarite Livesay (Captain)   Coach Mae Iddins
Crilla Campbell
Fay Bowman
Francis Higgins
Pig Bowman
Ethel Boyd
Neele Brown
Alene Ellison
Sis Bowman
Lucille Peck
Bernie Russell

## 1930 BASKETBALL TEAM

Players:   George Ellison   Coach Mae Iddins

Elsie Chesney
Doc Boyd
Bill Peterson
Una Livesay
Hazel Anderson

Wilma Jones
Muriel Nitch
Inez Davis
Polly Massengill
Jerry Vines
Gladys Livesay

**1931 BASKETBALL TEAM**

Wiggins          Coach Mae Iddins
Brown
Jones
Massengill
Hitch
Catlett
Anderson
Lane
McElveen

This was the last year for intercollegiate sports on the campus for women. Miss Mae Iddins began the Point System for the girls in which they could still have their athletic program and earn the school letter. They received a certain number of points for each sport they participated in and at the end of the year their points were totaled to see what they had earned. Beginning with the next page, a list of all the EAGLE, SWEATER, and LETTER girls.

*It Gets Foggy at Mossy Creek*

### 1931-1932 EAGLES

Florence Williams
Blanche Lease
Elsie Kirby
Mildred Collier
Virgie Davis
Edith Davis
Lucy Robertson
Armetta McElveen
Mildred Coram
Hazel Gossage
Lucille Wilson
Inez Hopson
Angaler Rymer
Sara Lana

### 1932-1933 EAGLES

Edna Shoun
Willie Moore
Virginia Fugate
Fern Carwood
Martha Boyd
Johnnie Bovard
Eva Ruth Wiggins
Nina Dossett
Margaret Newport
Wilma Stout
Mildred Bracy
Glenna Gegley
Lorene McDaniel
Carolyn Shull
SWEATERS
Hazel Gossard
Lucille Wilson

### 1933-1934 EAGLES

Ural Ogle
Mildred Hale
Jodie Brown
Lorene Buckner
Wanda Roberts
Hattie Brummitt
Thelma Eldridge
Mary Katherine Scarbough
Elizabeth Hardy
Mildred Iddins
Gertrude Hughes
Ruth Shields
Anne Smith ~
Lois Gatt
Stella Richardson
Sarah Shull
Norma Phillips
Illene Randolph
Elizabeth Gilmore

### 1935-36 LETTER

Catherine Strange
Mary Ruth Holt
Dean Cates
Bernice Craig
Maude Chambers
Mildred Kidd
Evelyn Kidd
LaVerne Willoughley
Winston Payne
Rebecca Stevenson
Doris DeVault
Dorothy DeVault
Eileen Hill
Eleanor Mchan
Virginia Root
Flo Wallace
Katherine Green
Helen Moulton
Pattie Kettle
Louise Cantrell

# *A History of Sports at Carson-Newman College 1851-1974*

**1933-34 SWEATER**

Sarah Lane

**1934-35 LETTER**

Mildred Hale
Jodie Brown
Inez Hopson
Elizabeth Hardy
Mildred Iddins
Gertrude Hughes
Ruth Shields
Anne Smith
Lorene McDaniel
Elizabeth Gilmore
Ilene Randolph
Carolyn Shull
Norma Phillips

**EAGLES**

Doran Craig
Mary Ella Wallace
Lucille Thomas
Johnnie Sharp
Geneva Ratcliffe
Bill Rhymer
Joyce Epley
Louise Brown
Frances Burkitt
Louise Hol
Nora Mae Catron
Lou Berid
Mary Ellen Woodward
Ruth Lovelace
Una Deakins

Maude Townsend
Philomene Miller
Maria Hughes
Irene Reynolds
Reba Reynolds
SWEATERS
Doran Craig
Mary Ella Wallace
Lucille Thomas
Johnnie Sharp
Sarah Shull

**1936-37 EAGLES**

Pansy Creswell
Virginia Kemmer
Virginia Shull
Florence Shull
Una Ratcliffe
Gladys Lee
Norma Lawes
Marjorie Cates
Manella Woody
Virginia Garland
Willie Floy Fox
Lon Davis
Marie Hughes
Gladys Price
Ruth Emore
Mary Elanor McDowell
Reba Reynolds
Pauline Rymer
Ruth Cole

# *It Gets Foggy at Mossy Creek*

**1936-1937 Eagles continued**
**LETTERS**

Louise Brown
LaVerne Willoughly
Winston Payne
Philomene Miller

**SWEATER**

Eileen Hill
Mattie Lou Ladd
Virginia Root
Flo Wallace
Katherine Greene
Doris De Vault
Dorothy De Vault
Frances Burkett

**1937-38 EAGLES**

Lady Kate Allen
Elizabeth Buckner
Sallie Ledbetter
Helen Morton
Pauline McGuffin
Louise Myers
Mary Wall
LaVerne Garrison
Wilma Ruth Thornton
Mildred Sampson
Sarah Sullenburgar
Marie Robinson
Bernice Robinette
Mildred Myers
Edith Anderson
Margaret Eledge
Helen Wilson
Ruth Sharp
Anna Beth Hardin
Mary Myers
Georgia Myers

**LETTER**

Catherine Strange
Florence Shull

Ruth Cole

**SWEATER**

LaVerne Willoughlby
Winston Payne
Louise Brown
Philomene Miller

**1938-39 EAGLES**

Elizabeth Franklin
Margaret Grubb
Mary Jarnigan
Helen Kinder
Lillian Martin
Ramona Mitchell
Catherine Monroe
Betty Lou Roberts
Wilmina Trent
Blanche Price
Virginia Pope
Margaret Ivy
Johnny Hardy
Elizabeth McNabb
Eleanor Seahorn
Sue Belle Begley
Bill Parker
Phanoy Tallent
Blanche Hardy

**LETTER**

Lady Kate Allen
Elizabeth Buckner
Saddie Lidbetter
Helen Morton
Pauline McGriffin
Louise Myers
Mary Wall
Ruth Sharp
Anna Beth Hardin

**SWEATER**

Pansy Creswell
Virginia Kemmer

# *A History of Sports at Carson-Newman College 1851-1974*

Gladys Price
Norma Lawes
Mary Ruth Holt
Bill Rhymer
Joyce Epley
Virginia Shull
Virginia Kemmer
Pansy Creswell
Ruth Elmore
Mary Eleanor McDowell
Pauline Rymer

Virginia Shull
Ruth Elmore
Mary Eleanor McDowell
Pauline Rymer
Ruth Cole Frances Sharp
Anna Love Sullivan
Ruth Brown Moffett
Constance Mynatt
Betty Davis
Betty Crovett
Emma Knight
Lellah Begley

## 1939-40 EAGLES

Frances Sharp
Anna Love Sullivan
Ruth Brown Moffett
Constance Mynatt
Betty Davis
Betty Crovett
Emma Knight
Lellah Begley
Ada Allen
Edna James
Adelle Reynolds
Alma Stout
Anna Ruth Culverhouse
Lucille Woodward
Dorothy Jarman
Ota Ka King
Edith Pope
Dot Evans
Geraldine West
Lola West
Lola Wilson

## 1939-1940 LETTERS

Eleanor Seahorn
Edna James
Sue Belle Begley
Dorothy Jarman
Margaret Eledge
Ota King
Bill Parker
Emma Knight
Helen Wilson
Catherine Monroe
Blanche Hardy
Constance Mynatt
Johnny Hardy
Alma Stout
Georgia Myers
Anne Sullivan
Blanche Price

PINS
Irene Reynolds
Ruth Sharp

## SWEATER

Ruth Sharp

## 1941-42 EAGLES

Ruth Begley

## It Gets Foggy at Mossy Creek

Anna Beth Hardin

**PINS** Ruth Elmore
Mary Eleanor McDowell
Pauline Rymer
Virginia .Kemmer
Pansy Creswell
Ruth Cole

**1940-41 EAGLES**
Mary Barrarly
Elizabeth Barnett
Rosalie Beeler
Dathyne Brown
Delsie Mae Carver
Ruth Coffey
Nita Coker
Fay Cullum
Marilee Davis
Mary Louise Elkins
Margie Goans
Gladys Honeycutt
Sue Kemmer
Dorothy Layman
Dollois Layman
Gladys Longley
Maude Lyon
Sally Myers
Gladys Owenby
Phyllis Rankin
Jane Ridley
Kathleen Skeen
Helen Shipe
Marie Spears
Grace Tallent
Janie Tallent
Mildred White
Betty Jane Talley
Emma Knight

**1940-1941 SWEATER**
Sue Begley
Margaret Eledge
Bill Parker

Mary Lou Cross
Dorothy McNabb
Evelyn Parker
Marguerite Taylor
Jane Crovatt
Linnie Etta Adkins
Mabel Walker
Phyllis Lowe
Lucille Knight
Colleen Keebler
Mabel Hill
Mary Kathryn Graves
Kathern Frink
Lida Eskew
Bill Dickson
Mary Emma Primm
Gertrude Parrott
Grace O'Donovan
Mary Lynn
Ruth Hill
Aileen Ezell
Lena Bowen
Grace Bailey

**LETTER**
Margie Goans
Janie Tallent
Dathyne Brown
Nita Coker
Dorothy Layman

**1941-42 LETTER**
Janie Ridley
Gladys Owenby
Dellois Layman
Mary Baggerly

**SWEATER**
Constance Mynatt
Ada Allen

PIN
Eleanor Seahorn

**1942-43 EAGLES**
Eleanor Seahorn

Betty Bowen

# A History of Sports at Carson-Newman College 1851-1974

**LETTERS**

Ada Allen
Lillah Begley
Rugh Brown
Betty Crovatt

Helen Hodges
Mildred Knight
Betty Litton
Clyda Proffit
Betty Standifer
Lucille Winker
Betty Jo Blalock
Jean Brooks
Iris Fries
Vera Ruth Rule
Emmalee Winegar
Deane Wallace
Lola Davis
Louise Owenby
Caroline Sullivan
Yvonne Parham
Mildred Ogle
Lulabelle Hardy
Mary Jo Carroll

**LETTERS**

Rugh Begley
Fay Cullom
Mary Louise Shultz
Gladys Longley
Mabel Hill
Lida Eskew
Dorothy McNabb
Mary Lou Cross

**1942-1943 SWEATER**

Margie Goans
Anna Love Sullivan
Dathyne Brown
Nita Coker
Dorothy Laymen

**1943-1944 EAGLES**
Jean Wardrop
Grainger Holt

Lydia Bray
Christine Cates
Helen Jo Dodson
Rosemary Edens
Betty Hayes

Marjorie Smith
Helen Formby
Aurelia Crawford
Christine Cates
Alla Atchley
Mildred Ball
Betty Brewer
George Anna Ford
Rue Franklin
Martha Standifer
Tommie Hitch

**LETTERS**

Dorothy McNabb
Betty Hayes
Mildred Knight
Iris Frees
Marguerite Taylor
Betty Bowen
Alla Atchley
Lucille Winkler
Helen Hodges
Helen Jo Dobson
Aurelia Crawford
Betty Standifer
Rosemary Edens
Christine Cates

**SWEATER**

Dorothy McNabb
Ruth Begley
Betty Bowen
Marguerite Taylor

**PIN**

Dathyne Brown

# It Gets Foggy at Mossy Creek

Nita Coker
Dorothy Layman
Dorothy McNabb

**1944-45 EAGLES**

Kathyrn Ault
Mary Nell Brooks

Rue Franklin
Elizabeth Helton
Frances Swann
Pauline Bowers
Dorothy Bettes
Thelma Thatch
Juanita Larew
Loretta Mason
Eloise Huff
Nell Edwards

**LETTERS**

Alla Atchley
Christine Cates
Aurelia Crawford
Helen Jo Dodson
Rosemary Edens
Mildred Knight
Helen Formby
Martha Standifer
George Anna Ford

**SWEATER**

Betty Bowen

**PIN**

Betty **Bowen**

**1945-46 EAGLES**

Helen Ward

1945-46 LETTER

Juanita Larew
Louise Ownby Crews
Nelle Edwards
Donna Jean Layman
Loretta Mason

**1946-47 EAGLES**

Shirley Birchfield
Carolyn Cate
Iva Lou Castell
Ruby Cavin
Ruth Drinnen
Joan Easterly
Louise Emmert
Mary Jane Houston
Margaret Lee
Jamie Masengill
Elouise McCarrol
Ruth Ownby
Ruby Price
Frances Roden
Edna Sheucraft
Imogene Stevens
Jane Strauss
Jean Strauss
Lucille White
Mary Ruth Wofford

**LETTER**

Joyce Duffield

# *A History of Sports at Carson-Newman College 1851-1974*

Joanne Larew
Claire Lovell
Shirley Morris
Kathryn Ault Watts
Muriel Bennett
Helen Bowers
Betty Burns
Merle Campbell
B. J. Corum
Betty Alice Cowan
Ulene Deweese
Madge Deel
Pearl Drinnen
Joyce Duffield
Helen Ingersol
Mary Jackson
Dorothy King
Don Lawson
Lois Liner
Doris Overbey
Jo Reeves
Katherine Sylar
Mary Thornton
Betty Gay Walden
Carolyn Woodward

### LETTERS

Helen Bowers
Iva Lou Casteel
Ruby Cavin
Joan Easterly
Louise Ernrnartt
Jamie Massengill
Jane Strauss
Jean Strauss
Lorenna Riddle
Mary Ruth Wofford

### SWEATER

Katherine Sylar
Doris Dorian

### PIN

Gerry Ellis
Mary Jackson
Don Lawson
Lois Liner
Doris Overby
Kathryn Sylar
Jo Reeves
SWEATER
Nelle Edwards
Loretta Mason

### 1947-48 EAGLES

Arlene Cate
Martha Chunn
Marguerite Close
Ruby Crayton
Mary Green
Dorothy Knicely
Jean Knicely
Vernita Lee
Helen Oglesby
Jo Rives
Fredda Shoun
Joy Staley
Mary Tollett

Polly Meredity
Polly Meredith
Jodell Oakes
Eloise Osborne
Lyndall Overby
Sally Pangle
Kathryn Parker
Betty Peck
Jama Rubin
Janie Talley

### LETTER

Helen Bowers
Arlene Cate
Martha Chumn
Ruby Crayton
Mary Green
Dorothy Knisley
Jean Knisley

261

*It Gets Foggy at Mossy Creek*

**PIN**

Nelle Edwards
Loretta Mason

**1948-49 EAGLES**

June Allen
Betty Bales
Wanda Bramlett
Betty Ruth Bryan

**SWEATER**

Bille Ruth Buttrey
Lou Henry Cates
Bobbie Jeanne Cooper
Ruth Eden
Betty Jo Hudson
Donna Lawson
Doris Overby
Lyndall Overby

**1949-1950 EAGLES**

Nancy Curtis
Jean DeCoursey
Joyce Drinnen
Tiny Green
Betty McNabb
Eloise Quarles
Pat Riggs
Velma Sword
Joann Welchance
Jolene Warren

**LETTER**

Betty Jo Hudson
Jodell Oakes
Lyndall Overby
Betty Peck
Janie Talley
Sally Pangle

Eloise Osborne
Polly Meredity
Marilyn Logan

June Allen

**SWEATER**

Vernita Lee
Helen Oglesby
Jo Rivas
Carol Woodward

**SWEATER**

Joan Easterly
Jamie Massengil
Lorene Riddle
Mary Ruth Wofford

Betty Jo Hudson

Bette Peck
Janie Lee Talley

**PIN**

Dorothy Knisley
Jean Knisley
Vernita Lee

**1951-52 EAGLES**

Evelyn Anderson
Martha Brown
Betty DeFoe
Charlotte Drinnen

Sue Shanks
Joyce Sharp
Floy Sims
Jo Ann Tyre
Betty Worthy
Bobbie Jean Catlett

**LETTERS**

Esther Fite

Sarah Ford

# *A History of Sports at Carson-Newman College 1851-1974*

    Dorothy Frost
    Dorothy Knisley                        Dot McBride
    Jean Knisley                          Polly Morris
    Vernita Lee                           Mary Tollett
    Carolyn Woodward            Joan Wilson
    Ruby Cavin                           Judy Jordon

**PIN**    Jamie Massengil       **SWEATER**
            Joan Easterly                     Jean DeCoursey

                                          Joyce Drinnen

## 1950-1951 EAGLES

Anna Burkhard
Dorcus Bush                **PIN**      Betty Peck
Esther Fite                            Janie Talley
Sarah Ford                        Lynndale Overby

Dorothy Frost            **1952-53 EAGLES**
Nancy Green                        Ann. L. Cate
June Jordan                         Earlene Hull
Dorothy McBride             Si Longmire
Willa Raye Miller   .             Joyce Neighbert
Pauline Morris                  Loreata Phipps
Agnes Roach                   Earnestine Sharp
Maxine Turner               Alice Sutherland

Gerry Walker                    Ruth Fite
        Joan Wilson               Katy Garner
Geraldine Worthy
Patsy Hickman          **LETTER**    Charlotte Drinnin
Carolyn Woodward
Betty Defoe
Nancy Curtis                       Floy Sims
Jean DeCoursey     **SWEATER**
Joyce Drinnen                   Betty McNabb

Tiny Green                       Mary Tollett
Betty McNabb                   Betty Worthy

Eloise Quarles            **PIN**
Jama Rubin                     Jean Decoursey

Velma Soard                   Joyce Drinnin
Jodell Oakes

*It Gets Foggy at Mossy Creek*

**1953-1954 EAGLES**
Mary Ann Bearden
Charlotte Duckette
Billy Mathews
Bobby Mathews
Bennie Norwood
Wanda Smith
Sara Smith
Bettye Ruth Fite
Gerry Tommey
Mary J. Knisley
Georgia Morris
Bobbie Sorrill
LETTERS
 Earlene Hull
Si Longmire
Joyce Nieghbert
Loretta Phipps

Earnestine Sharp
Alice Sutherland
Katy Garner
SWEATER
 Charlotte Drinnen
FIoy Sims
Joan Wilson
**1954-55 EAGLES**
Sara Depew
Nancy Duncan
Jean Ellis
Sylvia Fuller
Shirley Harris
Charlese Jones
Cleo Lawson
Anita Morrell
Nancy Jo Norton
Pat Smith
Tracie Sutherland
Marianna Taylor
Vivian Duggan
Betty Lou Underwood

**LETTERS**
Mary Ann Bearden

**1955-56 LETTERS**
Sylvia Fuller
    Charlese Jones
Cleo Lawson
Anita Morrell
Georgia Morris
Tracie Sutherland
    Marianna Taylor

**PINS**   Earnestine Sharp
Siothia Longmire
**1956-57 EAGLES**
Ann Allison
Carolyn Barnette
Sara Huy
Patsy Line
Beth Orr
Nelda Smith
Jan Weasner
**LETTERS**
Mary E. Allen
Bobbie Bagley
Shirley Boyd
Rachel Joyce
Gloria Torrance
Sadie Tatum
**SWEATER**
Sylvia Fuller
Cleo Lawson
Marianna Taylor
1957-58 EAGLES
 Peggy Evans
Irene Forrester
Leah Maxwell
Carol Alular
Jane Roberson
Toni Thacker
    Priscilla Thomas
Betty Wells

**LETTERS**
Carolyn Barnette
Patsy Line

# A History of Sports at Carson-Newman College 1851-1974

Charlotte Duckette
Billy Mathews
**SWEATER**

Bobby Mathews
Bennie Norwood
Wanda Smith
Bettye Ruth Fite
Berry Toomey

**SWEATER**
Earnestine Sharp
Loretta Phipps
Joyce Neighbert
Si Longmire

**PINS**

Charlotte Drinnen

**LETTERS**
Peggy Cline
Irene Forrester
Nancy Lawson
Priscilla Thomas
Betty Wells
**SWEATER**
Patsy Line
Betty Winters
**PIN**
Mary E. Allen
**1959 -1960 EAGLES**
Ellen Hall
Edna Marled
Virginia Moore

Nelda Smith

Mary E. Allen
Sadie Tatum
**1958-59 EAGLES**
Evelyn Jo Brown
Betty Chute

Julie Davis
Brenda Ferguson
Sandra He skill
Nancy Lou Lawson
Barbara Northcutt
Libby Ownby

Phyllis Pettit
Faye Rogers
Edna Smith
Sandra Tombaugh
Joyce Walker
Sandra Wright

Judy Phillips
Shirley High
Jan Taylor
Janice Thompson
**LETTERS**
Nancy Lawson
Barbara Northcutt
Libby Ownby
Sandy Tombaugh
Joyce Walker
Gail Warren
Sandy Wright
Faye Rogers
Betty Wells
**SWEATER**
Peggy Evans
Betty Wells
Peggy Clines

265

## *It Gets Foggy at Mossy Creek*

Below are listed some of the outstanding girl athletes in the physical education department. The Point System continued during the 1960's and 1970's but complete records were not kept.

**1960**

Shirley Rich
Sandy Wright
Peggy Cline
Thelma Rodgers

**1961**

Sandy Wright
Shirley Rich
Barbara Northcut

**1962**

Barbara Northcut
Joyce Walker
Ellen Ball

**1963**

Judy Hudson
Gail Verble
Ellen Ball
Janice Thompson

**1964-1965**

Judy Hudson
Sharon Eggers
Libby Hudson
Reba Sue King
Julia Jones

**1965-1966**

Sharon Eggers
Pat Morgan
Julia Jones
Libby Hudson
Reba Sue King
Judy Duncan
Ruth Ann Johns

**1966-1967**

Pat Morgan
Judy Duncan
Libby Hudson
Reba Sue King
Julia Jones
Ruth Ann Johns
Janice Kirby

**1967-1968**

Becky Black
Libby Hudson
Pat Morgan
Jenny Lynn Quarels
Ruth Ann Johns
Janice Kirby
Janet Miller
Judy Duncan

**1968-1969**

Becky Black
Lynn Cosson
Janet Miller
Pat Morgan
Jenny Lynn Quarels
Madge Susong
Ruth Ann Johns
Dianne Elliott
Betty Mason
Grace Woolwine
Carol Lowry
Jean Jones

**1969-1970**

Madge Susong
Becky Black
Jenny Lynn Quarels
Jean Jones

# A History of Sports at Carson-Newman College 1851-1974

Jeanne Duchemin
Bitha Creighton
Sharon Brown
Gracie Wool wine
Betty Mason
Carol Lowry
Dianne Elliott

**1970-1971**

Madge Susong
Becky Black
Jeanne Duchemin
Betha Creighton
Sharon Brown
Dianne Elliott
Betty Mason

Gracie Woolwine

**1971-1972**

Jean Jones
Carol Lowry
Hazel Wilkie
Gracie Wool wine
Beitha Creighton
Sharon Brown

**1972-1973**

Bitha Creighton
Sharon Brown
Hazel Wilkie

# CHAPTER VII

# OUTSTANDING ATHLETIC TEAMS IN THE HISTORY OF CARSON-NEWMAN SPORTS

1. 1895 Baseball Team--The first athletic team in Carson-Newman's history to participate in intercollegiate competition. On April 27, 1895, they played against The University of Tennessee and won the game 4-3. This team was led by James Floyd at shortstop and Luther Beeler at second base (ALUMNI BULLETIN, 1948).

2. 1895 Football Team--The first organized football team in Carson-Newman's history. It was led by quarterback, captain and assistant coach, James Floyd. Luther Beeler was the head coach (Carr, 1959: 260).

3. 1903-1904 Basketball Team--The team was recognized as Carson-Newman's first intercollegiate basketball team. Luther B. DeArmond, president of the athletic association was responsible for its organization. Ed "Tip" Lawrence was the captain and leading scorer (Carr, 1959:261).

4. 1911-1912 Basketball Team--Called the "Untouchables," with a perfect 10-0 record. It was listed in THE SWANN (first annual) as the team that was never beaten. Some of the team members were Dana X. Bible, B. C. Reece, Clyde Hale, Roy Shipley, Theron Sams, and Hugh Hayworth (THE SWANN, 1912:12).

5. 1912 Baseball Team--The team was called the "Invincibles" and had an undefeated 8-0 record. It was led by Dana X. Bible and John Kilpatrick (THE SWANN, 1912:13).

6. 1913 Football Team--The best record for a football team up to that time with a 7-2-1 season. The team was led by fullback, Paul Squibb; center, Charles Sullivan, and quarterback, Clay Bunch (CARSON- NEWMAN COMMENCEMENT, 1914:64-69).

7. 914 Baseball Team--It had a 10-1 record and was led by Captain C. N. Wheeler and Coach John Kilpatrick (CARSON-NEWMAN COMMENCEMENT, 1914-1915:79).

8. 1914 Track Team--The first recognized track team in the history of the college. The team was led by Paul H. Squibb who was a sprinter and jumper (CARSON-NEWMAN COMMENCEMENT, 1914:77).

9. 1915 Tennis Team-An outstanding team which helped to increase the interest in the sport. Tennis was publicized as cine of the most enjoyable sports on the campus (Carr, 1959:263).

10. 1913-1914 Basketball Team--This team won fourteen games and lost one to the University of Tennessee. This was the best record since the undefeated team of 1911. The team was led by Captain Clyde Davis (CARSON-NEWMAN COMM~NCEMENT, 1915:73).

# *A History of Sports at Carson-Newman College 1851-1974*

11. 1917 Baseball Team--The team had a season of nineteen wins and four losses under the direction of John Kilpatrick who also played on the team. This was the best team since 1914 (Carr, 1959:268).

12. 1920 Girls Basketball Team--The team was undefeated and was led by Munsis Tittsworth and Grace Disney at the forward positions who combined for thirty-four points in one game (THE GRENADE, 1920: 141).

13. 1922 Football Team--The team won seven games and lost three. It was led by fullback John Hutchins and captain-quarterback "Frosty" Holt (APPALACHIAN, 1922: 136-140).

14. 1924 Football Team--A team led by quarterback, "Frosty" Holt; fullback, John Hutchins; center, "Mac" McNabb and guards, "Sunshine" Mudford and Tommy Taylor. The season ended with a 7-2 record (APPALACHIAN, 1925: 140-147).

15. 1922-1923 Basketball Team--The Smoky Mountain Athletic Conference champions with a 13-2 record. The squad was led by Captain "Frosty" Holt and center Russ Bebb. Coach Lake Russell was beginning to build a dynasty in basketball at this time (APPALACHIAN, 1923: 153).

16. 1923-1924 "Full House" Basketball Team--A season of twenty wins and only one loss, the team was led by "Frosty" Holt, Russ Bebb, Red Higgins, B. Blackstock and John Hutchins ended the season as Smoky Mountain Athletic Conference champions. This was the best basketball team since the undefeated team of 1911. They were called the "Full House" because of the 3 H's and 2 B's in the lineup (APPALACHIAN, 1924: 148).

17. 1924 Baseball Team--Undefeated with a 12-0 record. The team was again led by "Frosty" Holt, John Hutchins and Walter Haas. The highlights of the season were a 6-4 victory over Notre Dame and winning the Smoky Mountain Athletic Conference championship (APPALACHIAN, 1925:156). 298.

18. 1925-1926 Basketball Team--An 18-2 record and Smoky Mountain Athletic Conference champions. The only two games lost were by two points on the road. The club was led by 7' 3" "Slim" Shoun and the leading scorer, Andy "Russ" Bebb (APPALACHIAN, 1926:162-164). 1925-1926 Girls Basketball Team--The team was led by the captain, Mae Iddins, It won the conference with a 12-2 record--one of the best girls teams in the school's history (APPALACHIAN, 1926:165-167).

19. 1925-1926 Girls Basketball Team--The team was led by the captain, Mae Iddins. It won the conference with a 12-2 record--one of the best girls teams in the school's history (APPALACHIAN, 1926: 162-164).

**Baseball Team 1912**

# *A History of Sports at Carson-Newman College 1851-1974*

**Dana X. Bible**

**One of the forerunners of Carson-Newman College athletics who was a great athlete and later and outstanding coach.**

**Shown here in 1912.**

**Baseball Team 1914**

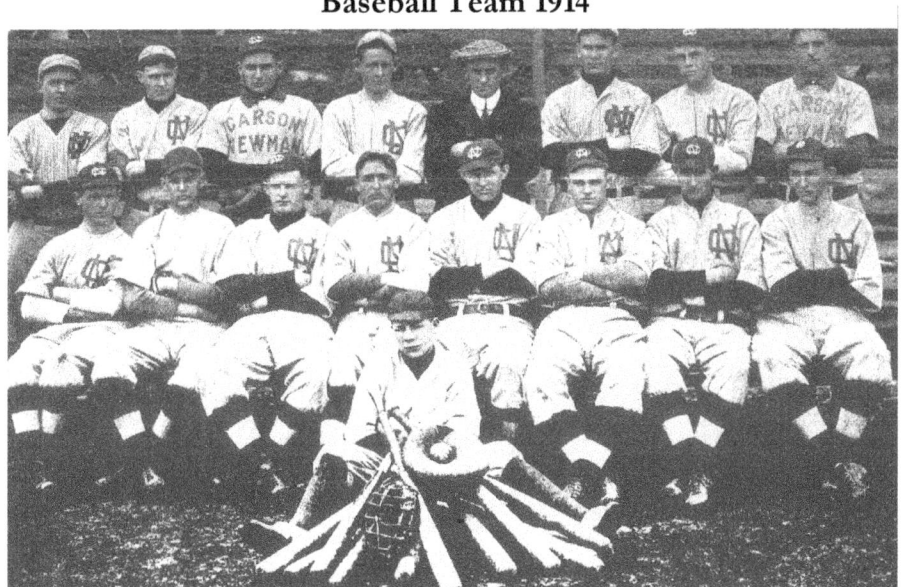

# *It Gets Foggy at Mossy Creek*

**Baseball Team 1912**
**Dana X. Bible is holding the ball**

# A History of Sports at Carson-Newman College 1851-1974

**The first recognized track team at Carson-Newman 1914**

**Girls Basketball Team 1920**

## It Gets Foggy at Mossy Creek

The 1924 Football Team

The Parsonettes
Girls Basketball Team 1924-1925

# A History of Sports at Carson-Newman College 1851-1974

WALTER HAAS, Capt. — Guard
BOB SNYDER — Guard
HAROLD McNABB — Forward
JONES HOWELL — Forward
BILL FARRIS — Forward
CLIBERT McHORRIS — Forward
RAY SHOUN — Forward
MILAS SHOUN — Center
GEORGE BALLARD — Guard
LESTER NEWTON — Guard
FRED HOLT — Forward
HARMON LOWRY — Forward

## *It Gets Foggy at Mossy Creek*

The undefeated 1924 Baseball Team

1924 Basketball Squad lost only one game
The was the famous "Full House" team called so because of 3 H's and 2B's —
Higgins, Holt, Hutchins, Bebo and Blackstock

# *A History of Sports at Carson-Newman College 1851-1974*

1931 Basketball Squad
SMAC Runners-Up

Bob "Dog" Watts
Famous barefoot tennis play of 1947

# It Gets Foggy at Mossy Creek

20. 1927-1928 Basketball Team--The team had an undefeated season with a 17-0 record and were Smoky Mountain Athletic Conference champions. They were led by captain, Walter Haas and "Slim" Shoun (7' 3" center) (Carr, 1959:274). This was one of the best teams to wear the orange and blue.

21. 1927 Baseball Team --Led by Captain P. Mulendore, the team ended the season with a 15-2 record. They were a fast hit and run team which easily won the Smoky Mountain Athletic Conference championship (APPALACHIAN, 1928: 112).

22. 1931 Basketball Team--The team was led by "Tip" Smith, the captain of the team and Ken Wood, 6' 6" center. They were Smoky Mountain Athletic Conference champions with a 17-3 record and runners- up in the conference tournament (APPALACHIAN, 1931: 135).

23. 1933 and 1935 Football Teams--The 1933 squad had a 7-1 record and the 1935 squad had a 7-3 season. Both teams were led by Wendell Henderson's great running and passing (Carr, 1959:275).

24. 1936 Football Team --Smoky Mountain Athletic Conference championships with a 10-0 record. This was the greatest record in football in Carson-Newman's history. The team was led by the outstanding halfback Wendell "Yankee" Henderson and All-Smoky Mountain Athletic Conference tackle, Frank Grubbs who was also the captain of the squad. The team was coached by "Frosty." Holt and his assistant, Fred Noe (APPALACHIAN, 1937: 124, 126).

# *A History of Sports at Carson-Newman College 1851-1974*

25. 1936-1937 Basketball Team--The team only lost one game and had a 16-1 record. The loss was to The University of Tennessee. It was also Smoky Mountain Athletic Conference champions led by the 3 H's (John Hudson, sophomore; Carl Hawkins, junior; and Charles Hamblen, sophomore). This was one of Carson-Newman's all-time great basketball teams (APPALACHIAN, 1937:139).

26. 1937-1938 Basketball Team--This was the tragic bus wreck team which killed Roy Roberts and Jim Grissom and broke the arm of the leading scorer, John Hudson. The team had started on the road to another conference championship when the tragedy struck. When the wreck occurred, the team was en-route to East Tennessee State to play a scheduled game (Interview with Coach "Frosty" Holt, March, 1972).

27. 1937 Football Team--The season was ended with an 8-1-1 record and the Smoky Mountain Athletic Conference championship. The team was led by T. J. Stafford, Folk Lamber, Captain H. Ramsey, C. P, "Doc" Wilson and Bill Catlett. This was known as one of the hardest hitting teams in small college football in the South (APPALACHIAN, 1938:123-127).

28. 1942-1943 Basketball Team--Led by Grant "Casey" Jones in scoring, Ben Booker (captain) and Fred Stroud at forwards, Wally Poteet and Charlie Moffett at guard, the team had a 17-3 record and won the Smoky Mountain Athletic Conference championship (APPALACHIAN, 1943: 119).

29. 1943 V-12 Football Team--With a 6-1 record, the team lost only to Vanderbilt University. Among the outstanding players were Queenie Clark, Cliff Vaughan, and "Bullhead" Garrott. This team had more talent than any in the history of the college since the members were from different universities and colleges assigned to the Navy Unit at Carson-Newman College. The team was under the direction of Coach "Frosty" Holt (Carr, 1953:277).

30. 1947 Football Team --This was the best team since the 1936 team. The season ended with an 8-0-2 record and the Smoky Mountain Athletic Conference championship. The team was led by Charlie Moffett, Buddy Cosson, Buster Jennings and Jack Wads. I the backfield with Captain John Murray and Milburn Atkins leading the line (APPALACHIAN, 1948:126).

31. 1951 Baseball Team--The Smoky Mountain Athletic Conference champions with a 17-4 record. It was led by Hubert Ashe in hitting and pitching, Joe Shipley and Tom Northern in pitching and Jerry Conner at first base. (APPALACHIAN, 1952: 173).

32. 1953 Tennis Team --Smoky Mountain Athletic Conference champions and undefeated in conference play. The team was led by Buddy Catlett and coached by J. O. Conwell (APPALACHIAN, 1954:212).

33. 1954 Baseball Team--As the Smoky Mountain Athletic Conference champions, they ended the season with an 18-3 record. Jerry Conner, Mac Lambert and A. G. Payne were among the outstanding players (APPALACHIAN, 1955:165).

34. 1954 Tennis Team--The Smoky Mountain Athletic Conference champions were led by Buddy Catlett, the conference singles champion. Under the direction of Coach J. O. Conwell, the team made a clean sweep of all conference matches (APPALACHIAN, 1955: 164).

35. 1957 Tennis Team--Under Coach J. O. Conwell, the team ended the season with a 16-1 record, 9-0 in the conference, and were the Volunteer State Athletic Conference champions. The team was led by Otto Spangler, Lesley Peek, and Herb Childress (APPALACHIAN, 1958: 151).

36. 1958 Tennis Team--With a 13 - 0 record, it was considered to be the best tennis team ever at Carson-Newman. It won the Smoky Mountain Athletic Conference championship, the Volunteer State Athletic Conference championship, and finished third in the Tennessee Intercollegiate Athletic Conference. Otto Spangler was the number one man followed by Les Peek (APPALACHIAN, 1959: 137).

37. 1959 Soccer Team--This was the first soccer team in the history of the college. It was led by Brazilian, Derrick Davis, as captain and Jimmy Sewell as co-captain. The season was completed with a 3-1 record (APPALACHIAN, 1960: 139).

38. 1960 Tennis Team--Volunteer State Athletic Conference champions with a 14-2 record, it lost only to The University of Tennessee and was undefeated in conference play. This was the first intercollegiate tea m to send players from Carson-Newman into national competition. Henry Dickenson was the coach (APPALACHIAN, 1961: 74).

39. 1960 Track Team --This was the first track team to be established at Carson-Newman in the modern era. There had been good track teams up to 1914-1915 but then only appeared periodically until Coach Roy Harmon and Charlie Bryant started the track program in the late 1950's. The 1960 team won the conference championship and was led by Martin Huckabee who broke many records in the sprints and high hurdles (APPALACHIAN, 1961:77).

40. 1961 Baseball Team--The team finished ninth in the nation in the final standings of the National Association of Intercollegiate Athletics with a 27-6 record. It was also Volunteer State Athletic Conference Eastern Division champion and Conference tournament champion, but lost to national Champion, Eastern Carolina, in District playoff (APPALACHIAN, 1962:72-73).

41. 1960-1961 Basketball Team--Under Coach Dick Campbell, the team was Volunteer State Athletic Conference Eastern Division champions, Volunteer State Athletic Conference tournament champions, and District 27 champions and had a 9-1

conference record. This was the first team (other than tennis) to re- present Carson-Newman in the National Association of Intercollegiate Athletics in Kansas City, Missouri. They were led by Chris Jones, Albert Mashburn, Gerald Ellington and Clark Bryan (APPALACHIAN, 1961: 60-64).

42. 1962 Cross Country Team--The first cross country team in the history of the college. They were led by Jerry Turley and followed by standouts Chip Mims and Jim Asher. The 1963 cross country team received credit in the annual and in several newspapers as being the first to compete but the 1962 team was the first organized team (Interview with Coach "Frosty" Holt, March, 1972).

43. 1961-1962 Basketball Team --Volunteer State Athletic Conference champion, Conference tournament champion, District champion and participated in the National Association of Intercollegiate Athletic tournament in Kansas City with a 29-7 record. The team was led in scoring by the captain and Most Valuable Player of the Conference, Chris Jones; Gilbert Luttrell, high scoring guard; Jerald Ellington All-Conference forward; Clark Bryan, forward and Albert Mashburn, the 6' 8" center (Mr. Rebound). The' 1962 team was called by many the greatest to ever represent Carson-Newman (APPALACHIAN. 1962: 165-169).

44. 1962 Baseball Team--Volunteer State Athletic Conference champions and ranked tenth in the nation. The team was led by pitcher Clyde Wright, Bobby Crumb, David Slagle and Roy Ratherdale. The hitters were Bill Kinser, Tommy Dihart, Lefty Greg and Jerry Murrell. They finished the season with a 27-7 record (APPALACHIAN, 1963:176-178).

45. 1962 Soccer Team--Coached by students Wayne Huling and Ernie Hill, it was undefeated with a 5-0 record. The team was led by soccer star, Derrick Davis from Brazil (APPALACHIAN, 1962:76-77),

46. 1963 Wrestling Team--Coached by Bob Davis, this was the first wrestling team to compete in intercollegiate competition from Carson-Newman in the history of the college. They were led by Dale Chrisman, Geno Magariti and Jerry Loveday (APPALACHIAN, 1963:180).

47. 1962-1963 Basketball Team--With a 27-5 record, it was Volunteer State Athletic Conference champions, tournament champions, District champions, and played in the quarter finals of the National Association of Intercollegiate Athletics. The team under Coach Dick Campbell was led by Clark Bryan, Albert Mashburn, Vie Arwood and All-American Gil Luttrell (APPALACHIAN, 1963: 169-174).

48. 1963 Baseball Team--With a 25-8 record and the Volunteer State Athletic Conference championship, the team under Coach "Frosty" Holt was ranked nationally for the fifth year in a row. They were led by pitcher David Slagle, Clyde Wright, David

Ratherdale, and Bobby Crumb. The leading hitters were Dave Hillard, Clyde Wright, and Leon Baird (APPALACHIAN, 1964:190-191).

49. 1964 Basketball Team --The team was Volunteer State Athletic Conference champions with a 10-0 record, tournament champions, District champions, and finished a 30-4 record which was the most wins ever recorded by a Carson-Newman basketball team. It was led by captain and twice All-American, Gil Luttrell; Jerald Ellington who was All-Conference and won many Most Valuable Player awards; Roy Hill, the Most Valuable Player of the Volunteer State Athletic Conference; Jim Shuler and Vic Arwood. This team was noted as one of the all-time great Carson-Newman teams (APPALACHIAN, 1964:180-187).

50. 1964 Baseball Team--Volunteer State Athletic Conference champions with a 27-8-1 record, some of the schools on their schedule were The University of Tennessee, University of Kentucky, South Carolina, Eastern Kentucky, East Tennessee State and Bowling Green. It was ranked seventh in the nation and led by Clyde "Chico" Wright who made All-American, the first in baseball; center fielder, David Holland who hit .360 consistently; second baseman, Roy Hill; and outfielders, Danny Pierce, Leon Baird and Gil Luttrell (APPALACHIAN, 1965:85).

# A History of Sports at Carson-Newman College 1851-1974

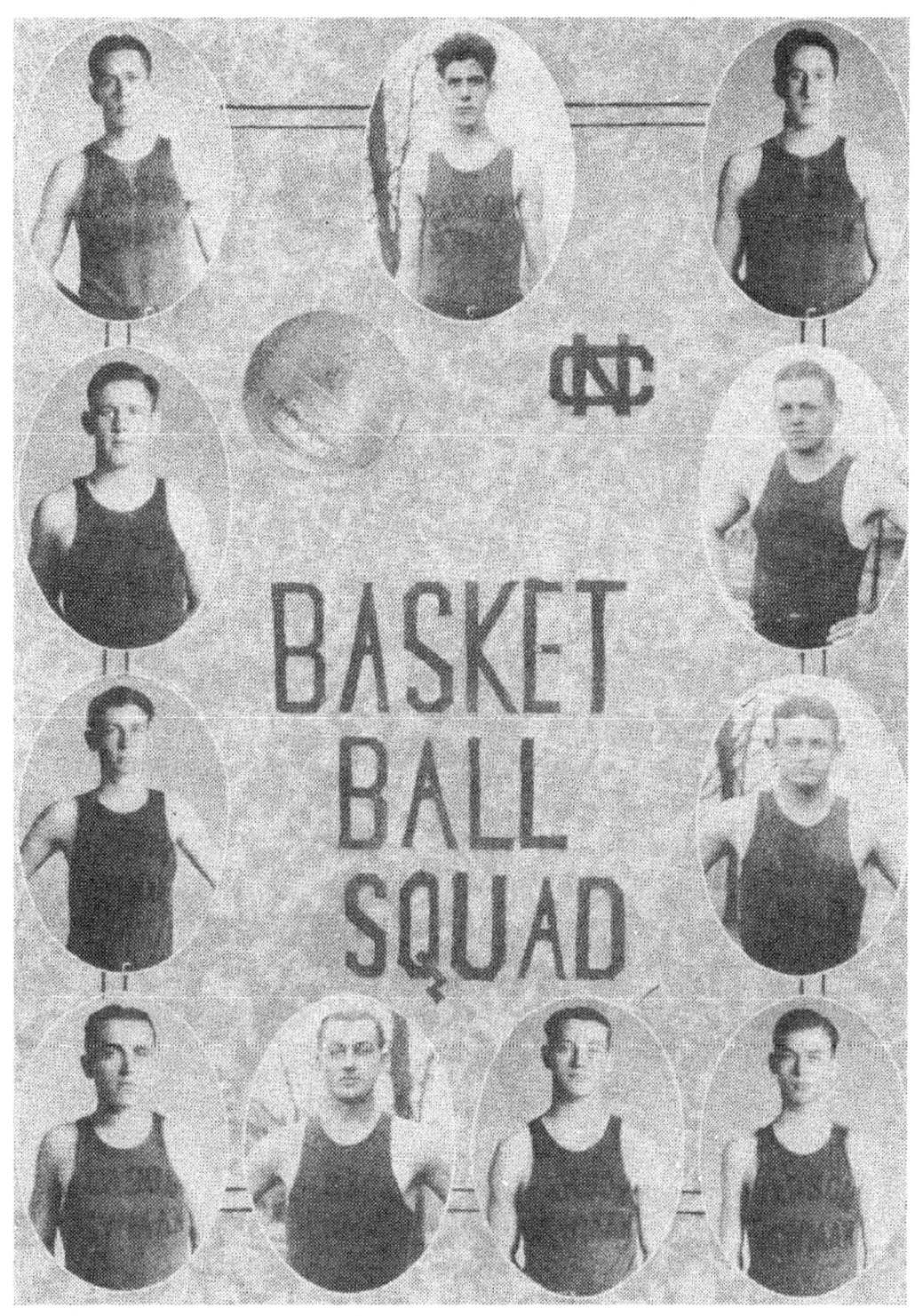

*It Gets Foggy at Mossy Creek*

Football Team 1932

The Great Team: These 1936-37 Eagles only tasted defeat once.

# A History of Sports at Carson-Newman College 1851-1974

1937-38 Bus Wreck Basketball Team in which Roy Roberts, #5, and John Grissom #6 were killed

# It Gets Foggy at Mossy Creek

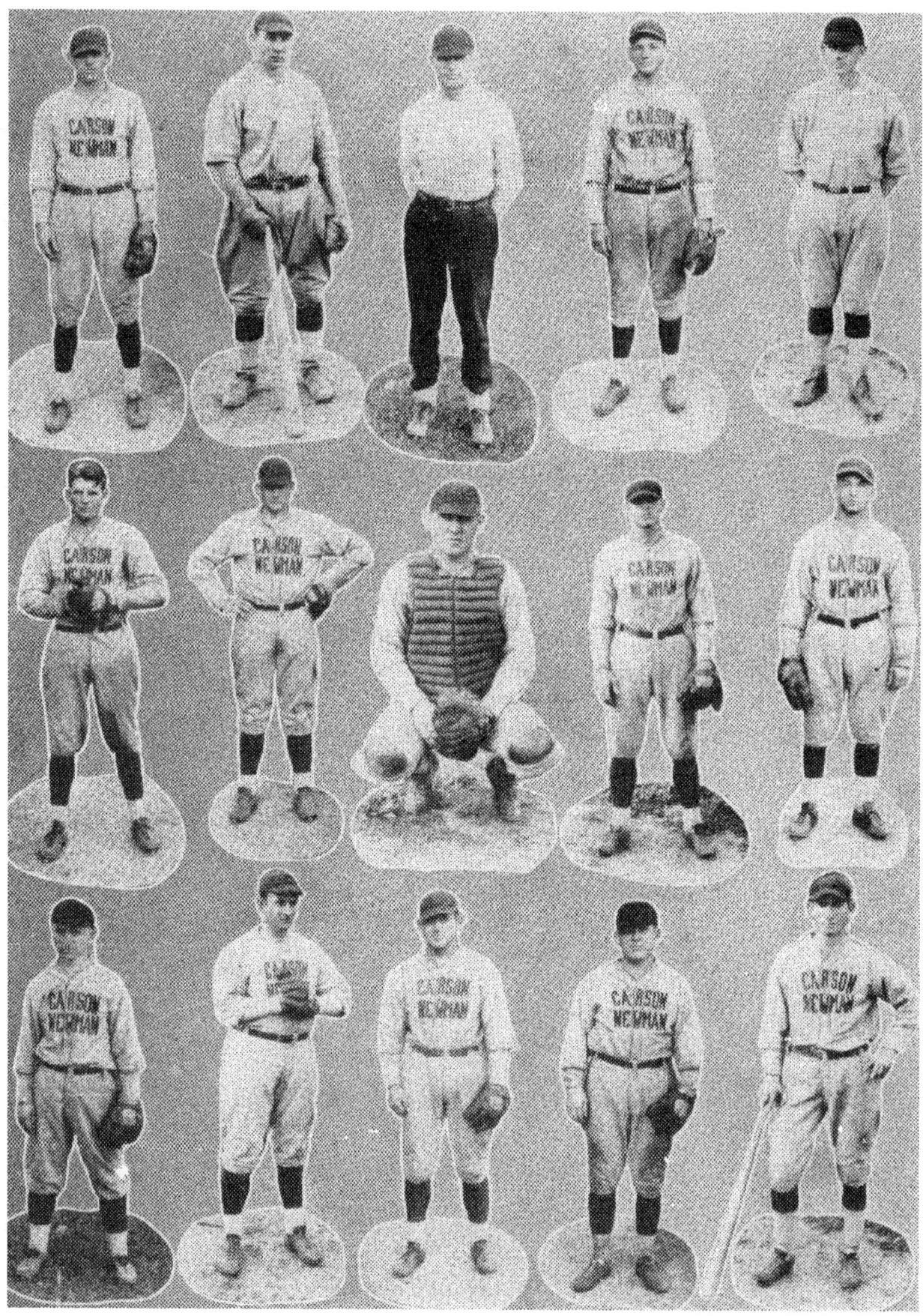

# A History of Sports at Carson-Newman College 1851-1974

**Football 1936**

**Basketball 1942-45**

**Basketball Team 1925**

# A History of Sports at Carson-Newman College 1851-1974

**Grant "Casey" Jones**

**V-12 Football Club 1943**

## *It Gets Foggy at Mossy Creek*

**The Undefeated Football Team 1947**

**1953 SMAC Champions**

# *A History of Sports at Carson-Newman College 1851-1974*

**Tennis Team 1952**

51. 1964 Tennis Team --With a 12-1 record, it placed second in the Volunteer State Athletic Conference tournament and was led by Dennis Haynes, Wilburn Taylor and Larry Ware (APPALACHIAN, 1965).

52. 1965 Basketball Team--With a 27-6 record, the team was Quincy Invitational champions, Volunteer State Athletic Conference Eastern Division champions, Lincoln Memorial University Invitational champions, tournament champions and District champions, The team was led by All-American Roy Hill, four year regular Vic Arwood, Jerry Cannon, Richard Perry, Jim Shuler, and Charlie Breazeale (APPALACHIAN, 1965).

53. 1965 Tennis Team--Eastern Division champions of the Volunteer State Athletic Conference, runner-up in the Volunteer State Athletic Conference tournament and a season record of 11-0. The team was led by Larry Ware; Wilbur Taylor; Joe Bill Sloan; Jimmy Chapman; Larry Conner; and Jim Shuler (APPALACHIAN, 1966).

54. 1965 Baseball Team--This was the most famous intercollegiate athletic team to be assembled in the history of Carson-Newman College sports. The 1965 baseballers won the Volunteer State Athletic Conference championship, tournament championship, District championship, and National championship. The team breezed through the national tournament undefeated and their final record was an unbelievable 36-3, the most wins by an athletic team at Carson-Newman College. The team was coached by Bobby Wilson. This team did not realize at the time but they had six All-Americans on the field--Clyde Wright, W. A. Wright, Roy Hill, Danny "Mac" Pierce, Gene Lively, Mike Levi (they all at one time in their college career made All-American) (A-PPALACHIAN, 1966:216-219). The 1965 baseball Eagles were assembled and - worked with through the years by Coach "Frosty" Holt-- Mr. Baseball. His dream had come true--a National Baseball Championship. Coach Bobby Wilson in his first year as head coach led this team to the title and was named the National Association of Intercollegiate Athletics Area & Coach-of-the-Year, but much of the credit must be given to the "old man" of baseball, "Frosty" Holt

55. 1966 Football Team --Under Coach Richie Gaskell, the Eagles had a 7-3-1 record and a victory in the Exchange Bowl with a 9-0 win over Georgetown University during his first year as head coach. This was the start of a fine football era in the late 1960's and early 1970's (APPALACHIAN, 1967:101-107).

56. 1967 Track Team--The Volunteer State Athletic Conference championship was won by the track team for the first time in Carson-Newman's history. The team was led by Jim Frost in the triple jump, Larry Campbell in the discus and shot put, Mike Lovett in the broad jump and hurdles, Ray Maynard in the one-half mile run and Leonard Markham in the two mile run and also the one mile run (APPALACHIAN, 1968:99).

57. 1968 Football Team--This was one of the highest scoring teams in Carson-Newman's history. With an 8-2 record, the team-was noted for scoring touchdowns in short periods of time. The team was led on offense by long passes from quarterback Dale Rutherford to wide receiver Tom Jones. The defense was led by Larry Lay and

Harold Denton led the line charges from his tackle position (APPALACHIAN, 1969: 88-95).

**SMAC Champions 1957**

**Tennis 1958**

# A History of Sports at Carson-Newman College 1851-1974

**Basketball Team 192**

**The Undefeated Soccer Team 1962**

## It Gets Foggy at Mossy Creek

Baseball Team 1912

Soccer Team 1959

# A History of Sports at Carson-Newman College 1851-1974

**1962 Basketball Eagles 30-4**

**First Cross Country Team 1962**

# It Gets Foggy at Mossy Creek

**VSAC Baseball Champions 1962**
**3rd Year in a row**

**Dale Chrisman puts the Eagle hold on opponent - 1964**

# *A History of Sports at Carson-Newman College 1851-1974*

**1971-72 Cross Country Team**

---

**1972 Track Team**

# *It Gets Foggy at Mossy Creek*

**1973 State Champions Cross Country**

# A History of Sports at Carson-Newman College 1851-1974

**C-N's First Wrestling Team 1962**

**1963 Basketball Eagles
You spell it "g-r-e-a-t"!!**

# It Gets Foggy at Mossy Creek

1964 Basketball Team

1965 Eagle Track Team

# *A History of Sports at Carson-Newman College 1851-1974*

**National Champions Baseball Team 1965**

**Track Team 1968**

58. 1968 Track Team--Under Coach Dal Shealy, the Volunteer State Athletic Conference championship was won in both 1967 and 1968 (APPALACHIAN 1968:99).

59. 1967 Baseball Team--The Eagles had a 27-11 record, were Volunteer State Athletic Conference champions, District champions, and runner-up in the Area 7 playoffs. Lowell Hagy, Mike Levi, John Maury, and W. A. Wright were some of the team leaders (Athletic Records, 1967)

60. 1968 Baseball Team--With a 28-11 season, the Eagles were led by All-American catcher, W.A. Wright. The team went to the District tournament before bowing to Pfeiffer (Athletic Records, 1968). 338

61. 1969 Baseball Team--The season ended with a 23-10 record despite injury to three key players, The Eagles won the Eastern Division of the Volunteer State Athletic Conference, the District championship and were runners-up in the Area I, National Association of Intercollegiate Athletics Playoffs. Led by the pitching of Frank Fillman, Tom Jones, and L. Pratter and the hitting of J. Crowder, E, Ogburn, Tom Jones, and Bill Stover, the Eagles had a strong team (APPALACHIAN, 1970:98-99).

62. 1970 Basketball Team--With a 28-8 record under Coach Gene Mehaffey, the team was Eastern Division champions and Volunteer State Athletic Conference champions. It was led by record-breaking, All- American Tommy Everette, "The Leaper" Tony Mills and Buddy Sivils. This was an outstanding team (APPALACHIAN, 1970:100). They were also runners-up in District 24 (Athletic Records, 1970).

63. 1970 Cross Country Team--The team finished with a 15-4 record and won the Volunteer State Athletic Conference for .the first time in the school's history (APPALACHIAN, 1971:38-39).

64. 1970 Baseball Team--The team had a 21-3 record, were Volunteer State Athletic Conference runners-up, District champions, and runners-up in Area V. Some of the team leaders were All-American pitcher, Tom Jones, Paul Bostic, catcher; Rick Privette, shortstop; and Johnny Crowder at third base (Athletic Records, 1970).

65. 1971 Football Team--Under Coach Dal Shealy, this was one of the best gridiron teams with an 11-1 record including a 58-3 victory in the Share Bowl held in Knoxville, Tennessee, The team was led on offense by All-American fullback, Rodney Wampler, Jimmy Sullivan, Tim George, Vince Dial, Clarence Sharp, Van Filligin, Bobby Gordon, and Mike Grass. The defense was led by the outstanding linebacker and captain, Billy Wilson, Bus Stokes, and John Thomas. Not many of the opponents went around the ends with players like Keith Reynolds, Herman Sanders and Jim Denton covering. The defensive secondary W3.S led by Nick Shook, Frank Gioscia, and Butter Hubbs (APPALACHIAN, 1972).

# A History of Sports at Carson-Newman College 1851-1974

**Sam Huffman, Steve Miller, Ron May and Rick Mix on**

**Golf Team 1969**

# It Gets Foggy at Mossy Creek

**1964 Baseball Team**

**A Great Eagle Team - 1965**

**1966 Football – Won 7 Game**

## *A History of Sports at Carson-Newman College 1851-1974*

**Benny blocks as Larry charges through for C-N yardage**

**Dale carries the pigskin down the grid as the defense closes in.**

# It Gets Foggy at Mossy Creek

**1964 Alumni Team – Undefeated and Coached by Frosty Holt.**

**Led by Arnold Mellinger and Chris Jones**

# A History of Sports at Carson-Newman College 1851-1974

**1968 Football Team 8-2 Record**

**1969 Eagle Baseball Team**

*It Gets Foggy at Mossy Creek*

Tennis Team 1969

VSAC Track Champions 1970

# A History of Sports at Carson-Newman College 1851-1974

**VSAC Cross Country Champions 1970**

**Basketball Team 1971-72**

## *It Gets Foggy at Mossy Creek*

**The Big "O" 1971**

**Skip Wyatt 1972**

**Steve William 1972**

**1972-1973 Eagles**

**This basketball team won more games in one season than any other basketball team up to that period.**

# A History of Sports at Carson-Newman College 1851-1974

**Tennis Team 1972**

**Football Team – Number 2 in the Nation**

# It Gets Foggy at Mossy Creek

**VSAC Eastern Division Champs 1973-74**

**Championship Track Squad 1974**

## A History of Sports at Carson-Newman College 1851-1974

66. 1971 Cross Country Team--Volunteer State Athletic Conference champions, Bryan Invitational champions, and second place in the Tennessee Intercollegiate Athletic Conference with an overall record of 22-4. This was the first cross country team to participate in national competition in Kansas City, Missouri. The team was led by the captain and number one man, Scottie Powers, who won many individual awards, Lee Owenby, Perry Horne, Danny Graham, Steve Thomas, Mike Robinette, Pete Nichols and Bill Neely also helped lead the team to many victories under Coach Chris Jones (APPALACHIAN, 1972).

67. 1972 Track Team --After winning the championship of the Volunteer State Athletic Conference for four consecutive years, 1967-1970, the trophy was again brought home in 1972. The team was led by David Johnson in the pole vault, hurdles and. the broad jump; sprints were led by Tony Smith; Tommy Mitchell led in the 440 while distance runner Lee Owenby won his event. The field events were led by Ron Hall with the javelin and Bucky_ Meade in the high jump (Interview with Coach Fred Sorrells, October, 1972) _. This was one of Carson-Newman's finest track teams under the direction of Fred Sorrells.

68. 1972 Golf Team--This was the first golf team to participate in the national tournament in New Mexico, With an overall record of 15-2, the Eagle linemen won the Volunteer State Athletic Conference and District' 24 without much trouble. Tommy Ducey and Bobby Vann led with back-up strength from Puggy Blackmon, David Whaley, and David Watts. The team was coached by Charlie King (Interview with Coach Charlie King, November, 1972).

69. 1972 Tennis Team--This team finished with a perfect 17-0 regular season record while winning the Volunteer State Athletic Conference, National Association of Intercollegiate Athletics District, Tennessee Intercollegiate Athletic Conference and finished eighth in the national tennis tournament. The number one player was Johnny Orr while Jack Tarr, David Brewer, Bob Rymer, Jim Myers, Tommy Dickerson, Bob Albritton, Mike Bales and Tommy Arnett were good back-Up men. The team was coached by Sam Green (Interview with Coach Sam Green, November 1972).

70. 1972 Cross Country Team--The team had a 17-1 record for the regular season winning the Bryan Invitational, Carson-Newman College Invitational, and was the first cross country team from Carson Newman to win the Tennessee Intercollegiate Athletic Conference championship for the state. Lee Ownby, the number one runner, participated in the National Cross Country Meet held in Kansas City, Missouri (Athletic Records, 1972).

71. 1972 Football Team--The team finished the regular season with a 9-1 record. In the playoffs, the Eagles played Livingston State of Alabama and the game ended with a 7-7 tie but the victory was awarded to Carson-Newman on penetrations. This advanced the Eagles to the Championship Bowl at Commerce, Texas against East Texas State where the Eagles were defeated 21-18. This was the first football team from Carson-Newman to participate in a national tournament, Under Coach Dal

Shealy and his fine staff, the Eagles ended the season with a 10-2 record (KNOXVILLE NEWS-SENTINEL, December 10, 1972).

72. 1972-1973 Basketball Team--This was one of the most exciting teams to watch in the history of the college. This team won the University of North Carolina at Asheville Invitational Tournament, the Eastern Division championship of the Volunteer State Athletic Conference, the Volunteer State Athletic 347 Conference tournament championship, and lost to Kentucky State (three times national champions) by one point in the District playoffs, Many team and individual records were broken during the season. Carson- Newman was led by Captains Steve Williams and Jim McGowan, Mike Ogan, Jay Cuny, Mark Mason, Pete Billingsley and David Mills. The team was coached by Dr. Gene Mehaffey and assisted by Coach Chris Jones, It won more games (thirty-one) than any basketball team in Carson-Newman history and lost only seven.

# CHAPTER VIII
# THE MODERN ERA AND FUTURE

The 1970's brought a new era in sports and one which showed great promise for the future, Many sports were represented in the program and all were growing stronger and more effective.

## FOOTBALL TEAM BECOMES NATIONAL CONTENDER

With the new era came a new head coach in football, Mr. Dal Shealy. Coach Shealy and his coaching staff- Charlie King (offensive line), Fred Sorrells (defensive line coordinator), Sam Green (defensive secondary), Ron Case (linebacker) and Bob Sanders (receiver)--took two years to bring the Eagles to one of their best seasons in the history of the college. The 1970 season found the coaches with a team characterized by youth and inexperience. One of the outstanding players on the squad, Tom Jones, became ineligible when he signed a professional contract in baseball. He had made All-American in football the previous year and his absence was felt by the squad. There were, however, several players who were very capable and demonstrated their leadership ability. They were Jimmy Sullivan and Butch Genoble at quarterback, Mike Souder and Tim George at split receiver, and defensively All-American Honorable Mention Billy Wilson, Buzz Stokes, and Bobby Gordon. The 1970 squad ended the season with a 4-6 record and. many close games, Under the leadership of this same coaching staff, a 1971 squad emerged that was the pride of the campus, The 1971 squad ended with an 11-1 record--the only record that could compare was the 1936 squad, coached by "Frosty" Holt, which had a 10-0 record. The Eagles were fifth in the nation in the National Association of Intercollegiate Athletics final poll of the regular season--the highest any Carson-Newman team has ever finished in the national rankings. The team finished the regular season with a 9-2 mark (Sports Release, November 22, 1971). This was later changed, however, as Samford had to forfeit their game because of an ineligible player which gave the Eagles a 10-1 season. In the Share Bowl, which was held in Knoxville, Tennessee, Carson-Newman faced Fairmont State of West Virginia and won this game by a score of 54-3 (Sports Release, December 13, 1971), The Eagles named to the 1971 District 24 (National Association of Intercollegiate Athletics) team were offensively George at end; Bobby Gordon at guard; Bob Small-wood at guard; Billy Horton at center; Van Filligim at running back; and Rodney Wampler at fullback. The defensive squad included Skip Bean at end; Curtis Atwell at tackle; Billy Wilson at linebacker; John Thomas at linebacker; and Gary "Butter" Hubbs at safety. Rodney Wampler, senior, was named All-American (1972 FOOTBALL PRESS GUIDE). The 1972 team finished the regular season with a 9-1 record. They were consistently rated in the top five teams in the nation, small college, during the regular season and going into the last game had the rating of the number one small college team in the nation; however, the final National Association of Intercollegiate Athletics rating at the end of the regular season made them the number two team. Their first play-off game was with the defending national champion of 1971, Livingston State of Alabama, The game ended in a 7-7 tie but the victory was given to Carson-Newman because they had more penetrations within the opponent's twenty. The team then advanced to the NAIA Champion Bowl at Commerce, Texas, where they were defeated by East Texas State, 21-18 (KNOXVILLE NEWS-SENTINEL, November 29. 1972). So the team returned to Carson-Newman with a number two rating, after the playoffs, in the National Association of Intercollegiate Athletics and a season record of 10-2 (KNOXVILLE NEWS-SENTINEL, December 10, 1972).

## *It Gets Foggy at Mossy Creek*

**Cheerleaders 1970's**

**Burke-Tarr Stadium**

# *A History of Sports at Carson-Newman College 1851-1974*

**Rodney Wampler – 1979
Great Running Back**

**Football Coach – Dal Shealy
1971**

*It Gets Foggy at Mossy Creek*

## CROSS COUNTRY SURGES

The cross country teams under Coach Haydon were also adding to the sports program at Carson-Newman with a Volunteer State Athletic Conference championship in 1971 and a record of 15-4. With the resignation of Coach Haydon, Chris Jones took over the coaching responsibilities. The 1971 team had a good year and ended the season with a 22-4 record and a trip to the National Tournament in Kansas City. The 1972 team also compiled a fine record of 17-1 for the regular season. They won the Bryan Invitational, Carson- Newman College Invitational and were the first cross country team from Carson-Newman to win the Tennessee Intercollegiate Athletic Conference championship for the state. Lee Ownby, the number one runner, participated in the National Cross Country Meet in Kansas City, Missouri (Athletic Records, 1972).

## BASKETBALL ADOPTS RACE HORSE STYLE

The 1970 basketball season under Coach Gene Mehaffey and his new assistant, Chris Jones, ended with an 18-16 record. In the Volunteer State Athletic Conference semi-finals in Nashville, the Eagles dropped an 85-83 overtime decision to LeMoyne-Owen but came back the next night to win the consolation game 101-86 over Lincoln Memorial University (BASKETBALL BROCHURE, 1971). The following year, the Eagles returned prepared to make a better showing and had a final season record of 42-13. Coach Mehaffey opened the season with eleven eligible players all of whom he felt were potential starters. Because of the depth of the squad, he instituted a system of rotating starters during the season. By Christmas the team was in full swing arid won their own Invitational Tournament by defeating Georgetown 99 to 85 in the final game. Defending national champions, Kentucky State Thoroughbreds visited Carson-Newman and took home an 87-86 victory--they had previously defeated Carson-Newman of their home court 77-76. Following this, Tennessee State, ranked number three in the national small college poll also visited the campus and walked off with a heartbreaking 78-77 decision in the last four seconds of play. This placed the team with a 14-10 worksheet (Sports Release, January 13, 1972). Going into conference play in Nashville, the Eagles were 12-12 and 8-1 in the conference. Tournament time proved revenge for the Eagles, however, as they had wins over Bethel and Belmont teams that had taken early season victories from the club. The team went on to win the Volunteer State Athletic Conference Championship and the right to meet Kentucky State in the District playoffs, marking the tenth time in twelve years Carson-Newman had earned the Eastern Division championship. Mike Ogan, sophomore, and Skip Wyatt, senior, were named to the first team of the Eastern Division and senior teammate Mike Morton was named to the second team. Ogan and Wyatt were also named to the All-Tournament team of the Volunteer State Athletic Conference tournament. Mike Ogan was also place-d on the first team of the National Association of Intercollegiate Athletics -District 24. During the first night of conference play, Ogan bettered Tommy Everette's 1970 season scoring mark of 746 points--at the conclusion of the tournament, Ogan had an even 800 points (Sports Release, February 28, 1972). After returning from the conference tournament victorious, the Eagles played Kentucky State to see which team would represent District 24 at the National Tournament in Kansas City. Kentucky State won and Carson-Newman's season ended 24-13 with several new records being set. Sophomore Mike Ogan led the team with three new individual single season records. Steve Williams, 5' 2" guard, the "smallest basketball player in college" led the team in assists with 300

# *A History of Sports at Carson-Newman College 1851-1974*

(News Release, March, 1972). A rugby team was formed in 1970 called the Mossy Creek Rugby Club. The team competed a few times, then was disbanded because of lack of interest.

**Football 1970's**

**1970 Letterman's Club**

## *It Gets Foggy at Mossy Creek*

**Henderson Hall**

**The Fog turns into snow**

# A History of Sports at Carson-Newman College 1851-1974

**Women's Basketball 1970**

# It Gets Foggy at Mossy Creek

**1970 Basketball Team**

**Managers 1971**

# *A History of Sports at Carson-Newman College 1851-1974*

### SOCCER EXPERIENCES UPS AND DOWNS

Soccer continued under Eric Dietz during the 1970 season and the players were members of the Tennessee Intercollegiate Soccer Association. The club finished with a 7-5-1 record and placed fourth in the Southeastern Soccer Classic held at The University of Tennessee. The team carried a roster of fourteen players (ORANGE and BLUE, September 28, 1970). The following year, 1971, the Soccer Club had a 2-5 season. The 1972 season, however, brought a better year as the club, coached by Sidney McGee, ended with a 5-3-1 record. Prince Atom and Pius Mosaic were the offensive leaders and Bola Soiree" and Graham Spencer were the defensive leaders with Gene Gooch as goalie (Interview with Pius Mosaic, November, 1972).

### BASEBALL RECORD SLIPS

The 1970 baseball team under Coach Bob Wilson ended the season with a 21-8 record. They were Volunteer state Athletic Conference runner-up, district champions and Area V runner-up. The following year, 1971, the nine had an 18-14 season record and in 1972, the record was 12-12-1 (Interview with Coach Bobby Wilson, November, 1972).

### TRACK TEAM DOMINATES VOLUNTEER STATE ATHLETIC CONFERENCE

The 1970 track team captured the Volunteer State Athletic Conference title for the fourth consecutive year (APPALACHIAN, 1971) and the 1971 team began the season hoping to make the fifth consecutive year. Of the 1971 squad, Coach Haydon said the team had speed as contrasted with previous teams whose strength was in the field events. The season ended with a second place in the Volunteer State Athletic Conference behind LeMoyne-Owen. This was the last year for Coach Haydon as he left to become Athletic Director at the Tennessee School for the Deaf in Knoxville (Athletic Records, 1971). The 1972 team under Coach Fred Sorrells captured the Volunteer State Athletic Conference title in Erwin, Tennessee, to make it the fifth conference title in six years for the Carson-Newman team. They finished the season with an 8-3 mark and the Volunteer State Athletic Conference championship. In Tennessee Intercollegiate Athletic Conference action, they finished fifth. The team bettered ten school records (News Release, 1972).

### NATIONAL RANKINGS FOR TENNIS TEAM

The 1970 tennis team had a 12-3 regular season record. They were District 24 champions and had a final rating of thirteenth in the National Association of Intercollegiate Athletics (Athletic Records, 1970). The 1971 squad under Coach Sam Green and captain, Jack Tarr, turned in a final rating of fourteenth in the nation according to the National Association intercollegiate Athletics standings. The team also finished second in the Volunteer State Athletic Conference and ended the season with a 16-1 record (Athletic Re- cords, 1971). The following year the 1972 team had a 16-0 record, won the Volunteer State Athletic Conference, Tennessee Intercollegiate Athletic Conference and District 24. In Volunteer State Athletic Conference play, they set several records. Their win marked the first time that a club had swept twenty-seven out of a possible twenty-seven points, Enroute to the championship the Eagles claimed wins in six Singles and three doubles matches. In the tournament, Carson-Newman's number one player, Johnny Orr

## It Gets Foggy at Mossy Creek

won the singles and doubles crown for the third time (1969, 1970, 1972) (Athletic Records, 1972). They competed in the national tournament action at Rockhill Tennis Club in Kansas City and had a final ranking of eighth in the National Association of Intercollegiate Athletics (TODAY MAGAZINE, 1972).

**Fog turns into snow at Holt Field House**

**"Double" Trouble. The Hightower twins plus Thomas and Raines**

# *A History of Sports at Carson-Newman College 1851-1974*

Hugh Clement 1971-72

Dave Whaley 1972

Jerry Brittingham

A "Will Be" with a "Has Been"!

# It Gets Foggy at Mossy Creek

**Jerry Brittingham and Bill Powell**

**Cross Country Action 1972**

# A History of Sports at Carson-Newman College 1851-1974

**Golf Team was Nationally Rank 1972**

Frosty Holt has helped a lot of Jefferson County boys. All-American Clyde Wright was one of them (pictured here). Frosty talks with future Eagles Jones, King and the Tiptons in 1971.

# *It Gets Foggy at Mossy Creek*

Bobby Vance

A close play
women's intramurals 1972

**Carson-Newman Maintenance Crew**

**John Walker shows the crew something about horseshoes**

# *A History of Sports at Carson-Newman College 1851-1974*

**Miss Pearl McHan (Miss "Mac") fed our athlete well – especially after the games.**

# *It Gets Foggy at Mossy Creek*

### GOLF RECORD ON THE RISE

The 1970 golf team had a 12-5 record and the following year improved this to 13-4 and a third place finish in the Volunteer State Athletic Conference. The 1972 team under Charlie King made history as they were the first Carson-Newman golf team to participate in a national tournament. They finished the season with a 14-1 record won the Volunteer State Athletic Conference and the District. The team then went to Roswell, New Mexico, to participate in. the national small college ~tournament where they had a final rating of twenty-fifth in the National Association of Intercollegiate Athletics (Athletic Records, 1970, 1971, 1972).

### SUMMARY

The 1970's brought with it a new era in sports and one which looked as though it was going to be even greater than the previous ones. Almost every sport was improving and a wide range was covered in the sports program. With the new era also came a new head coach in football, Dal Shealy. Coach Shealy and his fine coaching staff took two years to bring the Eagles to one of their best seasons in the history of the school. The 1970 team had a 4-6 record, but came back the next year to have a team with an 11-1 season and a 54-3 victory in the Share Bowl against Fairmont State of West Virginia. The 1972 team was the first football team in Carson-Newman history to participate in a national tournament. The regular season ended with a 9-1 record. They met an Alabama team in the play-offs and after a 14-14 tie, Carson-Newman was awarded the game on penetrations. The team travelled to Texas for the national championship where they were defeated by East Texas State.

The 1970 basketball season again under Coach Mehaffey and his new assistant, Chris Jones, ended with an 18-16 record. They came back in 1971 to have a 24-14 season, Volunteer State Athletic Conference championship and runner-up to Kentucky State in District 24. The 1972 season produced a 24-13 record and another runner-up position in District 24. Soccer continued under Eric Dietz during the 1970 season with a 7-5-1 record and fourth place in the Southeastern Soccer Classic. The following year the club had a 2-5 season, but the 1972 team, coached by Sidney McGee, had a better season with a 5-3-1 record (Athletic Records, 1971; 1972). The baseball team had a good year in 1970, ending the season with a 21-8 record. They were Volunteer State Athletic Conference runner-up, District champions and Area V runner-up. The 1971 team had an 18-14 record. Bill Stover was named small college All-American from that club. The 1972 season brought Coach Wilson an even season with a 12-12-1 record and another All-American in Carl Torbush (Athletic Records 1970; 1971; 1972). Rugby made a brief appearance on the campus in 1970. The Rugby Club was financed by the Physical Education Club and even though the only two games played were lost, the team members had a good time and enjoyed the year. The track team under Coach Troy Haydon captured the Volunteer State Athletic Conference title for the fourth consecutive year in 1970 and came back in 1971 with the hopes of making it the fifth but came in second to LeMoyne-Owen. The 1972 team under Coach Fred Sorrells finished the season with an 8-3 mark and again won the Volunteer State Athletic Conference (Athletic Records, 1970; 1971; 1972). The tennis team began the 1970's with a 12-3 record, District 24 championship and a final rating of thirteenth in the nation (small college). The 1971 team under Coach Sam Green turned in a 16-1 record and a second place in the Volunteer State Athletic Conference with a final rating in the National Association of Intercollegiate

# *A History of Sports at Carson-Newman College 1851-1974*

Athletics of fourteenth. The 1972 team proved to be one of the best as they had a 16-0 record, won the Volunteer State Athletic Conference, Tennessee Intercollegiate Athletic Conference and District 24. They attended the national tournament and finished with a final rating of eighth ill the National Association of Intercollegiate Athletics. The 1970 golf team had a 12-5 season and the 1971 team had a 13-4 record with only one returning letterman. The 1972 team under Coach Charlie King made history as it was the first Carson-Newman golf team to participate in a national tournament. It finished the season with a 14-1 record won the Volunteer State Athletic Conference and the District. The team then went to Roswell, New Mexico to participate in the national small college tournament where they had a final rating of twenty-fifth. The 1970's continued the surge for national recognition with football, cross country and golf entering national competition.

## THE FUTURE

By means of questionnaires sent to many alumni, to both present and past staff members, to friends of the school and to others who have had associations with the Carson-Newman athletic program evaluations were made as to the meaning of the program to the school and a projection of their ideas for the future. The response to the questionnaire indicated the depth of feeling for the school and its program by those contacted.

## GOLF

Record: 17-4
NAIA District 24 - 2nd place
Leading Players - Tom Ducey, Puggy Blackman, David Whaley, Bobby Vann
Coach Charlie King

## TENNIS

Record: 18-8
VSAC Eastern Division Champion
VSAC Champion
NAIA District 24 Champion
Participant in National Tourney
Leading Players - Mike Bales, David Brewer, Tommy Dickerson, Bob Albritton, Jimmy Morton
Coach - Sam Green

## TRACK

Record: 4-1
Leading Participants - Bucky Meade, Cedric Atkins, Lee Ownby, Jim Smith, Tommy Mitchell
Coach - Ken Sparks
The following school year of 1973 -1974 the mighty Eagles showed no signs of slowing down their winning pace. The over-all athletic record of this year was 117 wins and 36 losses. This resulting in a .765 winning percentage falling short of the school record set the previous year.

*It Gets Foggy at Mossy Creek*

## 1973 - 1974 AT a GLANCE

### CROSS COUNTRY

Record: 16-2
State Champions (TIAC)
NAIA District 24 - 2nd place
Leading runners - Chuck Rickards, Dean Ownby, Lee Ownby, Steve Thomas, Mike Jones
Coach - Chris Jones

### FOOTBALL

Record: 6-3
Leading Players - David Ward, Wally Shirrod, Carl Torbush, Sanders Shiver, John Thomas, Skip Johns
Coach - Dal Shealy

### BASKETBALL

Record: 23-10
VSAC Eastern Division Champion
Leading Players - Mike Ogan, Mark Mason, Jay Cuny, David Mills, Pete Billingsly
Coach - Dr. Gene Mehaffey

### BASEBALL

Record: 23-10
VSAC Eastern Division Champion
VSAC Champion
NAIA District 24 - 2nd place
Leading Players - Carl Torbush, Eddie Roberts, Larry Ledford, Craig Layman, Steve Blank, Robert Long, Bobby Brotherton
Coach - Bob Wilson

### GOLF

Record: 19-2
NAIA District 24 - 2nd place
Leading Players _ Tom Ducey, Bobby Varin, David Whaley, David Watts, Bob Cathy
Coach - Charlie King

### TENNIS

Record: 23-9
VSAC Eastern Division Champion
VSAC Champion
NAIA District 24 Champion
Participant in National Tournament - finished 10th
Leading Players _ Mike Bales, David Brewer, Steve Grossman, Sals Maharaj, Larry Denyes, Larry Berkheimer

# A History of Sports at Carson-Newman College 1851-1974

**Lee Ownby with Coach Jones**

**Lee Ownby**

**Steve Thomas**

**1972 Cross Country**

# *It Gets Foggy at Mossy Creek*

**Jimmy Sullivan 1972**

# *A History of Sports at Carson-Newman College 1851-1974*

**Football 1972**

# *It Gets Foggy at Mossy Creek*

**INTRAMURALS STILL GOING STRONG - 1973**

# *A History of Sports at Carson-Newman College 1851-1974*

## TRACK

Record: 7-0
State Champion (TIAC)
Leading Participants - Tommy Mitchell, Bill Herron, Chuck Rickards, Ronald McGee, Cedric Atkins, Jim Smith
Coach - Ken Sparks

## SOCCER CLUB

Although not sponsored by the athletic budget the Soccer Club led by such foreign students as Price Attoh and Pius Mozia had outstanding seasons.

## WOMEN ATHLETICS

The women athletic teams continued on a club type basis and were very successful in basketball, volleyball, softball and other sports. They were led by such stars as Sylvia Rhyne, Hazel Wilkey, Sandy Ramsey, Cathy Gibbons, Linda Gay Blane, Peggy Hudson, Deanne and Dianne Ross, Sharon Brown, and Bitha Creighton.


Among the former athletes whose questionnaire responses contributed to this section were:
Ben Booker
Malcome Brown
Wayne Burchett
Puggy Blackmon
C.B. Chesney
Ernest Cosson
John Dowling
Ralph Harmon
Mike Faulk
Carl O. Hawkins
Bill Horton
Dr. Charles Moffett
Powell Moore
John C. Murray
James K. Myers
Lee Ownby
Kenneth Reed
T. J. Stafford
Bill Tarr
Glenn Wade

From the present and past staff members, many reactions were received. Those whose responses are incorporated in this look to the future include:
Dr. Carl Bahner
Nat C. Bettis
Dana X. Bible

## *It Gets Foggy at Mossy Creek*

Dr. Clark Bryan
John Burton
Dr. Robert Burts
Dick Campbell
Issac N. Carr
Joe Chapman
Mrs. Freddie Clark
Earl Cleveland
Howard J. Cobble
J. O. Conwell
Dr. John Fincher
Dr. Harley Fite
Dr. Walter Guyton
Verner T. Hansen
Carey Herring
Dr. Gene Mehaffey
Thomas B. Milligan
William H. Roden
Dalmouth Shealy
Fred Sorrells
Martha Wilson


Women alumni who responded to the call for a look at Carson-Newman's athletic program and its influence on the school included:

    Becky Brown
    Jamie M. Couch
    Jean DeCoursey
    Ruth Ferguson
    Siothia R. Longmire
    Reba Sue Lowe
    Thelma Rogers

Others whose contribution assisted in the preparation of the section were:

    Travis Ball
    M. L. Bowers, Jr.
    Wayne Bowery
    Jerry Brittingham
    DeWayne Brooks
    Dow Brown
    Rev. Herman Ellis
    Millard F. Caldwell
    Dr. W. P. Clear

# *A History of Sports at Carson-Newman College 1851-1974*

Ben Collins
Buddy Godfrey
Jerry King
Samuel McDougal
Bill Rives
Guy Sexton

Mayford King
James Ray
E. Warren Rust
Alan Sharp

From these varied sources we look from the past to the future. The quality of the athletic program at Carson-Newman has always been outstanding and been an important part of the total program which has aided the progress of the college. Most colleges and universities depend on athletics for promotion of the school and a large number of students and alumni are involved in the program either as participators or spectators. Carson-Newman College is well known for its high educational standards, but many people know it because of its fine athletic teams. The athletic program has served to balance an over-all program, helped to keep a liberal arts approach and contributed to the public impression that Carson-Newman is a well-rounded institution. Costs at private colleges are normally higher than those at state schools and for this reason the private college must depend on its pride and tradition to attract students. Athletics have definitely added to the pride of Carson-Newman. The Christian ideals of the college have been enhanced and furthered by the success of its athletic teams. This success has given the college a reputation that is attractive to people regardless of where their interests lie. Carson-Newman has always taken a healthy and realistic approach to a strong athletic program. A successful athletic program is of benefit to any school if kept in the proper perspective and not allowed to encroach upon the primary purpose of the college or the university. The administration and coaching personnel have tried to place the proper emphasis on the athletic program. Athletics attract many people and many of the students on campus admit that one of the reasons they selected the college was because of its athletic program, Powell Moore, a student athlete, felt that without athletics Carson-Newman's name and enrollment would not approach what it is today. Another athlete, Puggy Blackmon, further stated that he never heard of Carson-Newman before he enrolled' except through the sports news. He felt that a large part of the enrollment on campus was because of the good athletic programs.

## ATHLETICS AID SCHOOL SPIRIT

Athletics have helped the school spirit on the campus which naturally helps to bring the student body closer together. The publicity that has been gained through the athletic program can never be measured. In his twenty-five years with the Federal Bureau of Investigation, John C. Murray related that he had had many inquires about Carson-Newman as a result of their athletics and fine reputation. He felt that this attracted students from a wide area--both athletes and non-athletes, Carson-Newman's reputation has brought many good athletes to the campus. Athletes like to be winners and Carson-Newman is known for winning. The sports program has given much in return for what it has received from the individual athletes, Sports develop character and responsibility as well as physical fitness. The body needs stimulation and challenge just as much as the mind. There would be little school spirit without competitive sports. Good players and

## It Gets Foggy at Mossy Creek

good teams, along with dedicated coaches, make a finer student body. It has also aided in developing young men and women into total personalities, many genuine experiences have resulted in and through athletic endeavors.

**Legendary Frosty Holt coached all sports for 40 years**

**Dal Shealy receives the trophy for finishing Number 2 football team in the nation.**

# A History of Sports at Carson-Newman College 1851-1974

**Keith Craig and Doug Moody**
**"Voices of the Eagles"**

**Carl Tipton Public Relations**

**Coach Holt 1973**

# *It Gets Foggy at Mossy Creek*

**Henderson Burns**

**Remains of Henderson Hall after 1972 fire**

**Player Committee 1973**

# *A History of Sports at Carson-Newman College 1851-1974*

**Ruins of Administration Building
After Fire of 1916**

**Basketball 1974**

## It Gets Foggy at Mossy Creek

David Brewer

Blank, Wilson and Torbush

Cross Country Bicycle Team 1974

# A History of Sports at Carson-Newman College 1851-1974

**Cheerleaders 1973-74**

**Cheerleaders 1974-75**

## *It Gets Foggy at Mossy Creek*

BASKETBALL ACTION 1973-74 SEASON

# A History of Sports at Carson-Newman College 1851-1974

**Women's Volleyball 1973**

## It Gets Foggy at Mossy Creek

**Women's Intramurals 1974**

# A History of Sports at Carson-Newman College 1851-1974

**Carl Torbush, Henry Blank and Mike Ogan**

**Managers 1974**

## *It Gets Foggy at Mossy Creek*

**Managers 1974**

# *A History of Sports at Carson-Newman College 1851-1974*

**Fans 1973**

**Football Team 1973**

# It Gets Foggy at Mossy Creek

**1972 Eagles**

**Ken Sparks**

**Mark Mason**

# A History of Sports at Carson-Newman College 1851-1974

**Mike Ogan and Steve Williams**

**David "Oscar" Mills 1974**

**Mike Ogan**

**1973 Eagles**

# *It Gets Foggy at Mossy Creek*

**Golf Action 1973**

**Tommy Mitchell and Buckeye Meade 1974**

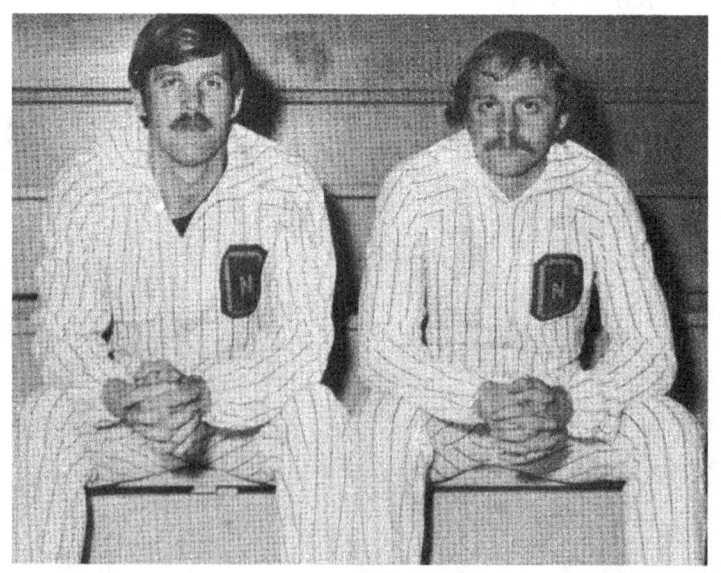

# A History of Sports at Carson-Newman College 1851-1974

Women's P. E. Club 1974

Women's Basketball Team 1973-74

# It Gets Foggy at Mossy Creek

**Libby Hudson and Volleyball**

**Women's Action Going Strong 1974**

# A History of Sports at Carson-Newman College 1851-1974

**Football Coaches 1974**

**Frosty Holt and Football Team**

*It Gets Foggy at Mossy Creek*

## HOLT AND IDDINS PROVIDE EXCELLENT LEADERSHIP

The staff who make up the back bone of the athletic program at Carson-Newman deserve much credit as they have guided the athletes who have been on campus down through the years. They have provided Christian training and tried to create the proper team spirit. Much credit is due to Coach Holt in this area as he gave more than forty years of his life to the athletic program at Carson-Newman. This is shown by the coaching positions at Carson-Newman being filled by the men who were under his leadership and later returned to be leaders themselves. Because of the excellent leadership given the athletes, both men and women, hundreds of other students have come to Carson-Newman. C. B. Chesney stated that he knew of many boys who attended Carson-Newman because of the program offered and the fine people on the faculty. This holds true for the women also. Mae Iddins did for the women what Coach Holt did for the men--they worked together to provide excellent leadership. The school does not offer many social activities; therefore the athletic program has been a strong factor in school spirit and a focal point of campus activity. Student interest for the college would decline strongly without athletics. The school spirit has influenced many students to attend the college and has done much to bring a unity to the student body and community. Athletics bring people, money, and recognition to the college and in this way they are important along with providing excitement and entertainment. Athletics has probably accounted for many donations to the operating fund of the college.

## ATHLETICS AID IN RECRUITING

Athletics add to the life, traditions and history of the college and this helps recruit students and develop school spirit. The program also helps to hold some of the school spirit and interest in the college after graduation. It tends to serve as a conversation piece and therefore supplies an opportunity for the Carson-Newman name to be aired--alumni always like to rehash old memories. Carl Tipton, the Public Relations Director at Carson-Newman, stated that athletics is a rallying point for alumni and students. It is a common avenue for building school pride and spirit. Many people have attempted to keep in touch with the college throughout the years and Malcolm Brown felt this had enhanced their interest and the college received eater support as a result.

Dr. John A. Fincher, the president of Carson-Newman, further stated that athletics is an essential component of a well-balanced program of education and activities. All of these factors help in recruiting students by drawing them together in one common cause which also helps in keeping the morale high. Sports have provided public relation tools and student emotional outlets. Given the degree of isolation in which the school exists and the high quality of the athletic programs through the years, Robert Burts stated that the athletic program has been a drawing card for students. It has complemented a fine academic program to make a strong college community. Dr. Clark Bryan, Dean of Students at Carson-Newman, more or less summed it up when he stated that athletics helped with public image, public relations, community support and recruiting.

# *A History of Sports at Carson-Newman College 1851-1974*

## FUNDING BECOMES ISSUE

Our society is marked by changes and naturally these changes would have an effect on the college and its programs. There are many changes taking place at Carson-Newman and will be many to come in the future years. This change is good if it does not interfere with the basic principles of the small Baptist College. Probably the greatest concern at Carson-Newman can be found in the area of finances and is also the same problem facing many other small private colleges. This is true in the area of sports as the cost of everything has increased. There will have to be an increased budget in order to meet the rise in costs. The smaller college has to compete with other colleges with larger budgets and more scholarships and they cannot do this year in and year out. The larger squads naturally are more expensive and some feel that it is too expensive in relation to the total academic cost. There also seems to be a trend in some of the larger colleges to cut back their budgets and base scholarships on need. This would give the smaller colleges a better opportunity to get the good athletes.

Some of the smaller colleges are dropping out of certain sports altogether; an example of this is football. This is done because of the financial cost which many feel benefits only a few students. Unless some restrictions can be agreed on by small colleges, football on a small scale may become impossible and thus ...rive Carson-Newman out of the sport. As many of the smaller colleges drop football, it may well be that scheduling of colleges within reasonable distances will become more difficult for Carson-Newman. This brings to light another problem which all athletic teams must face and that is one of travel and equipment cost. It seems that along with everything else in the system, the costs in these areas are also rising. Carson-Newman has worked in this area of travel cost by purchasing in 1971 two Sports Vans which are used by the athletic teams in place of the rental of buses. (These vans are used by all athletic teams except football.)

In having to deal with the cut back in athletics (as in other programs of the college), the small college has to deal with recruiting the good athlete. They must deal with other colleges and universities who are able to offer more "fringe" benefits than Carson-Newman such as money and cars. Because of the complexity of the universities, however, many young people many young people may feel less individuality. This is an advantage the small college must capitalize on and offer a good program on a smaller scale. The small college with good athletic programs and a good academic program may be able to recruit good athlete$ not interested in larger schools.

## TREND TOWARD PROFESSIONALISM

There seems to be so much pressure and emphasis on having a winning team that many fine coaches and young people are lost in the current. Because of the pressure on coaches to win at all costs, the trend is to use more coaches in order to compete which adds to the budget. The trend from teacher-coach to full-time coach or to reduced teaching responsibility will adversely affect Carson-Newman athletic programs.

Some feel that commercialism of the "college sports" is a justified criticism in many universities and colleges where players are really professional entertainers rather than students. There is a trend toward professional as the average student cannot participate in all sports as the young people did perhaps fifteen years or so ago. The small college must also compete with television, professional athletics and with larger colleges. There also seems to be interest in intercollegiate athletics for women in gymnastics, the scientific approach to adult fitness, and competitive swimming. More emphasis is being placed on the "minor sports" of golf, tennis and track which give more students an opportunity to participate in athletics. A basic characteristic of man is competitiveness and since Carson-Newman is getting larger it will have to provide a greater variety of ways to allow its students to compete.

## BALANCE IN SPORTS PROGRAM NEEDED

When asked in the questionnaire about the future of Carson-Newman College athletics, most answering thought that there was a role for athletics in the small private college in our society. This would be true as long as the policies do not become too strict along church-related or religious lines and a sound philosophy of the role of athletics is continued. Dr. Harley Fite, who was president of the college for approximately twenty years, said he felt the future was good, provided the school keeps a balance between the literary and athletics and provided the college keeps a balance in the several areas of sports--not go overboard to be big time in anyone sport. Samuel McDougal, a local resident, added that he also felt the future is good provided the college not play out of their league too much. It was also felt that a solid conference for all sports was needed and that the "national title" emphasis should be dropped if all sports were to be continued. It was added that too much pressure should not be put on players to win, and coaches should not try to push small college teams beyond their capacity. There is definitely a place for small college athletics if they are handled correctly.

## FINANCES DETERMINE FUTURE

When looking into the future of Carson-Newman athletics the foremost problem seemed to be the same one it has always been one of finances. Money to support athletics in church-related schools is limited; therefore, continuing the present program could be a struggle. The future depends upon the amount of financial aid; Bill Horton felt the program will remain at a relatively high standard but it will not be much better until it has more money and outside support. Enrollment is a vital factor to progress of the college athletic program and also to the college as a whole. With the continuous growth of the student body attracting outstanding athletes, there is no limit to the future of Carson-Newman athletics. Athletics will grow as the college grows but how the money is used is of utmost importance in this growth. It was brought out that if the money distribution is not modified some of the spring sports will continue to decline; more money and support should be provided for all sports and not just one or two. In regard to athletics, the point was brought out that more money will have to go into scholarships or athletes will turn to the larger schools where they can get more diverse educational opportunities and financial aid. The "pros" and universities will make recruiting difficult for the small private colleges who cannot compete. J. O. Conwell, a retired professor and tennis coach at Carson-Newman, more or less summed up the feeling of many of the alumni and faculty when he stated that Carson-Newman must offer something different from what state schools offer. If they cannot be different, distinct and unique, then there is not a reason for them to exist. Carson-Newman continues to produce

# A History of Sports at Carson-Newman College 1851-1974

well-rounded individuals and athletics is certainly a wholesome outlet for both men and women. Reba Sue Lowe suggested that athletics gives one a wonderful chance to witness for Christ and also to advertise the college. Discipline and self-discipline is a great factor for the future of Carson-Newman which has the momentum to attract good athletes. Since there are more and better athletes eager to play, the future should be bright for Carson-Newman. The athlete must remember that he is a student first and an athlete second and if it is kept in this perspective then athletics will continue to grow, according to James K. Myers. One alumnus claimed Carson-Newman is one of the few places left where a top athlete can develop into a top person as well.

## DEDICATED LEADERSHIP VITAL

Athletics will play an important part in the life of the college as long as they have a full and strong program. A well balanced athletic program is a necessity if any school wants to attract and hold students. The program should be under the control of the trustees and faculties with good sensible coaches--ones who are dedicated. As long as those involved in directing the athletic program exhibit the Christian attitude of doing one's best in an atmosphere of fair play, it seems it would only result in progress and support from the community and alumni which would, in turn, help the financial problem. John E. Dowling stated that he felt education, religion and athletics should be the foundation of the American way of life. This would mean that the schools' future would be based on the basic principles found in the early history of the American way of life. Man will try many new and different things, but the basic principles set down in early times are always the foundation.

## EDUCATIONAL VALUE OF SPORTS

Athletics are important to the college and the individual. Dana X. Bible, former Carson-Newman coach, who has been involved in sports both as player, coach and spectator has written what he considers to be the educational value of sports. This is appropriate in concluding the history of athletics at Carson-Newman College.

> I have often been asked what there is of educational value that sports have to teach. I recognize, of course, the value in improving the physique of a growing boy. I recognize also, the value in affording an outlet for the natural human desire for the playing of games, but my faith in sports is not based on either of these grounds. It is based upon the conviction that athletics, properly supervised and properly developed, afford a laboratory training for the development of character such as is not afforded elsewhere in the life of a growing boy. His character is being developed by a struggle against himself--a struggle against his own inability--but there is, I believe, a third phase of education in which character must be developed and made strong, not only by competition against himself, but by competition against others. It is in this field that our modern system of sports fulfills so important a function. Nothing is more important than that a boy should learn during the formative years to control and command his own powers, to focus them upon a single end, to mobilize them quickly and completely, to think fast and realistically, to coordinate one's activity with the activity of others engaged in the same task, to call up and expand in an emergency, last reserves of

strength and courage, to pour out all one's energy in furious effort and at the same time with a chivalrous regard for the rights of others, the rules of the game within limits dictated by decency and sportsmanship. This is a training it seems to me, that lies at the heart of all development of an individual toward good and useful citizenship.

Now it is possible in the classroom to preach all this to a boy, to show him the need and importance of it, but it is vital and imperative that he should have a laboratory training in carrying out the precepts we give him. Sports furnish such a laboratory. Sports not only teaches him the will to win and the way to win, but it teaches him something else. It teaches him how to meet defeat. He cannot win all the time. When he is defeated, what is his attitude? Does he curl up and quit? Does he attack the sportsmanship and ability of his opponents, or does he keep his chest out, with clear eyes and, above everything else, self-respect?

If he has learned to do that he has learned something that life can never take from him. If any system that furnishes such as training as this, is not very directly serving an educational purpose, then certainly many of us are in error as to what the ends of education should be in the case of a growing boy.

The duty of the coach, it seems to me, is to make these habits a part of the current ideal of the average student. In order to do this he must drive himself and his team. There must be no affectation about not caring for victory. He must care for victory and fight for it hard and cleanly. He must seek to make the game a thrilling exhibition of skill and technique. But in his ambition to win, he must never forget that victory is a means and not an end – which fundamentally his duty is to make sound, keen, decent men.

In summarizing the athletic program at Carson-Newman, four basic factors have been found.

1. The first organized event held on the campus was a Field Day which was encouraged on an intramural basis, Two years later, 1895, the first intercollegiate athletic event was found on the campus-a baseball game played against the University of Tennessee. This was followed in the fall with football which was instituted by Luther M. Beeler of Jefferson City and James S. Floyd, a student at Carson-Newman at the time.

2. The athletic program has grown from its first two intercollegiate sports to include an extensive sports program on a varsity or club basis at the present time.

3. Fine Christian leadership has been given to the athletes through Coach "Frosty" Holt and Miss Mae Iddins and many other outstanding coaches who followed them. Coach Holt and Miss Iddins returned to their alma mater in the late 1920's and stayed until their retirement. They are credited with the fine athletic program found on the campus today.

# *A History of Sports at Carson-Newman College 1851-1974*

4. Carson-Newman entered national competition in 1960 and has continued to return periodically in many sports. Those sports qualifying for national competition are tennis, basketball, baseball, football, cross country and golf. In 1965 the baseball team won the national championship.

The findings in this study warrant the following conclusions:

1. Athletics at Carson-Newman College have grown from a meager beginning in 1895 to a very important place in the total college program.

2. The athletic facilities have improved at the college and have helped with the fine athletic program found on the campus today.

3. In the persons of Sam B. "Frosty" Holt and Mae Iddins, Carson-Newman has had excellent leadership for over forty years.

4. The Athletic program at Carson-Newman has been supported by the faculty, students, alumni and community.

5. Carson-Newman has been recognized throughout the nation for its outstanding athletic program through teams, coaches, and athletes who represented the school.

6. Intercollegiate athletics at Carson-Newman College has implications, suggestions and ideas for other small private colleges to follow


The title of this book "It Gets Foggy at Mossy Creek" is dedicated to Coach Frosty Holt, KING of all the Eagles. I can remember as an athlete and now as a coach at Carson-Newman, Frosty's famous words it gets foggy at Mossy Creek. We would lose a game at another school and Frosty would come into the locker room and say "Remember boys, they still have to come to the creek and it will be too foggy for them."

This meant that it was almost next to the impossible to beat the Eagles on their home court or field. It meant that it was hard to shoot baskets in a goal that had fog around it, it was hard to tackle an Eagle in the fog especially in the fourth quarter and in baseball, why it was like trying to hit a B. B. with all that fog in the 9th inning. Then fog began to appear on the Eagle tennis courts, golf courses, track, wrestling mats and soccer fields. Why, I heard of a boy from a visiting cross-country team run all the way to Knoxville from Jefferson City because he got lost in the fog. Now, I believe you understand Frosty's meaning a little better. I have written an Epic to tell the history of Carson-Newman College athletics since 1851. Now that you have read this book, you can appreciate the true meaning of this epic and hopefully will recognize the people and places involved. The English and grammar have a lot to be desired in this epic, and Shakespeare would roll over in his grave if he read it, but nevertheless; this epic tells the true story of Mossy Creek:

## *It Gets Foggy at Mossy Creek*

*It was in 1833 that some preachers felt the need*
*To build a Christian college where they could study, write and read.*
*They toiled, labored, and prayed; it was god's will they did seek,*
*So in the fall of 1851 they opened the doors of mossy creek.*

*For many long years there after it was all work and no play.*
*Until the spring of '83 when Mr. Henderson came to say,*
*"Mental, moral, and spiritual traits we have strived for hard and long,*
*But it's time to dwell on the physical and keep our bodies strong."*

*April of 1895 CN was challenged to a baseball game,*
*It was the mighty university of Tennessee with all their fortune and fame,*
*It looked like the UT nine would surely get the victory,*
*But the fog rolled in and CN won by the score of 4 to 3.*

*It was a rough and tumble type of game they called it football,*
*But it wasn't too tough for CN, so they played it the very next fall.*
*Many teams came to town and a victory they would seek,*
*But Carson-Newman scored with ease, running through the fog at mossy creek.*

*Many sports were added to the Baptist school as the century turned,*
*And not many outside teams could win, so they learned.*
*The "invincibles' and "untouchables" of 1911-12 brought the college a lot of fame,*
*These teams were led by a great player, Dana X was his name.*

*It happened down in Athens in the fall of '21.*
*That football playing preacher was going to have a little fun.*
*Ira Dance, Ira Dance, why'd ya hit that man so hard,*
*Every bone and tooth in his body was completely jarred.*

*From that day on, the teams were not quite the same,*
*Because the fighting parsons was their new name.*
*They became meaner, stronger, and faster with each passing year,*
*And when a visiting team came to the creek, they shuddered with fear.*

*He was tough, strong, and smart-fast as a lightning bolt;*
*There wasn't a sport he couldn't play, his name was Frosty Holt.*
*He led the fighting parsons to victory again and again;*
*He captained every team, he was truly a leader of men.*

*The players in the early 20's thought they ought a' be paid;*
*So the college committees met and gave them athletic aid.*
*Also, Butler Blanc was built, a gym that wouldn't leak,*
*But the visitors still couldn't win, cause it gets foggy at mossy creek.*

# *A History of Sports at Carson-Newman College 1851-1974*

*There was a great coach, his name was Lake Russell,*
*If his teams couldn't win on talent, they would win on hustle.*
*He won so many games it got to be a bore,*
*He coached undefeated teams; basketball in '28, baseball in '24.*

*In 1924 everything had come to a head,*
*Carson-Newman College was using "ringers" they said*
*But ole' mighty C-N wasn't anybody's fool,*
*These ringers had been used by every other school.*

*In 1929 the college was very concerned,*
*They couldn't find a coach, but young Frosty returned.*
*Baseball in the spring, basketball in the winter and football in the fall;*
*It didn't matter to Frosty cause he could coach them all.*

*For the next 40 years he was a Caesar to a Rome;*
*He put in many long hours, Holt Fieldhouse was his home;*
*He changed the blow of a fighting parson to the sting of the Eagles beak,*
*He would say "you might beat us over there; but it'll be foggy at the Creek."*

*Eaglettes, Parsonettes, sure those girls can play;*
*It all came about because of Miss Mae;*
*Sweaters, pins, and sports clubs, she worked hard and long,*
*For more than 40 years she, sang her song.*

*It happened on a cold February the first in 1938.*
*The most tragic accident in CN history, it must a' been fate;*
*Jimmy Grissom and Roy Roberts on that day they would die;*
*Now they've soared with other Eagles up to the sky.*

*Country was fighting country in the year of '44.*
*Most of the Eagles went to fight in that horrible war.*
*Carson-Newman couldn't have a team, no men were there to play;*
*But the Navy V-12 boys came in to save the day.*

*Soccer, basketball, golf, and football,*
*Those mighty Eagles were champions in all.*
*Wrestling, tennis, cross country and track,*
*There wasn't anything the Eagles did lack.*

*Frosty was a baseball coach deluxe, he was the "man",*
*He had some of the best teams in all the land.*
*With a hitch of his britches, a jerk and a spit,*
*Why, he could teach any boy how to bunt, slide, and hit.*

## *It Gets Foggy at Mossy Creek*

*In basketball he brought the Eagles national acclaim.*
*He was the little general, Dick Campbell was his name;*
*At Carson-Newman they always won, and only lost a few away,*
*It was a little foggy around the visitors goal, so they say,*

*The name of Eagles flashed across the nation in the 1960's*
*Because in all sports, they began to pile up the victories.*
*Many honors came to the players because team losses were few,*
*So finally C-N had their first All-American in 1962.*

*Things at Mossy Creek really came alive;*
*When the Eagles won a National baseball title in '65.*
*The opposing teams emotions turned from love to hate.*
*Because in all sports the Eagles began to dominate.*

*Now, we wonder what the super 70's will bring;*
*Going to a National tournament is just an everyday thing.*
*Among the league, the opposing teams began to sigh,*
*One was overheard to say, "That eagle still flies too high."*

*Already the football team has brought us national acclaim,*
*Cross country, tennis and golf have done the same.*
*We can't hardly count in the '70's all the victories we've won,*
*Why, basketball alone in '72 brought us 31.*

*In the seventies our country was changing and so was our school;*
*Alcohol, drugs, and sexual freedom seemed to be the rule.*
*The breakdown of our homes and morals would begin to take its toll,*
*But those eagles still had Christian principles deep down in their soul*

# *A History of Sports at Carson-Newman College 1851-1974*

QUESTIONNAIRE

Form 1: Persons Living in Jefferson City, Tennessee

Name_____    Address_____

1. How long have you lived in Jefferson City? Give dates.

2. What effect, if any, have Carson-Newman College athletics had on your community?

3. Have you ever been connected with Carson-Newman College athletics? How? (as spectator, player, coach, etc.)

4. How do athletics today compare with athletics when you first became associated with the college?

    Example: equipment used, talent of players, philosophy of sports, and psychology of coaches.

5. Do you feel that athletics have been an important factor in the progress of Carson-Newman College? Explain how.

6. What are some weak points of Carson-Newman athletics down through the years?

7. List some events that you remember most about Carson-Newman College athletics--good or bad (championships, accidents, records broken, etc.)

8. What are some of the changing trends in athletics that might effect a small church-related college such as ours?

9. What do you think is the future for athletics in a small church-related school such as Carson-Newman?

*It Gets Foggy at Mossy Creek*

QUESTIONNAIRE

Form 2: Former and Present Faculty Members of Carson-Newman

Name_____ Address
_____

1. How long have you been a Carson-Newman faculty member? Give dates.

2. Do you feel that athletics have been an important factor in the progress of Carson-Newman College? Explain.

3. As a faculty member, do you feel that too much emphasis has been placed on athletics at Carson-Newman? Explain.

4. What effect do you feel Carson-Newman athletics have had on:

    a.    Student body
    b.    Faculty members
    c.    Community

# *A History of Sports at Carson-Newman College 1851-1974*

QUESTIONNAIRE

Form 4: Former and Present Students Who Did Not Participate in Athletics at Carson-Newman College

Name_____ Address
_____

1. During which years did you attend Carson-Newman College?

2. Do you feel that athletics have been an important factor in the progress of Carson-Newman? Explain.

3. Has too much emphasis been placed on athletics at Carson-Newman?

4. While a student at Carson-Newman did you attend athletic contests? How often?

5. What is or was the feeling of the student body toward athletics?

6. What are some of the weak points of Carson-Newman athletics?

7. Did you participate in the Carson-Newman intramural program? Did you enjoy it? Tell why or why not.

*It Gets Foggy at Mossy Creek*

QUESTIONNAIRE

Form 5: Former and Present Athletes of Carson-Newman

Name_____ Address _____

1. During which years did you attend Carson-Newman?

2. What did athletics mean to you personally at Carson-Newman?

3. Do you feel that athletics have been an important factor in the progress of the college? Explain.

4. What are some of the weak points of Carson-Newman athletics?

5. Would you have attended Carson-Newman College if you had not been involved in athletics?

6. What do you think the future holds for athletics at Carson-Newman?

7. List some events that you remember most about Carson-Newman College athletics--good or bad (championships, accidents, records broken, etc.),

8. How does someone not involved in athletics feel about the college athletic program?

9. Will athletics always play some part in your life? Explain.

# *A History of Sports at Carson-Newman College 1851-1974*

PERSONS ANSWERING QUESTIONNAIRES IN CONNECTION WITH THIS STUDY

Bahner, Dr. Carl T., Professor of Chemistry, Carson-Newman College, Jefferson City, Tennessee.

Bailey, Dean C,' Head Basketball and Baseball Coach and Athletic Director, Lincoln Memorial University, Harrogate, Tennessee.

Bailey, Jesse A., Penrose, North Carolina.

Baker, Jean A., Winter Park, Florida.

Ball, Travis, Jr., Professor of English, Wolfeboro, New Hampshire.

Bass, Thomas, Macon, Georgia.

Bettis, Nat C., Professor of Religion, Carson-Newman College, Jefferson City, Tennessee.

Bible, Buford A., Knoxville, Tennessee.

Bible. Dana X... Retired Athletic Director, University of Texas, Austin, Texas

Black, Becky, Graduate Student, 1972, University of Tennessee, Knoxville, Tennessee

Blackmon, Puggy, Member of 1972 Golf Team, Carson-Newman College, Jefferson City, Tennessee.

Booker, Ben, Kingsport, Tennessee.

Bowen, W. A., Jefferson City, Tennessee.

Bowers, M. L., Jr., Newport, Tennessee.

Bowery, Wayne, Social Worker, Student during the early 1960's, Blountville, Tennessee.

Brittingham, Jerry, Director of Student Activities, Carson-Newman College, Jefferson City, Tennessee.

Brooks, DeWayne, Graduate Student, 1972, University of Georgia, Athens, Georgia.

Brown, L. Dow, Clinton, Tennessee.

Brown, Malcolm E., Shelby, North Carolina.

Bryan, Dr. Clark, Dean of Students, Carson-Newman College, Jefferson City, Tennessee.

Bryant, Charlie, Head Track Coach, Erwin, Tennessee.

Buhler, Franchot, Silver Springs, Maryland.

Fite, Dr. D. Harley, Retired President, Carson-Newman College, Jefferson City, Tennessee.

Freels, Edward T., Jr., Associate Professor of Geography, Carson-Newman College, Jefferson City, Tennessee.

Godfrey, Buddy, Newport News, Virginia.

Guenther, Mrs. Monique, Oak Ridge, Tennessee.

Guyton, Dr. Walter, Academic Dean, Carson-Newman College, Jefferson City, Tennessee.

Hall, Ron, Football Player, Carson-Newman College, Jefferson City, Tennessee,

Hamblen, Charles H., Jr., Atlanta, Georgia.

Hansen, Verner T" Assistant Professor of Mathematics, Carson-Newman College, Jefferson City, Tennessee.

## *It Gets Foggy at Mossy Creek*

Harmon, Ralph, Football Player, Carson-Newman College, Jefferson City, Tennessee.
Hartley, Maurice, Raleigh, North Carolina.
Hawkins, Carl O., Richmond, Virginia.

Herring, Carey R., Assistant Professor of Mathematics, Carson-Newman College, Jefferson City, Tennessee.
Hines, Doug, Basketball and Baseball Coach, Bethel College, McKenzie, Tennessee.
Horton, Bill, Talbot, Tennessee.
Honeycutt, Freda, Carson-Newman College, Jefferson City, Tennessee,
Hudson, John, Jefferson City, Tennessee.
Johnson, David, Student, Carson-Newman College, Jefferson City, Tennessee.
    Johnson, Jerry C., Head Basketball Coach and Athletic Director, Lemon-Owen College, Memphis, Tennessee.
Jones, Grant L., Sevierville, Tennessee.
Joyce, Maurice, Student, Carson-Newman College, Jefferson City, Tennessee.
King, Jerry C., Pastor, Raleigh, North Carolina.
King, J. Michael, Chattanooga, Tennessee.
King, Mayford, Jefferson City, Tennessee.
Laing, R. Lamar, North Miami Beach, Florida.
Lawson, H. F., Crossville, Tennessee.
Lee, Joe N., Graduate Student, 1972, University of Tennessee, Knoxville, Tennessee.
Litton, Robert B., Birmingham, Alabama.
Longmire, Siothia R., Winder, Georgia.
Sexton, Guy Jr., Plant Engineer, Carson-Newman College, Jefferson City, Tennessee.
Sharp, Alan, Student, 1972, Carson-Newman College, Jefferson City, Tennessee.
Shealy, Dalmouth, Head Football Coach, Carson-Newman College, Jefferson City, Tennessee.
Sorrells, Fred, Assistant Football Coach, Carson-Newman College, Jefferson City, Tennessee.
    Smith, Mary Elizabeth, Associate Professor of Education, Carson-Newman College, Jefferson City, Tennessee.
Stafford, T. J., Jr., Maryville, Tennessee.
Stephenson, Bob, Head Basketball Coach, Christian Brothers College, Memphis, Tennessee.
Sweet, Fletcher; Knoxville, Tennessee.
Tallent, Jep, Jefferson City, Tennessee.
Tallent, Reece, Photographer, Jefferson City, Tennessee.
Tarr, Bill, Tarr Chevrolet, Jefferson City, Tennessee.
Tipton, Carl K., Director of Public Relations, Carson-Newman College, Jefferson City, Tennessee.
Vance, Carl T., Morristown, Tennessee.
Wade, Glenn C., Louisville, Tennessee.

# *A History of Sports at Carson-Newman College 1851-1974*

Weinkle, Robyn C., Baseball Player, Carson-Newman College, Jefferson City, Tennessee.

Whitney, Bruce, Assistant Professor of French, Carson-Newman College, Jefferson City, Tennessee.

Wilson, Martha, Assistant Professor of Physical Education, Carson-Newman College, Jefferson City, Tennessee.

Wright, Eugene, Harriman, Tennessee.

Wright, W. A., Baseball Coach, Tennessee Tech, Cookeville, Tennessee.

## PERSONS INTERVIEWED IN CONNECTION WITH THIS STUDY

Bowen, W. A., Member of 1937 Basketball team, Jefferson City, Tennessee.

Bryant, Charlie, 1960 Track team at Carson-Newman, Erwin, Tennessee.

Glover, Edward W., Director of Alumni Affairs, Carson-Newman College, Jefferson City, Tennessee.

Graves, Bobby, Member of 1962 Carson-Newman Golf team, Knoxville, Tennessee.

Green, Samuel B., Carson-Newman Football and Tennis Coach, Jefferson City, Tennessee.

Holt, Sam B. ("Frosty"), Retired Athletic Director of Carson-Newman College, Jefferson City, Tennessee.

# *It Gets Foggy at Mossy Creek*

### Appendix B

### I-SONGS

"Alma Mater"

Carson-Newman, how I love thee,
Alma Mater, Hail!
Orange and Blue wave high above thee,
Through the calm and gale.

Chorus

Long thy sons have sung thy promises
And they name adored,
While thy heart in Jubal raises,
Carson-Newman evermore.

Years have crowned thy head with glory,
An thy sons have told
All the great and thrilling story
Of thy deeds of old.

Chorus

Upward was thy grand endeavor
Which thy founders knew;
Hail the victors, doubting never,
Hail the Orange and Blue.

### II -- SYMBOLS

In 1921 a ministerial student, Ira Dance, was a member of the football team. The Carson-Newman football team had traveled to Athens, Tennessee, to play the Athens School of the University of Chattanooga. During the course of the game, Ira Dance at the home of the opponents so hard in regular play that it was necessary to take the player out for the remaining part of the contest. This incident so aroused the injured player's teammates that the coach and captain of the Carson-Newman team had to confine Ira to his hotel room for the night. From this incident the newspapermen began to identify the Carson-Newman team as "The Fighting Parsons." This designation remained for ten years, until 1931 when Coach "Frosty" Holt proposed that the name be changed. The idea was approved and Coach Holt offered a cash prize of one silver dollar to the person suggesting the best name, the decision to be made by a committee of students and faculty, Miss Tennessee Jenkins, Professor of History, was the winner. She had suggested that "Eagles" be adopted as the new name. This action was taken in 1931 and the new name was applied to the members of all athletic teams immediately. This name has symbolized Carson-Newman athletes in general; and on occasions the student body has also

# A History of Sports at Carson-Newman College 1851-1974

been identified as "Eagles." The women in the physical education and intramural programs have been referred to as "Eaglettes."

### III - MONOGRAMS

The "block style" was first used as the college monogram. This practice was continued until 1930 when the circular C-N was woven into the fabric of the monogram. Often the letter form used is a large "C" with "N" placed within the "C". This form is popular today and is used by the team members and also the cheerleaders. Once the monogram has been awarded, they are worn on sweaters or jackets with great pride. Such awards always represent an important achievement, and the student having earned one merits the respect of his fellow students.

Those eligible for college monograms are varsity athletes, girls through the point system and cheerleaders.

### IV - MOTTOES

The college motto - "Truth, Beauty, Goodness' - which is emblazoned on the beautiful seal in general use by the college. It can be found on publications, stationery, and any material relating to the college. The motto appears in a beautiful design with the seal over the front of the platform in the college auditorium. It is beautiful in design and symbolizes not only an academic institution but features the hills of the famous East Tennessee Valley. Its design is given below:

CARSON-NEWMAN COLLEGE

### V - CHEERS AND YELLS

The yells used around the twenties were (Carson-Newman College Pamphlet, 1921-1922):

EXECUTION!
1-2 -3 -4 -3 -2 -1
Who on earth are we for?
Carson-Newman!
(Clap Hands)
(Pat Feet)
Rah! Boom!!!

CHEER GANG
Cheer, gang, cheer

## *It Gets Foggy at Mossy Creek*

Carson-Newman has got the ball
Cheer, gang, cheer
Old Athens is going to fall
For when we reach that goal
There will be no goal at all
There'll be a hot time
On the campus tonight
Rah! Rah!

VARSITY FIGHT!
Varsity, fight!
Varsity, fight!
Fight-fight-fight-fight, fight!
Tear'em up!
Smash'em up!
Fight -fight -fight -fight-fight!
Varsity, fight!

The yells used during the late fifties and early sixties were (Carr, 1959):

EVENING BRETHREN
Evening brethren
Meeting time.
How are you feeling?
Feeling fine.
Who are you going to yell for?
C-N-C
Well, fifteen rahs for C-N-C
Rah, rah, rah, rah, rah,
Rah, rah, rah, rah, rah,
Rah, rah, rah, rah, rah,
C-N-C

YEA ORANGE, YEA BLUE
Yea Orange, Yea Blue,
Yea Eagles,
We're betting on you!

# *A History of Sports at Carson-Newman College 1851-1974*

## BIBLIOGRAPHY

ALUMNI BULLETIN (issued three times each year by the Secretary), October, 1948.

APPALACHIAN (student annual or yearbook, on file in Maples Library, Carson-Newman College), 1922-1972.

Athletic Records (records involving the athletic program of Carson-Newman College), 1923-1972.

Billington, John E. "A Biography of Sam B. Holt." Unpublished Master's thesis, Springfield College, Springfield, Massachusetts, 1953.

Bledsoe, Joseph C. ESSENTIALS OF EDUCATIONAL RESEARCH. Ann Arbor, Michigan: Edward Brothers, Inc., 1963.

Bucher, Charles A., and Ralph K. Durpree. ATHLETICS IN SCHOOLS AND COLLEGES. New York: The Center for Applied Research in Education, Inc., 1965.

Carr, Isaac Newtown. HISTORY OF CARSON-NEWMAN COLLEGE. Jefferson City, Tennessee: The Trustees of Carson-Newman College, 1959.

CARSON AND NEWMAN MAGAZINE (published monthly by the literary societies of Carson-Newman College)-Volume 1, 1896.

CARSON INDEX (published by the literary societies of Carson College), 1882; 1883; 1884.

CARSON-NEWMAN COLLEGIAN (a magazine published by students of Carson-Newman College), 1912-1915.

CARSON-NEWMAN COMMENCEMENT (published monthly by students of Carson-Newman College), 1913-1915.

CATALOGUES OF CARSON-NEWMAN COLLEGE, 1886-1893; 1914-1915; 1919-1920.

Cozens, Frederick, and Florence Stumpf. SPORTS IN AMERICAN LIFE. Chicago: University of Chicago Press, 1953.

Cubberly, Elwood P. THE HISTORY OF EDUCATION. Boston, New York: Prentice-Hall, 1953.

Dewitt, R. T. TEACHING INDIVIDUAL AND TEAM SPORTS. New York: Prentice-Hall, 1953.

Durant, John, and Otto Bettmann. PICTORIAL HISTORY OF AMERICAN SPORTS. New York: A. S. Barnes, 1952.

Hall, William F. "A History of Carson-Newman College." Unpublished Master's thesis, The University of Tennessee, 1937.

KNOXVILLE JOURNAL, THE. Sports items, October 17, 1924; November 12, 1924; November 22, 1924. KNOXVILLE NEWS-SENTINEL, THE. Sports items, October 17, 1924; September 29, 1929; February 15, 1938: April 30, 1962.

Materials on Dana X. Bible (private possession of Mrs. Ted Shipley, sister of Dana X. Bible) Jefferson City, Tennessee,

Menke, Frank G. THE ENCYCLOPEDIA OF SPORTS. New York: A. S, Barnes, 1953 and 1960.

Minutes, Board of Trustees, Carson-Newman College, Jefferson City, Tennessee, 1889; 1917; 1924.

News Release (releases sent to the newspapers on file in the Public Relations Office of Carson-Newman College), 1960-1972,

ORANGE AND BLUE (student newspaper), October 15, 1918; November 1, 1918; February 15, 1920; May 1, 1920; October 12, 1923; February 15, 1924; October 15, 1924; November 22, 1930; September 29, 1931; September 10, 1935; November 24, 1936; February 8, 1938; March 15, 1938; September 13, 1938; February 17, 1943; March 30, 1943; April 23, 1951; February 18, 1967; May 13, 1967; October 27, 1968; May 12, 1969; September, 1969; October, 1969; November, 1969; December 5, 1969; May 12, 1970; November 13, 1970.

Presidential Report to Trustees, Carson-Newman College, 1924.

Report of Executive Committee, Board of Trustees, Carson-Newman College, 1924.

Rice, Emmett A., John L. Hutchinson, and Mabel Lee. A BRIEF HISTORY OF PHYSICAL EDUCATION. New York: Ronald Press, 1969,

Scott, Harry A. COMPETITIVE SPORTS IN SCHOOLS AND COLLEGES. New York: Harper, 1951.

Scrapbook on Physical Education and Sports for Women (Private possession of Mae Iddins), Jefferson City, Tennessee).

THE EAGLE (student handbook), Carson-Newman College Volumes I-XII: *1946-1958*.

THE GRENADE (student yearbook, on file in Treasury Room of Maples Library, Carson-Newman College), 1920.

THE LARKER (second student yearbook, on file in Treasury Room of Maples Library, Carson-Newman College), 1917.

THE SWANN (first student yearbook, on file in Treasury Room of Maples Library, Carson-Newman College), 1912.

THE WANEHI (student yearbook, on file in Treasury Room of Maples Library, Carson-Newman College), 1921.

WASHINGTON HERALD (now TIMES-HERALD), Sports item, February 5, 1924.

Williams, Jesse F., and William L. Hughes. ATHLETICS IN EDUCATION, Philadelphia: W. B. Saunders Company, 1930.

*It Gets Foggy at Mossy Creek*

## ABOUT THE AUTHOR

The author is an East Tennessee native being born and raised in Cocke County. He was educated in the Newport Public Schools where he was an outstanding athlete. His all-round athletic talents brought him All-State honors in basketball, All-East Tennessee honors in football, and Most Valuable player awards in baseball.

He received his B. S. Degree from Carson-Newman College where he was honored as Carson-Newman's first All-American in any sport (1962). After graduation he played professional basketball for the Cincinnati Royals of the National Basketball Association and the Kansas City Steers of the American Basketball League. Later, after receiving his amateur status back he played in four consecutive National AAU basketball tournaments in Denver, Colorado. He participated in the World Cup basketball Tournament against other countries of the world and was named the Most Outstanding Amateur basketball player in the Southeast two straight years.

In 1967 he was again drafted back into professional basketball taking part in the Oakland Oaks training camp in California, and the Louisville Colonels camp in Kentucky.

He received his Master's Degree from the University of Mississippi in 1965 and his Doctorate from the University of Georgia in 1972.

From 1963-1968 he coached football, basketball, and golf in Griffin, Georgia. During that time he took his basketball teams to the State AAA tournament 3 years and his golf team won the District 4 years in a row.

He is currently Assistant Basketball Coach, Head Cross-Country Coach and Assistant Professor of Physical Education at his Alma Mater, Carson-Newman College. Under his leadership, the Cross-Country team has compiled a won-loss record of 58-6 and two State Championships.

His competitive spirit at the age of 34 is still high as he enjoys such sports as softball, golf, tennis, jogging, and weight lifting. His biggest goal in life is to help young people through sports and also help them find a Christian way of life.

Standard Publishing Company